MARKET

Wild Gyrations, Risks and Opportunities in Stock Markets

Second Edition

Also by the author
Hong Kong: China's New Colony
The Years of Living Dangerously

MARKET PANIC

Wild Gyrations, Risks and Opportunities in Stock Markets

Second Edition

Stephen Vines

WILEY

John Wiley & Sons (Asia) Pte Ltd

Other Wiley Editorial Offices

John Wiley & Sons, Inc., 111 River Street, Hoboken, NJ 07030, USA
John Wiley & Sons Ltd, The Atrium, Southern Gate, Chichester PO19 8SQ, UK
John Wiley & Sons (Canada) Ltd, 5353 Dundas Street West, Suite 400, Toronto, Ontario M9B 6H8, Canada
John Wiley & Sons Australia Ltd, 42 McDougall Street, Milton, Queensland 4064, Australia
Wiley-VCH, Boschstrasse 12, D-69469 Weinheim, Germany

Library of Congress Cataloging-in-Publication Data

ISBN: 978-0-470-82472-6

Printed in Singapore by Saik Wah Press Pte Ltd

10 9 8 7 6 5 4 3 2 1

Contents

Acknowledgements

MANY PEOPLE have provided advice and assistance in the production of this book. Their generosity and guidance is much appreciated. I only hope that in making these acknowledgements that I have not left anyone out.

This, new edition of the book, was produced with the enthusiastic encouragement of Nick Wallwork from John Wiley & Sons (Asia) and the help of Janis Soo on the production side. I am also grateful for the assistance of Alvin Siu, visiting scholar at the Hong Kong University of Science and Technology (HKUST), who helped me update the data for this edition.

This project, at its original stage, received active and extremely helpful support from Martin Liu formerly of Profile Books. It was edited with considerable diligence by Trevor Horwood who has an uncannily keen eye for spotting the inconsistent, the irrelevant and the missing.

It was not always easy to find the data contained in this book and I am especially grateful to Tim Adam for digging out a large mass of figures. Patrick Dunne furnished helpful advice on how to put this data into chart form. The splendid library at the HKUST, as ever, was my primary source of written material and the library's helpful staff provided considerable assistance in locating this data.

A number of people have supplied useful ideas and suggested sources which have helped considerably. Among them are Bill Mellor, Matthew Brooker, Bob Bunker, Jonathan Green, Andreas Kluth, Ilja Maynard-Gregory and Tony Measor.

John Carey and Warren Primhak, who are the subjects of the interviews in Chapter Six, gave up a lot of time for this purpose and showed great patience with repeated questioning. I am also grateful to Deutsche Securities Asia for permission to visit their trading room in order to gather additional material for this chapter.

The following people and organisations have generously permitted the reproduction of their charts: Gerald Dwyer and Gary Santoni for Figure 2.2, the copyright of which is held by McGraw Hill Education, which also gave permission. Hugh Fasken, the editor of the former *FT Expat* magazine gave permission for use of Figure 8.1. The Publications Department of the International Monetary Fund kindly assisted in obtaining permission for the material used in Figures 5.2 and 8.2. Robert Shiller gave permission for use of Figure 1.2, 1.3 and 9.1, based on material contained on his www.irrationalexuberance.com website.

Once again, I really appreciate all this help.

List of Figures

Preface

THE APPROACH of a market panic can be compared to the approach of a herd of marauding elephants. It is clear where they are headed, certain that destruction will be left in their wake and, yet, until their advance starts to gather pace it is hard to tell when they will arrive. And, because they are so bulky and fast once in motion, it is difficult for on-the-spot observers to describe what's happening because most sensible people in this situation are busy getting out of their path.

Having watched the approach of the market panic of 2008 I would like to claim that I predicted when it would arrive and what impact it would have but even though I, like others observing the markets, noted the warnings signals, I cannot claim such prescience. It is one thing to spot a trend but quite another to get the timing exactly right. Bearing in mind this difficulty, it seemed like a better idea to keep out of the prediction game and to focus on understanding the trends in the stock market, especially when they veer to extremes and produce both panics and impressive rebounds. So, readers looking for precise predictions are likely to be disappointed but anyone interested in the underlying causes of market panics, and the opportunities they produce, will, hopefully, not be so disappointed because this is what the book is about.

I happened to be in New York, in September 2008, when the panic erupted with full force. Flicking through the myriad of television channels available in this city, where choice is a form of religion, I watched announcers yelling into the cameras about how share prices were tumbling, how banks were collapsing, and how everyone was blaming everyone else. The women with big hair, who seem to populate these television channels, bobbed their impressive manes up and down as new tidbits of information flowed in their direction. Male TV announcers, in their duller uniforms of monochrome shirts and dark suits, reached out for job lots of adjectives to describe what was happening, as though somehow the unfolding story in 2008 was unprecedented and totally bewildering. As we shall see later in this work, this is far from the truth.

Yet, there can be no underestimating the gravity of the 2008 stock market crash. Unlike the last great worldwide market panic in 1987, the panic of 2008 has been accompanied by a full blown recession with all the advanced economies heading towards negative growth, leaving only the newly industrialized nations to pull the international community out of a global recession. However, this does not mean that the two biggest powerhouses of economic growth, China and India, are immune from the carnage taking place on the stock markets. On the contrary, their equity markets have suffered even more profoundly than the rest. In other words, it is very hard to understate the enormity of the panic of 2008.

Fortunately, or maybe unfortunately, for an author of a work on market panics, this book was first published in 2003 when equity markets were performing strongly and talk of market panics was far from most people's minds. By 9 October 2007 the Dow Jones Industrial Average hit an all time high of 14,164 points. A remarkable piece of serendipity ensured that in the space of exactly five years share prices had almost doubled from a new low set on 9 October 2002 when the Dow hit 7,286 points. Not only had share prices doubled in New York but, as ever, markets around the world followed America's lead and did so in a sufficiently gradual manner to suggest that this time everything would be different and share prices had truly reached a new plateau from which they were unlikely to be dislodged.

The immutable truth is that in a bull market investors and other market participants do not want to read about sharp declines in share prices, let alone about market panics. The wealth and prosperity produced by bull runs makes negative news and information very unwelcome, so it was a somewhat unrewarding business appearing on television shows and doing interviews about a book which both warned of the dangers of a new panic and confidently asserted that this need not be a cause of despondency because panics provided fantastic opportunities for investors. It was a message better tailored for the current period of 2008, when interest in the negative is heightened, albeit to an exaggerated extent. But I should not complain because it means there is now a more receptive audience for information about market panics. However, there remains a high degree of scepticism towards people like myself who believe that panics are times of unprecedented opportunities. The sceptics seem to lack any kind of historical perspective – they prefer not to know that over time there has never been a form of investment which has consistently produced returns as high as those found in stock markets. And when stock prices are depressed the opportunities for serious wealth creation emerge in ways that are rarely seen.

In both the short term and the longer term, market panics can be wonderful times for skilful investors. All the biggest gains on the Dow have come during the periods of greatest panic in the last one hundred years – the panic of 1929, the panic of 1987, and it can be said with some confidence that this applies to the panic of 2008, even though it is hard to be optimistic in the conditions that prevail at the time of writing. It could also be argued that this scenario ignores the years 1927 to 1974, which was a period with a tremendous bear market, though it did not originate with a sudden sharp slump in prices of the kind that marks out a true market panic. On the contrary, the fall in share prices was more gradual, albeit ultimately nonetheless damaging. And here's the point: there were less opportunities in the 1970s precisely because there was no full blown panic. There was certainly nothing like the record breaking one-day fall on the Dow seen in 1987 which, at a stroke, wiped 22.6 per cent off share prices on 19 October. Nor was there a repetition of the 12.8 per cent slump on the Dow seen on 28 October 1929, followed by two other comparable one-day market slumps in that year. It was not until 15 October 2008 that a one-day slump of this kind was seen again when prices on Wall Street tumbled by almost 8 per cent, eclipsing the 7.13 per cent plunge on Wall Street when the market re-opened following the terrorist attacks on New York in 2001. It should also be noted that the October 2008 share price falls on Wall Street were echoed by even bigger slumps in share prices on other markets. (It is also be worth noting, although the significance of this observation may not be important, that all but one – 11 February 1932 – of the biggest one-day declines on the Dow, from 1929 to the present day, occurred in the last quarter of the year).

The biggest price fall since the beginning of the new millennium came, as noted above, on 15 October 2008 but an earlier price collapse of 7.3 per cent on 9 October, gave way to one of the biggest one-day price rises in history when the Dow soared by over 11 per cent four days later. It was, of course, a false dawn but nevertheless could have secured considerable profit for anyone holding shares for a mere four days. Much of this book focuses on taking advantage of spectacular movements in stock price history but these come about rarely.

On the whole, however, it is not too healthy to dwell on one-day index records – it is far more useful to look at the evolution of cycles which provide the basis for a share trading strategy. The lengths of cycles vary considerably but they follow an entirely consistent pattern of overreaction and underreaction to events that move share prices. And, of course, every cycle heading one way moves in the other direction, usually with some speed once the reversal begins.

Practically everyone investing in shares knows this but every time the cycle changes direction investors seem to behave as if something startling and new is underway. The first edition of this book was written in the shadow of the 9/11 events, when markets all over the world behaved in an alarming but perfectly predictable manner. I simply could not understand why so many people were lining up to sell their shares on 17 September 2001 when it was pretty obvious that the market would overreact on the downside and there would be plenty of upside in the near future. I am not writing this with hindsight because I was an active equities buyer at this time, spoilt for choice over the range of offerings of high quality stocks at bargain prices.

Why could I be so certain of a recovery, while so many people were lining up to sell their shares? Thinking about this persuaded me to undertake the research which forms the basis for this book. I wanted to know why what appeared obvious to me, and many other people, was apparently not so obvious to those who in this instance, and at all other times of market panic, were persuaded that they needed to get out of stocks.

The answer lay in understanding how the market worked. To reach this understanding required a study of how the stock market behaved when it went to extremes, when the pressure affecting the market was most acute and when both the strengths and weakness of the market were mostly likely to be laid bare.

The more I read and the more I studied the data one thing became staggeringly clear – it is far easier to know what to do when a market falls into crisis than it is to know when to buy and sell shares at other times. An article in the *Wall Street Journal*, of 9 August 2004 started with a paragraph that exemplifies the common dilemma facing investors at times removed from panic but full of uncertainty: 'With major US stock indexes at their lowest levels since last year, many investors are fretting whether this is a nasty "correction" or the start of a real bear market. It isn't an easy question to answer: many of the variables are almost impossible to measure.'

E.S.Browning, the author of this article, then went on to list the variables and study their implications. He quoted market analysts giving a range of views, all of which seemed perfectly reasonable, even though contradictory. Anyone reading this would be left with the conclusion that, all in all, it might be better to postpone investment decisions. However, there is always a case to be made for postponing a plunge into the stock market on grounds of uncertainty. If everyone were to postpone indefinitely taking a decision, trading would dwindle to nothing. This does not happen; but uncertainty is a constant factor of stock market investing. Yet, being the perverse people that they are, investors tend to become more active in periods of uncertainty when prices are rising, while behaving in strange ways as prices fall during periods of panic, when history teaches us that a number of certainties arise for investors.

The basic certainty is that any market suffering a profound fall will, often quite quickly, enjoy a substantial recovery. It could even be said that market crises are almost designed as buying opportunities, yet much of the literature on investing is devoted to telling investors how to avoid getting burned at times of crisis.

Starting from a diametrically opposite point of view, I have set out to explain why crises are times of great opportunity and have been proved to be so for at least 100 years. While there was clear evidence of the money making opportunities to be gained by turning away from the stock buying herd at its most bearish, most of what I read focused on the fabulous prospects offered by the stock market when prices had reached their highest levels.

Obviously, good money can be made in bull markets. The temptation to wait for the market to go higher and yet higher persuades otherwise quite sensible people to buy more and more shares when prices are at a peak. When these bull markets slam sharply in reverse, as they always do, many of the people who have made large sums of money lose all or some of their gains.

No one knows where that peak may be, nor do they know where the troughs are to be found. Therefore, the sensible investor should conclude that there is no point looking for that which cannot be found. Yet the search for the elusive goes on, while the search for the obvious is ignored. Thus most investors are loath to buy shares after panics set in because they are still looking for the new trough. A more sensible approach is to ignore the trough and be satisfied with the bargains that emerge and act accordingly, usually at the point when volatility decreases. Investors who do so are more than likely to make a profit.

As shares have proved to be by far the most profitable asset class over time, buying them when they are cheap seems to be a rather obvious thing to do. However, markets are not places where rationality reigns supreme. Eventually, stock markets behave rationally but there are enough periods of irrational behaviour to ensure that the brave investor can make a lot of money out of other people's follies.

The ideologues who believe in markets as the most efficient and sensible way of measuring economic activity and allocating resources to support economic growth greatly dislike suggestions that stock markets are little more than casinos – in other words, places where money can be made and lost with little reference to the underlying activity and value of the assets which are supposed to be reflected in the operation of markets. The truth lies somewhere between these two extreme positions because there is most certainly a casino-like quality in stock markets; but they also perform a serious role as capital raising centres.

I have written about stock markets and business for quite some time, but I now realise that I only really started to understand what I was writing about in the past two decades when I established some businesses of my own and learned what it is really like to earn money by buying and selling goods and services. Before then the reality of business consisted of looking at the accounts of listed companies and following their progress on the stock market. This was supplemented by talking to senior members of management, government officials and their intermediaries whose job it is to tell the world how wonderfully they are performing. Naturally, a diligent journalist tries to balance all this talk by seeking out those with a different point of view and by searching for data to provide some concrete evidence for the assertions that are made. Yet all this activity is far removed from the reality of business.

In some ways, operating a business has made me more cynical and sceptical about stock markets; in others, it has helped me understand what happens.

This cynicism seemed to be the prevalent mood among the investment community when the first edition of this book was published as corporate scandal piled on corporate scandal, at one point destroying Arthur Andersen, one of the world's biggest accountancy firms; at other points obliterating companies such as Enron, WorldCom and Tyco, which rode the crest of the 1990s bull market wave. And now some of the world's biggest investment banks have disappeared or been forced into shotgun mergers. Lehman Brothers passed into history with a whiff of scandal wafting over its demise while Bear Stearns and Merrill Lynch were forced into humiliating takeovers, as was AIG, an insurer that had seemed so impregnable in the days before its had bailout.

The effect of these scandals, and the collapse of household names, has placed a heavy dent in investor confidence. There is a lack of trust in published figures, a feeling that statements by companies cannot be taken at face value and that institutions, such as auditors and investment banks, which had once been seen as guardians of shareholders' interests, have become compromised to a great extent.

Companies themselves and regulatory bodies have moved to try and restore trust. In the United States, for example, the Sarbanes-Oxley Act, was introduced to give the force of legislation to improve corporate governance in the wake of the early 2000's failures. Yet, as the bear market gave way to the bull market of the mid-2000s, the memory of these corporate scandals quickly evaporated and the Bush administration committed itself to removing regulatory barriers that curbed corporate freedom.

Investors have a habit of turning against markets when they fall, often with good reason, but not always with logic because what bubbles to the surface is a revulsion against companies and the other bodies which are seen as having contributed to the losses that accumulate as markets tumble. Yet most businesses and companies that have secured stock market listings do not operate in a manner that justifies such widespread investor cynicism. Nor, incidentally, do they suddenly become paragons of virtue when markets start rising again. Their activities are more mundane and hardly focused on what is happening to the company share price.

What I have learned from running companies is that operating a business is largely a matter of tackling day-to-day problems of management. Very large companies can afford the luxury of having departments devoted to strategic planning for the future but nine times out of ten, the people in charge of the companies will be focused on the present and they will only pay occasional attention to their hired visionaries. Seen from the ground level of corporate management, the financial markets are really quite distant. They might occasionally intrude, and do so with some bluster, but their operations are very much detached from the business of business.

Professionals in financial markets, such as stock markets, are mainly individuals who have very little idea about what it takes to make a dollar by selling some products. They inhabit a world where spreadsheets are their guidebooks, PowerPoint presentations their graven images and the occasional meeting with the people who actually run companies provides the light relief. It may be thought that this crude characterisation of market professionals is slightly unfair. Many market participants are shrewd and perceptive but their trade is fueled by large amounts of hot air and contagious irrationality that certainly helps to move markets along but is of questionable assistance to the business of actually making and selling things.

This book is not intended to be some sort of moralistic critique of stock markets. I am more interested in discovering how they really work, especially when they are under pressure. Whether they are a force for good or evil is a matter given some consideration in Chapters Five and Nine but the bulk of the book is more concerned with two big questions. First, how are investors most likely to benefit from stock markets? Second, how are they likely to react?

The first question is important not just for those with direct investments in shares but for a far larger group of people who have pensions, saving schemes and investments in stocks made through unit trusts or mutual funds, as they are known in the United States. Generally speaking, there is no better way for individuals to preserve wealth and increase it than by investing in stocks. What happens in stock markets is therefore of more than mere academic interest to a large swathe of the world's population that looks to stocks to secure a comfortable retirement and to ensure that earnings are not eaten away by inflation.

I appreciate that it is somewhat unconventional to be writing a book of this kind from a base far removed from the world's biggest financial markets. However, living in Asia, which is home to some of the world's fastest growing stock markets, has helped me gain at least one valuable form of perspective. Traveling around the region I have come to appreciate the extent to which stock markets embody the hopes and aspirations of people who have managed to move from earning enough money to merely feed themselves to a situation where they are able to accumulate wealth and pass it on to their children. They still have the memory of a subsistence-level existence and therefore marvel at the opportunities arising from being able to save and accumulate wealth. For these people, stock markets are beacons of hope, they are symbols of modernity and, in a very real sense, places that provide the means to lift their lives onto another plateau.

Most importantly, stock markets give individuals access to participation in the profits of big businesses and a chance to increase their wealth by trading their holdings in these companies. Some people would describe this as a way of giving ordinary people a stake in capitalism. What is striking about the world's emerging stock markets is that they have been so enthusiastically embraced by those of modest means. The developed markets of the West now count a fair number of low income shareholders among their participants, but in their early stages of development they were very much trading centres for the well off. In emerging markets, widespread popular participation has been an important feature from day one. This does not mean that stock markets have become some kind of egalitarian instrument helping to secure an even distribution of wealth, but it does provide an avenue for wealth enhancement among those who will never own their own businesses and are unlikely to be seriously rich.

With this in mind, I hope this book will be of interest to non-specialist readers who want a better understanding of the markets where their money is invested. More specialist readers will, I trust, be interested in some of the new perspectives and ideas offered here and I hope they will bear with me if at times they find some issues spelled out which are already clear to them.

Some of my interest in stock markets is derived from being a small-time investor. I enjoy the whole business of share picking, making a play and then, if all goes to plan, taking a profit. I find that much of what I read about stock markets is written either by those who appear not to be actively involved in the markets on their own behalf or are moving such large amounts of money for clients that their participation in the markets has become almost impersonal. This is a pity because for most individual stock market investors there is a real sense of excitement, and anything written about the markets should reflect this.

Self righteous market participants will object to the idea that playing the stock markets contains elements of a game; but they are wrong. This is a vital element in the make up of markets and helps explain how they move. If I have failed to convey some of this excitement in this book, I apologise in advance. This is because no one should ever forget that stock markets are places where dreams are hatched, where a great deal of emotion is expended and where the extremes of euphoria and depression emerge in quick succession.

As for the structure of this book, the first chapter tries to shed some light on the most recent and dramatic market panic, the crash of 2008, and shows how very little this panic differs from those in the past. The second chapter sets out the basic contention of this work and looks at how booms develop and burst and panics ensue. This is followed by an attempt to classify the types of panics affecting stock markets. This categorization moves into new territory and should be helpful in promoting a better understanding of what causes panics and how they are likely to develop. Chapter 4 contains a more detailed consideration as to how the panic cycle develops and describes its main characteristics. This is followed by an examination of how panics are changing, primarily as the result of the growing separation between stock markets and the underlying economies and companies they are supposed to reflect.

Chapter 6 looks at market panics through the eyes of two market professionals who have been engaged in handling very large sums of money at times of crisis. Their experience and insights say a lot that cannot be contained in statistical summaries. From there, I move onto the fraught subject of market psychology, a key issue because markets are run by human beings and without understanding how they behave there is no hope of understanding markets.

Moving on, I have attempted to challenge the generally held assumption that investors are best protected by diversification. This seems to be a dubious proposition and leads to a lot of wasted effort, not to mention lots of wasted investment opportunities. Chapter 9 considers why markets are structurally imperfect and structurally troublesome. The concluding chapter can be seen as an attempt to apply these many theories and ideas to a practical end when unique opportunities arise from market panics.

When I wrote the original version of this work I was urged by friends to complete this book with great speed because, at the time of writing, the world's stock markets were in a state of frenzy. By the time the book was published markets had settled down again and it seemed as though a book entitled *Market Panic* belonged to another era and might even be of little more than historical interest. Lamentably, this has not turned out to be the case because, as the panic of 2008 showed, history has a habit of repeating itself, never exactly but with enough recognizable characteristics to provide the basis for a work that helps make sense of these frenzies, whenever they emerge.

Stephen Vines
February 2009

MARKET PANIC

1

The panic of 2008

IT IS ALMOST CERTAINLY of little comfort to investors, who saw their portfolios slashed to shreds by the market panic of 2008, and of even less comfort to those who lost their jobs and homes during the carnage, but the plain fact remains that this crash was predictable and barely differed, in essence, from any of the major crashes seen in the past century or before.

It may be argued that this crash spread faster and wider than past crashes and a case could be made that the proliferation of financial derivative instruments accelerated the pace of the crash and made the whole mess even more complex. Moreover, in some ways, the panic of 2008 had a greater ability to shock because it came after a period of sustained economic growth, engendering a false sense of security fortified by the growing acceptance of an ideology asserting the supremacy of free markets and their ability to be sufficiently resilient to cope with any shocks to the system. However, as the crisis developed, the ideologues were cowed into an awkward silence as it became clear that markets alone could not solve their own problems and that even the most fervent free marketers were seeking state intervention at levels rarely seen in history.

So, there is some validity in attempts to seek exceptional circumstances for the crash of 2008 but the differences are not to be exaggerated. The effect of this bout of market panic is undoubtedly larger in cash terms than the losses incurred in any previous panic but that is simply because financial markets have got much bigger. Also, nations, notably Asian nations, have developed large stock markets which have joined the global financial system and become subject to the contagion that is part and parcel of globalization. However, in percentage terms, markets fell more sharply during the crash of 1987 and the contagion from market to market spread with equal speed back then. That said, it is true that there are far more derivative financial products around today and that they have become increasingly removed from the underlying assets they are supposed to represent. In the 1920s, banks were busy repackaging loans they had made for highly speculative purposes, in a manner similar to what we now describe as the securitization of credit, and their activities did much to contribute to the crash of 1929. So, it would be a mistake to believe that there is something fundamentally different about the crash of 2008.

And, because memories are incredibly short, there has been much ill-informed talk of unprecedented government bailouts in the wake of the 2008 crash. Here too, there has been little fundamental departure from ground covered in the past. There was considerable state intervention in the immediate aftermath of the 1929 crash but most of it turned out to be counterproductive. In 2008, the impressively rapid response by governments does not look as though it will be similarly counterproductive, indeed the emphasis on infusing liquidity into financial systems and preventing the collapse of key financial institutions has a fair chance of ameliorating the worst consequences of the crash. In cash terms, more money is being poured into corporate rescues, loan guarantees and bank deposit guarantees than at any time in the past and it is more than interesting to see the return of nationalization as a means of supporting the economy. Additionally, it is also almost certainly true that the global spread of rescue plans from the United States, to China, to Iceland and so on, occurred at a speed and a level of geographic diversity never seen before. However, who can pretend that, in terms of scale, what happened in 2008 was smaller than, say, Franklin D. Roosevelt's New Deal program that followed the 1929 crash. Or even the $293.3 billion rescue of the failed saving and loans companies that was launched as one of the first acts of George W. Bush's presidency and related to just one set of financial institutions, as opposed to a rescue of the entire sector. In the last big regional crash which preceded the events of 2008, the Asian financial crisis of the mid-to-late 1990s, Hong Kong's acutely self-conscious free market government plunged into the stock market spending $15 billion to buy blue-chip shares in a scheme designed to prevent further market falls. The South Korean government, which espouses capitalism as its reason for being in contrast to the communist government that rules North Korea, spent even more on rescue packages.

In 2008, there were indeed new forms of rescue, initiated by the administration of Prime Minister Gordon Brown in Britain and widely emulated in other countries, including the United States, that involved the partial nationalization of banks. However, these were not novel methods of rescue – on the contrary, they hark back to the period following the end of World War II.

So, in essence, what happened in 2008 fitted neatly into the cycle of past panics rather than breaking new ground. This is not to suggest that the panic of 2008 was somehow trivial and lacked distinctive features but it is to say that its overwhelming characteristic was recognizability. In Chapter 4 we shall see how panics occur in cycles. Although the chapter was written in 2003, there is nothing in its general description of cycles that does not fit the circumstances of 2008. To emphasize this point it is worth going through the stages of the cycle that brought about the crash of 2008.

What led to the 2008 crash?

A case can be made for tracing the origins of the 2008 crash back to the development of the Black-Scholes formula in 1973 which, in essence, provided a mathematical equation for pricing risk.[1] It was originally devised as a means of pricing stock options but the authors, and a host of their followers, quickly came to realize that the formula was applicable across a whole range of derivative products, including the securitization of loans, which were then bundled together with what were, in effect, option positions and leveraged on the original asset, that is, the loans. The authors of the formula were not advocates for the development of ever more sophisticated derivative products. But they provided the tools which gave confidence to those in the financial community who devised these products, even if they were often only dimly aware of the origin of the tools they were using. What they grasped was the fundamental idea that once a value could be placed on risks it was possible to package and repackage loans.

Armed with these tools, US financial institutions and their counterparts in Europe (but to a lesser extent) borrowed vast sums of money from 2004 to 2007 and, in particular, made investments in mortgage-backed securities. This period marked the height of this business, although securitization of loans in the US can be traced back to the 1970s – a process greatly assisted by guarantees provided to investors by the government-supported Federal National Mortgage Association (Fannie Mae) and the Federal Home Loan Mortgage Corporation (Freddie Mac).

Underlying this flurry of loan securitization was the assumption that home values would continue to appreciate and that mortgages would be repaid. It looked like a classic no-brainer – borrowing at low interest rates to invest in higher yielding products. In 2004, the US Securities and Exchange Commission (SEC) fueled the borrowing frenzy by granting permission for investment banks to increase their debt levels, which they did with enthusiasm and proceeded to buy larger and larger numbers of mortgage-backed debt securities. Before the SEC changed the rules, banks were obliged to keep their leveraging ratios within $10 - 15$ times of their core holdings. Once these rules were relaxed leveraging ratios more than doubled in a staggeringly short space of time. This relaxation also meant that United States global corporations and financial institutions intensified their search for ways of moving their business either into the US itself or to offshore locations where restrictions were similarly relaxed or even more so. And in Britain, according to the Bank of England, the banks headed into the crisis of 2008 with outstanding loans of some £6 trillion, supported by a capital base of just £200 billion – in other words, a ratio of 1 to 30 in terms of capital base to lending.[2]

The net result of all this in the US, Britain and elsewhere was both to greatly boost loan portfolios and to do so in a way that seemed less risky as the widespread securitization of loans appeared to shift risk from the lenders onto a much wider base of investors.

A World Bank research paper correctly points the finger of blame at US government policy for "supplying an unprecedented expansion of Federal Reserve liquidity facilities and Federal Home Loan Bank advances which helped some of the most blameworthy institutions to avoid asset sales that might otherwise have triggered net-worth write downs punishing enough to force them out of business". But it was not government alone that was responsible because, as the authors proceed to show, at every stage of the process those involved had a vested interest in ensuring that the gravy train stayed on the tracks, regardless of its unstable cargo: "Lenders collected upfront fees for originating and selling poorly underwritten (and sometimes fraudulently documented) loans and passed the risks along to investors and securitizers without accepting responsibility for subsequent defaults. Securitizers sliced and diced the cash flows from questionable loans without demanding appropriate documentation or performing adequate due diligence. Insurers and credit-rating organizations used poorly tested statistical models and issued (along with accountants) aggressive judgments about whether a non-recourse "true sale" of the underlying loans had actually taken place. Finally, servicers accepted responsibility for working out troubled loans without as-sembling an appropriate information system or training a staff large enough to deal with the delinquencies and defaults they might (and did) eventually face".[3]

By 2007, US banks had issued $922.1 billion worth of mortgage-backed securities. Because these securities were so profitable there was little incentive for the people making the underlying loans to be particular about the repayment capabilities of their loan customers. Without the underlying loans there could be no assets to rebundle and without this booming business there would be far less scope for earning the ever-rising bonuses paid out on Wall Street. According to the New York State Comptroller's Office, these bonuses totaled $23.9 billion in 2006.

The gravy train appeared to be smoothly trundling along the tracks and this flurry of activity set equity markets alight. On 19 July 2007 the Dow Jones Industrial Average (DJIA) closed above the record 14,000 mark for the first time in history. Major markets elsewhere in the world moved in tandem with Wall Street, as they generally do, but this time even Japan's Nikkei 225 Index joined the trend after operating in a sphere of its own following the Japanese crash two decades previously (see Figure 1.1).

The classic conditions of a pre-crash scenario were clearly in play. And, as always happens when markets are poised to crash, the disparity between stock price movements and price-earnings ratios grows. Previous stock market crises have been the product of excessive valuations of companies but the 2008 crisis can be said to be about earnings. Figure 1.2, produced by Robert Shiller, the Yale University academic who authored the best-selling book *Irrational*

Figure 1.1 **World markets move in tandem with the US**

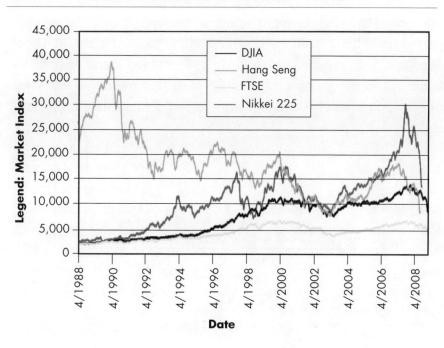

Source: Robert Siller, *Irrational Exuberance* 2nd ed. Princeton: Princeton University Press, 2005.

Exuberance, shows this rather clearly and, as ever, provides a good warning of overheating which was generally ignored by those who insisted that 'this time it will be different'. Shiller, himself, was among the minority who, in 1996, looked at his data and concluded 'it is hard to come away without a feeling that the market is quite likely to decline substantially in value over the succeeding ten years; it appears that long run investors should stay out of the market for the next decade'.[4] This was a very early call for caution and could be ignored by those who saw the markets rising to record levels and were confident that price-earnings ratios were incapable of telling much of the story.

Figure 1.2 **The gap between share price growth and price-earnings ratios blooms**

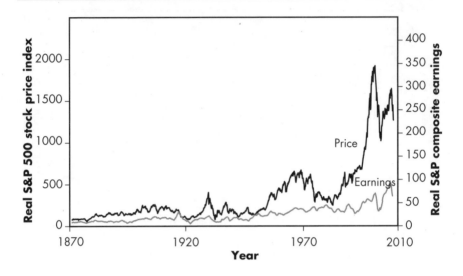

Source: www.irrationalexuberance.com

However more attention was paid to Warren Buffett, America's most famous investor, who, in 2003, expressed considerable alarm about the impact of derivatives on financial markets, describing them as 'financial weapons of mass destruction'. But even Buffett could be ignored as the stock market continued to soar and the sharp young traders asserted confidently that 'the old guy has lost his touch'.

There is, however, a very interesting wrinkle in the development of this boom and crash which was identified by Shiller and his colleagues at Yale. They found, as Figure 1.3 shows, that in this crisis it was private, as opposed to institutional, investors who were quicker to lose confidence in market valuations. In most crises, the professionals are first to identify reasons for caution and are more nimble in heading for the market exit as conditions deteriorate but, since 2007, it has been private investors who have been the biggest sceptics.

Figure 1.3 **Valuation confidence index**

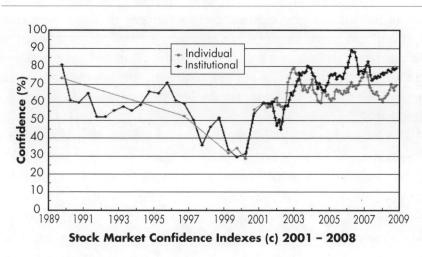

Stock Market Confidence Indexes (c) 2001 – 2008

Source: The Yale International School of Management

It is also worth noting, in passing, that the poor performance of fund managers cannot be overemphasized. Most surveys show that, on average, they never manage to achieve better results than the overall performance of the markets that are home to their funds – indeed most underperform benchmark indexes. Yet, investors in mutual funds pay a heavy price to these managers for handling their investments when they could achieve better results at lower cost by investing in index-linked funds that simply track the markets. Little wonder then that so few managers invest money in the funds they manage. A 2008 survey of 6,000 US-based funds showed that 46 per cent of their managers had not a single investment in the US stock funds they manage; 65 per cent stayed away from their own taxable bond funds and an even higher 70 per cent did not invest in their own balanced funds.[5] It is not possible to discover whether this is merely a recent phenomenon because the data only became available after a 2005 SEC ruling requiring fund managers to disclose their stock holdings in funds they run. Anyone who is dismayed by these figures is likely to be even more dismayed by the staggering lack of fund managers' experience in emerging markets. Research by the China-based brokerage, Galaxy Securities, showed that the average length of experience among Chinese mutual fund managers was a mere 1.7 years. Clearly few people in this position had even seen a bear market in China, let alone gained experience of how to handle it.[6]

The consequences of falling confidence, based on solid reasons to be wary, started to become apparent very rapidly. However, even at the beginning of 2008, many investment houses were pushing out predictions for the year that were sounding a cautiously optimistic note. Credit Suisse, for example, issued a research note on 10 January 2008 headed 'Buy US stocks with expected positive earnings surprise against the S&P 500'. The research report predicted that a recession was unlikely and that equities would reach new lows but that as early as the end of the year's first quarter the authors saw 'the equity bull market resuming as the economic and earnings uncertainty fades'.[7] It is not really fair to single out Credit Suisse for lack of foresight because its views were generally in line with the prevailing opinion which was that although the markets were in a bad way there was no cause for real alarm.

This impression was reinforced by the International Monetary Fund's (IMF) economists who are conservative and largely stick to consensus estimates. As late as April 2007, they were still confidently saying that 'overall risks to the outlook seem less threatening than six months ago' and they remained hopeful that growing signs of a downturn in the US would be unlikely to spill over to the rest of the world.[8] In other words the IMF, like the overwhelming majority of institutions and individuals in the forecasting business, did not see the storm ahead and were shocked as it gathered pace in the third quarter of 2008. It is always easier to criticise such failures of prediction with hindsight. Yet, even though there were high levels of concern about an economic slowdown at the beginning of 2008 it was hard to appreciate quite how rapidly or severely the recession would develop.

The bubble bursts

Although the crisis of 2008 is often described as 'Made in America' it is worth pointing out that the probable ignition point for panic came from France in August 2007 when BNP Paribas revealed that it was deep trouble, a revelation that immediately pushed up the cost of credit. As rates rose, house prices fell, especially in the United States where the sharp incline in borrowing rates led to a high level of defaults, particularly on sub-prime loans and among clients who, almost certainly, should never have been allowed to borrow the sums they received from eager bankers. By October 2008, some 6 per cent of all mortgage loans in the US were in default. This is more than two thirds higher than the level of defaults customarily experienced by the banks.

The problems of individuals struggling to make loan repayments rapidly started affecting the banks themselves. In 2007, America's five largest investment banks reported that their collective debts had risen to $4.1 trillion, equivalent to approximately 30 per cent of the US economy. By 2008, three of these banks were in crisis. Lehman Brothers went bust while Bear Stearns and Merrill Lynch (the bank with the bull as its symbol), resorted to fire-sale mergers to keep afloat. History is likely to record that the fall of Lehman Brothers on 15 September provided the trigger for the development of a full blown crisis. The bankruptcy of Lehman was the biggest in US history and came despite speculation that the US authorities would be prepared to launch a rescue as the bank's leaders had confidently expected. At this point, the crisis came forcibly to the attention of the American public and prompted the mood of panic.

And, while Wall Street was busy putting out fires, an even bigger fire fighting operation was underway in Europe where Fortis, one of Europe's largest banking and insurance corporations, had to be rescued by the Netherlands, Belgium and Luxembourg at a cost of €11.2 billion ($16.1 billion) in return for partial nationalization. All squeamishness about a return to the days of nationalization quickly faded across Europe as the British government injected a total of £37 billion ($55.5 billion) into three retail banks to prevent them from going under and secured partial ownership in return. Germany quickly followed suit by rescuing its banks and, in tiny Iceland, where the banking sector had expanded to a remarkable degree, the entire nation was faced with fiscal collapse as a result of their banks' exposure.

Elsewhere in the world, it soon became clear that the credit crisis on Wall Street was in fact a global crisis, or to be more exact an American and European crisis, although nations in Asia and Africa were rapidly drawn into the vortex even though their financial institutions were not brimming with toxic debts. Their problem was that they were trading with the West, were recipients of investment funds from the West and were themselves investors in the US and Europe. That delicate instrument, market sentiment, having swung into negative territory was also impacting on the confidence of local investors in Asia. The irony was that, in some cases, like China, their stock markets suffered even bigger falls than the markets in the West because they were already dangerously overvalued but, in others, such as Hong Kong, they suffered simply by being an open and liquid market which enabled investors to get their hands on badly needed cash to settle positions acquired elsewhere.

In mid-November 2008, Jim Rogers, the fund manager who made his name by predicting the commodities boom of 1999, estimated that more than $28 trillion had been wiped off global equity prices, accompanied by $690 billion in credit losses and write-downs.[9] The Bank of England put that figure higher at $2.8 trillion[10] but in reality all these figures are little more than 'guesstimates', albeit useful for conveying some idea of the magnitude of the crisis.

As stock prices declined, average global price-earnings ratios, based on the MSCI All Country World Index, fell from a high of around the mid-30s in the late 1990s to around 10 as the crisis took hold in 2008. It should be noted, however, that this is far from being an all time low – that dubious distinction was achieved in the mid-1970s.[11] Most striking is the fact that volatility in the stock markets returned to levels not seen since the 1929 crash. This increase in volatility is viewed by many analyists as an unprecedented opportunity for trading. However, while markets are in such a state of flux the prudent investor is almost certainly best advised to stand on the sidelines.

A real panic

In Chapter 3 we consider the various types of panic that occur in stock markets; by any standards the panic of 2008 can be considered to be a real panic, as opposed to one stimulated by mindless contagion or even false alarm. This is a panic accompanied by a severe economic downturn which inevitably has the effect of pumelling corporate profits – the underlying source of shareholder value.

In a background paper produced by the IMF's researchers for the November 2008 G20 summit of leaders from the world's 20 leading economic nations, the IMF forecast world economic growth declining by 1.5 percentage points to 2.2 per cent in 2009. However, the most advanced economies, the US, the Eurozone and Japan, were seen as suffering their most significant economic decline since World War II with a collective 0.3 per cent fall in growth. Every single major European economy was either in recession, or headed that way, by the last quarter of 2008. In November, Japan joined the nations in recession. The United States was hesitant about admitting that it was in the same situation but as Japan made their admission, the US administration was already conceding it was in the position but delayed using the 'r' word. It was said, with reason, that this was the worst economic situation since 1929.

The only reason that the world as a whole was not forecast to go into recession was that the two powerhouses of China and India were maintaining impressive growth levels in 2008, and were forecast to maintain growth in 2009, albeit at a slower pace than in the previous year. China's economic growth was forecast to decline from 9.7 per cent in 2008 to 8.5 per cent in 2009, while India was forecast to see its economy expand by 6.3 per cent in 2009, compared to 7.8 per cent the previous year. Possibly for the first time in history, we saw global economic growth being sustained by the so called developing world while the advanced economies were busy dragging down the overall growth picture.

At the November 2008 G20 meeting, called to find ways of tackling the crisis, the leaders struggled to explain what had happened. It is worth quoting in full their explanation of the root causes of the crisis. Their statement said:

"During a period of strong global growth, growing capital flows, and prolonged stability earlier this decade, market participants sought higher yields without an adequate appreciation of the risks and failed to exercise proper due diligence. At the same time, weak underwriting standards, unsound risk management practices, increasingly complex and opaque financial products, and consequent excessive leverage combined to create vulnerabilities in the system. Policymakers, regulators and supervisors, in some advanced countries, did not adequately appreciate and address the risks building up in financial markets, keep pace with financial innovation, or take into account the systemic ramifications of domestic regulatory actions.

Major underlying factors to the current situation were, among others, inconsistent and insufficiently coordinated macroeconomic policies, and inadequate structural reforms, which led to unsustainable global macroeconomic outcomes. These developments, together, contributed to excesses and ultimately resulted in severe market disruption."

Unusually for a statement of this kind, and albeit couched in the type of diplomatic language to be expected from such gatherings, this provides a reasonable summary of how the crisis arose. The solutions offered by the national leaders were less specific but there was a strong commitment to continued funding for economic bail-out packages and declarations of intent to reform the IMF. Also, there was to be focus on the urgency of global trade talks, essentially stalled since the 2001 launch of the Doha round of discussions on trade liberalization. Lastly, the leaders talked of plans for greater co-ordination between central bankers and others responsible for fiscal policy.

By the end of November, the financial newswire, Bloomberg, calculated that the total sum of guarantees, loans and other support measures, given by the US government alone, exceeded $7.76 trillion.[12] A significant amount of this sum includes credit and bank deposit guarantees but much of this is real cash coming out of national treasuries. At the time of writing it is hard to forecast what the total international bill will come to once the debris has been cleared, optimists even see the figures falling sharply as the recovery comes around and money given to institutions in the form of payment for equity is returned at a profit.

The left-wing American academic, Noreena Hertz, describes the panic of 2008 as 'the first full crisis of globalization, a recognition that in a tightly interconnected world, one country's troubles become each and every one's. It is the first collective "lose, lose".[13] This may appear to be the case but it cannot be overemphasized that the kind of contagion seen in 2008 was only really more global in the sense that there are now financial markets in every corner of the world. Back in 1929, when markets of this kind were mainly, but not exclusively, confined to Europe and North America, the contagion spread only marginally slower than in 2008 but the Wall Street crash was replicated on every single other financial market existing in the world at that time. And what is most remarkable is the way in which the panic of 2008 spread to markets like the Chinese stock markets, which has relatively few international investors, with every bit as much force as in markets where international trading was a far more significant factor.

Stages of the 2008 panic

The panic of 2008 showed that little has changed or, to put it another way, this crash follows the pattern of its predecessors in a remarkably consistent fashion. The cycle described in Chapter 4 shows how markets start with a period of euphoria, usually prompted by a significant development. In this instance the origins of the 2008 crash can be traced to the beginning of the new millennium when there was an enormous supply of cheap and plentiful credit to business and individuals.

In all cycles, developments of this kind are followed by an expansion of money supply, which in turns stimulates heavy speculation and borrowing. Then, novices start pouring into the market and are easily persuaded to get involved in speculations that they barely understand. And, as they do so, news of market matters moves from the business pages to the main pages of newspapers – this is a major warning signal at all times, and at all times largely ignored. Then, as we have seen above, more concrete warning signals emerge as price-earnings ratios reach quite unrealistic levels and yields on stocks become derisory. But these warning signals are also ignored because there is much talk about new paradigms and rejection of so called 'old fashioned thinking' which focuses on indicators which are dismissed as being no longer relevant. Another stage is reached when companies realize that there is near insatiable demand for new equity issues and new forms of debt instruments to cater for this investment appetite.

Generally, at this point in the crisis cycle, another rash of warning signals start flashing as dubious practices come to light and a number of scams are exposed. In the 2008 crisis, there was a flurry of excitement in June when the US Federal Bureau of Investigation arrested 406 people from Lehman Brothers over allegations of mortgage frauds. At around the same time, two former officials from the investment bank, Bear Stearns, were charged with criminal offenses related to the collapse of two hedge funds linked to sub-prime mortgages. But, back in June 2008, it was still thought that maybe these problems were little more than aberrations.

It is around this time that the more savvy investors started heading for the market exit. As they did so, lending institutions became more insistent about repayment of loans and made conditions of repayment more onerous, thus forcing sales of assets, which led to greater downward pressure on prices. The next stage of the panic cycle emerged as the plunge in prices turned to full flight and the price of good assets tumbled alongside the weak. Usually, there is a specific incident that greatly exacerbates this flight. History may well record that the tipping point for the 2008 crisis was, as pointed out above, the collapse of the US investment bank, Lehman Brothers, on 15 September, having posted a loss of $3.9 billion for the three months to August and then slowly revealing its large basket of toxic debts.

What happened after the Lehman failure was what happens in all market panics at this stage of the cycle. Markets appear to be in free fall and widespread revulsion develops towards the very assets which once basked in the sunlight. Hence, in 2008, phrases such as 'subprime lending' and 'hedge funds' became terms of investor abuse, much as odium attached itself to the word 'dotcom' at the end of the 1990s Internet boom. And, in the same way that it proved wrong to consider all dotcom companies as being beyond the pale, as memory of the bust fades, it will surely be the case that aversion to hedge funds will dissipate because there will always be a place for hedging in the investment world, there will always be derivative products and, of course, there will always be leveraging of investments. This is also a time for reviewing heroes and anti-heroes. When the markets were booming at the beginning of the new millennium those who made the most money were adoringly featured in numerous newspaper stories and invited to pontificate on TV and radio shows. But, as the markets plunged, sentiment towards these people turned with equal venom. The *Wall Street Journal*, the house publication of free marketers, ran an interesting story on 21 November, 2008 describing how, just ahead of the crash, the heads of 120 major US corporations, including those hit hardest by the bust, had swiftly pocketed over $100 million in cash compensation and stock sales.[14] Stories like this provoked a wave of anger against the failed heroes who were once able to command wide public respect.

What happens next is the most problematic stage of the panic cycle as markets remain intensely depressed yet some minds turn to thoughts of recovery as seemingly irresistible bargains start to emerge. This stage of the panic cycle contains a number of false dawns when, because of the extreme volatility of markets, it appears that the carnage is over. On 13 October 2008, for example, the DJIA rose by 11 per cent, the fifth-biggest percentage rise in the history of the index – all-time records were set in 1929, 1931 and 1932 (see Figure 2.1). In London meanwhile, on the same day, share prices rose by 8.3 per cent, the second-biggest gain since 1987. Note these dates because, as ever, the most spectacular share price gains came during the depths of past crises – in America it was during the panic that started in 1929 and in London the price rise followed the Black Monday collapse of 1987.

The 2008 panic in perspective

The 1987 panic was remarkably severe but, equally. remarkably short lived and, unlike the panic of 2008, it was not accompanied by a full blown recession. In this sense, it contained many elements of a phony panic of the kind discussed in Chapter 3. The biggest worldwide panic before the events of 1987 came in the mid-1970s, triggered by an enormous hike in oil prices engineered by the oil cartel of the Organization of Petroleum Exporting Countries (OPEC) and was greatly exacerbated by the collapse of the Bretton Woods agreement, forged in the aftermath of World War II, to stimulate economic recovery and bring stability and liquidity to the international financial system. The 1973–4 crisis delivered a nasty shock to the system and forced stock markets into trading on even lower price-earnings ratios than have been seen in the crisis of 2008, yet it was less severe than its predecessor, the crash of 1929, which is now viewed as the closest counterpart to the crash of 2008.

Such is the severity of this crash that some people seem to think that crashes are a more pronounced feature of financial markets today than they were in the past. This is not so, there were more crashes during the nineteenth century but there was one every decade in the twentieth century which was also a millennium that witnessed 30 bear markets on Wall Street and 25 in London. The generally recognized definition of a bear market is a 30 per cent decline in prices over a 50-day period.

But, in the last century, and in the current millennium, the most notable aspect of market panics is that they are either localized or sector specific. The biggest of the sector specific crashes was the dotcom bust of 2000 which was mainly seen on New York's NASDAQ, cutting share prices in half and then pummeling them again to produce a further decline of the same order in the space of a month. The NASDAQ Composite Index has, at the time of writing, never recovered, indeed it languishes at around 30 per cent of its peak of 5,048 points, reached on 10 March, 2000. The dotcom crash was essentially centered on hi-tech stocks but, as the NASDAQ crashed, other sectors were affected and the wave of destruction swept around the world; it was probably the biggest sectoral crash since the great railway-related crashes of the mid-nineteenth century. Meanwhile, the most distinctive crashes of the last century have been regional; the Asian markets crash of 1997–98 was the most significant and spread to both Brazil and Russia but this was less severe than the Japanese crash of 1990 which has led to problems that have lingered for two decades. Mexico had its very own crash between 1994–5 and a number of smaller nations have also suffered nasty slumps which remained confined to their borders.

Although it may appear that globalization and the enormous power of international capital residing in an ever shrinking number of hands has made markets more unstable and, thus, more prone to panics, the evidence is thin on the ground. What happened in 2008 has happened before and, as we shall see, there is a remarkably well-defined pattern to market panics which is the subject of the rest of this book.

2

Preparing for panics and profiting from them

O N 19 OCTOBER 1987, 1.2 billion shares were purchased on the New York Stock Exchange, by any standard this was an impressive day of trading. The following day's newspaper headlines spoke of a massive share sell-off, but this is nonsense because for every share sold there had to be a buyer. It would have been equally true for the headlines to have read: 'Massive Share Buying on Wall Street'. Journalism does not work that way, though, and so the headlines said nothing of the kind because the point of the stories was that the New York stock market had recorded its biggest-ever single-day percentage fall. The Dow Jones Industrial Average (DJIA) suffered a 22.6 per cent decline as the index dropped 508 points and over $500 billion was wiped off the value of shares. Incidentally, it is interesting to note that on Black Thursday, 28 October 1929, when Wall Street plunged 12.8 per cent, the second biggest one-day fall on record, it triggered subsequent price declines up to 1931 which in total knocked 'only' $50 billion off the value of share prices.

John Kenneth Galbraith, the author of the definitive work on the 1929 crash, has observed that 'of all the mysteries of the stock exchange there is none so impenetrable as why there should be a buyer for everyone who seeks to sell'.[1] Sometimes buyers and sellers are not matched and make the connection only after prices slump further and further, but slump they do when investors really want to sell, which usually means when they are panicking. In other words there is always a price at which buyers are prepared to enter the market. Thus the mystery Galbraith speaks of is not really quite that mysterious.

This explains why, in both 1987 and 1929, a large number of investors saw through the carnage and spotted a great opportunity in moving into the market while others were scuttling to get out. Practically every shred of historical evidence shows that their confidence was justified. In the period immediately after the great market collapse of 1987 and in other subsequent periods of sharp market falls it has been repeatedly demonstrated that those who bought at the height of the carnage were rewarded for their audacity.

This is because markets are splendidly schizophrenic in being both rational and deeply irrational. They are irrational in their extreme response to events and new information and rational in the sense that the extreme responses do not last, allowing profits to be made by those who have not been swayed by panicky responses.

It pains the advocates of rational markets to admit to the failings of investors who behave in an extreme manner. Ironically, it is these true believers who blame investors for undermining the purity of the market. They get themselves tied into knots with this argument because they end up saying that the market is rational and logical but market participants are not. A classic example of this thinking was supplied by Irving Fisher, the famous Yale University professor whose bullish view of the market before the 1929 crash and subsequent apologia for that view made him something of a laughing stock in certain quarters. In his post-crash analysis he wrote, 'my own impression has been and still is that the market went up principally because of sound, justified expectations of earnings, and only partly because of unreasoning and unintelligent mania for buying'.[2]

Figure 2.1 **Ten biggest one-day gains on the Dow**

Rank	Date	% change
1	15/03/1933	15.34
2	06/10/1931	14.87
3	30/10/1929	12.34
4	21/09/1932	11.36
5	13/10/2008	11.08
6	28/10/2008	10.88
7	21/10/1987	10.15
8	03/08/1932	9.52
9	11/02/1932	9.47
10	14/11/1929	9.36

Source: Dow Jones indexes

This almost amounts to saying that the market got it wrong when it came down, which cannot be true because the only level that is correct for a free market is the level at which it stands. Analysing in retrospect what level the market should have reached is irrelevant; buyers and sellers are the only people in a position to make that determination and, once they have made it, it matters little whether their judgement is right or wrong because they have made the market. It is another matter altogether to predict where the market might be heading because, until it gets there, there is room for debate.

Bear markets yield the biggest gains

The debate over the correct level for share prices intensifies when markets move to the extremes and share price movements become more erratic. Most people take the simple view that the biggest share price gains occur in bull markets while the reverse occurs in bear markets. This is not quite right.

The biggest ever single-day price rises on Wall Street came during bear markets. Until 1987, all the biggest single-day percentage gains in the US stock market occurred from 1929 to 1932 (see Figure 2.1). This means that these massive price hikes occurred during the longest period of share price falls in history. The biggest of these gains was 15.34 per cent registered on 15 March 1933. The only other times which saw price rises to match those of the post-1929 period were the 10.15 per cent rise in the DJIA on 21 October 1987, two days after the Black Monday crash, and again in 2008 as the latest crash took hold in October.

Lest anyone should believe that impressive share price rises in the midst of bear markets are somehow a uniquely American phenomenon, it is worth considering the experience of the worst bear market in recent memory, namely the decade-long depression in Japanese share prices. From a peak of around 38,900 points at the end of 1989, the Nikkei 225 Index lost around two-thirds of its value as the century ended. However, it was in the 1990s that seven of the ten biggest one-day rises ever recorded on the Nikkei occurred. The biggest one-day rise, a gain of 13.2 per cent, came on 2 October 1990, at a time when the prevalent attitude towards Japanese stocks was one of extreme pessimism.

One reason why the most dramatic price increases occur in the wake of market panics is that the volume of trading declines sharply as a bearish mood takes hold. As volumes decline the market becomes more sensitive to the activities of a small number of players. These bargain hunters quickly translate their bottom-scraping activities into higher prices.

The beneficiaries of these large price rises are the 'mysterious' share buyers mentioned by Galbraith. However, it is not only opportunistic traders who enter markets at times of sharp falls. Some of the most rational people operating in the stock market at these times are those who either buy the shares of their own companies or refuse to sell them simply because the market has entered into a period of frenzy. They know how much these companies are really worth and know a bargain when they see one.

By the end of the week which started with Black Monday in 1987 more than 100 US corporations announced they would be making share repurchases. Many of the companies were blue chips, including Citicorp, Bristol-Myers, Ford Motor Company, General Motors and Merrill Lynch. Without exception their faith in their own stock was vindicated, at least until the panic of 2008 struck.

Bring on the crises

It is not really necessary to be brave about buying shares when gloom is the prevailing sentiment. History stands firmly on the side of those prepared to take a gamble on recovery and history demonstrates that the risks are not quite as big as they may appear to be.

The Ned Davis Research organisation has reviewed the impact of twenty-nine major American crises since 1940 and found that the initial impact of these events was to cause an average 7 per cent fall in share prices. However, the average recovery period was a mere seven months, and within six months markets were showing even greater strength than in the pre-crisis period. A report compiled by researchers at the Bank of America in 2001 surveyed stock market crises over the past six decades and found that the DJIA registered an average gain of 15.5 per cent within a year of the crises emerging.

These averages are slightly misleading because they include the consequences of what I call phoney panics, which are discussed in the next chapter. Whether the panics are phoney or based on well-grounded fears about company profits, the crises surveyed by these two organisations were sufficient to cause prices to crash.

If there is a single message in this book, it is an incredibly simple one: stock market panics are the best time to make money. Because markets always overreact, they always correct themselves. There are few other certainties in the world of investment and although it is as well to remember that history will not necessarily repeat itself, it has shown an entirely consistent record of doing so in the wake of stock market panics.

This idea cannot be described as original. Many of the most successful investment managers have consistently advised profit seekers to adopt a brave strategy which goes against the mood of the crowd. Sir John Templeton, founder of Templeton Investment Management, was famous for encouraging investors 'to buy when others are despondently selling and to sell when others are greedily buying'.

Buying panics

When most people think of market panics they think in terms of severe downturns in stock prices. However, as a friend of mine who was a stockbroker in London back in the 1970s pointed out, there is also such a thing as buying panics. Significantly, no one describes them as periods of market madness, a description, as we shall see, that is commonly applied to severe market falls. Buying panics generally occur when markets are falling and big fund managers find themselves seriously underinvested in the market. This was the case in London in 1972, when share prices were dropping through the floor. In these circumstances a large number of fund managers thought it prudent to keep a substantial part of their portfolio in cash but at the merest whisper of a market upturn they were forced into a scramble to buy shares. This produced a buying panic, causing temporary surges in share prices. The result was that the average number of bargains struck on the London Stock Exchange each day rose from 20,784 in 1971 to 26,476 in 1972, although share prices remained depressed.

Nowadays most big fund managers are fully invested and there are tighter rules controlling the management of funds, most of which do not permit the keeping of large cash positions. However, private funds and hedge funds operate in a different way. This may well give rise to situations in which the fund managers embark on a buying panic.

Why are investors bargain-averse?

Interesting as they may be, buying panics are not the real concern here. Even more fascinating is the response of otherwise sensible people to falling share prices. Investors who are anxious to offload their shares at the first sign of market weakness are usually the same people who bluntly declare that they will stay well away from the market while so much uncertainty persists and when prices seem to be in free fall. Yet these very same people might well be among the crowds that descend on department stores when they hold sales. Their logic for queuing to buy cut-price goods cannot be faulted because they are flocking to buy things they need or products they cannot usually afford unless they are offered at bargain prices.

Shares are not that different. Assuming that buyers are committed equity investors and believe that a substantial part of any portfolio should contain shares, there must be a case for buying equities when they are cheap.

Yet when it comes to shares these born-again, bargain-averse investors take an opposite view and declare that they only want to buy shares when prices are high and the market is rising. This partially explains why volumes of trading are typically far higher in bull markets than at times when prices are falling.

Warren Buffett, the chairman of Berkshire Hathaway and widely regarded as one of the shrewdest investment managers of recent years, shares the puzzlement over this lack of logic. In his typically folksy way he wrote about his great love of hamburgers. 'I'm going to buy hamburgers the rest of my life,' he declared. 'When hamburgers go down in price, we sing the "Hallelujah Chorus" in the Buffett household. When hamburgers go up, we weep. For most people, it's the same way with everything in life they will be buying – except stocks. When stocks go down and you get more for your money, people don't like them anymore.'[3]

The reason people do not act rationally lies more on the fear rather than the greed side of the equation that drives all stock markets. There is a tremendous fear of being caught in a vortex dragging prices down even further. Yet logic suggests that if the shares of a world beating company, with a solid earnings record, can be had at a considerable discount to its previous price, the discount must be worthy of consideration.

A simple strategy for success

There is always a temptation to make investment strategies complex when they are really very simple. The concluding chapter considers ways of dealing with stock panics and avoiding their consequences. However, let me outline the arguments at this stage as they form the basic contention of this book.

It is quite possible that in the wake of a panic stock prices will not return to the heady levels reached when the market was buoyant, but that is not a problem for the canny investor who has made a purchase of blue chip shares at bargain prices. This is because the investor has acquired a valuable asset by entering the market when prices are much lower than their historical level. In so doing the share buyer has created a much greater potential for gain. Some investors are mesmerised by comparing pre- and post-crash share price levels. However, this is relevant only to those holding shares purchased before the crash. Those buying shares at their depressed post-crash levels need only concern themselves with price movements following the crash, when the scope for gain is impressive.

Everyone in the stock market would love to have a crystal ball that can tell them exactly when to get in and when to get out of markets. But no such crystal ball exists, so the best a share buyer can do is cease worrying about where the peaks and troughs lie and simply concentrate on what works for the individual investor. It is nothing short of folly to try to forecast these extreme points of the market spectrum.

It is far more important for investors to learn discipline. This means they should set targets for the profits they wish to achieve and set targets for the toleration of loss. If, for example, an investor considers that a 10 or a 20 per cent gain is reasonable, they must sell once this has been achieved and have no regard for subsequent price rises. A profit will have been made that is considered to be reasonable and the time will have come to move on. The setting of targets must be tailored to individual tolerance of risk and individual expectations of rewards; there can be no general rules here. However, it is advisable to establish targets in line with the overall performance of the market. For example it may have been feasible to establish ambitious targets during the bull market period of the 1990s. In the decade as a whole, annual gains on share prices averaged out at some 18 per cent and rose even more sharply, by a staggering average of 50 per cent between 1994 and 2000. The 2008 crisis depressed annualized returns, for the ten-year period to 2008, down to a level just below 2 per cent.

Discipline in setting targets and keeping to them is especially important in fast-rising markets because they float on a wave of exaggerated expectations, leading investors to delay selling in the hope of securing dazzling gains. This means investors are quite likely to get caught when the bubble bursts.

In bull markets the wise investor will be turning over their portfolios, taking profits and reinvesting them either in equities or in other assets. In bear markets, ironically, it may be harder to make a lot of small gains but easier to make big gains at moments of exceptionally sharp share price declines.

Value investors, i.e. investors who seek out companies with solid earnings records and are prepared to hold the stocks over the long term, are not looking for stocks making price gains resulting from rumours and other factors that are not derived from the fundamental performance of the listed company's business. They may be reluctant to churn their holdings during periods when markets are rising. While their reluctance is understandable it is not entirely logical because they can always take their profits on stocks they view as offering good value and then buy them back again when they are cheaper.

One strategy widely advocated by financial advisers at times of market weakness is to move into so-called defensive stocks. This usually means utilities or other kinds of boring stocks that are known to be steady but dull performers. This notion is examined in greater detail in Chapter 8. At this point it is sufficient to say that recourse to defensive stocks is generally misguided precisely because at times of market declines when good bargains are to be found elsewhere in the market, defensive stocks tend to hold their price and start looking expensive.

All this begs the question of what investors should do if they have failed to extricate themselves once panic sets in. Almost always the answer is to do nothing. Certainly it would be foolish to sell at the height of a panic, unless this is unavoidable. However, it may not always seem to be wise to sit on losses. The experience of the 1929 crash might well suggest that an investor sitting on a portfolio purchased before the crash would feel more than justified in not wanting to wait twenty-five years for prices to return to their previous levels. In these circumstances none of the options is particularly attractive. An investor might think about accepting a certain level of losses and selling at moments when the market flickers back to life. Alternatively they may wish to sit tight in the knowledge that, generally speaking, when stock prices fall, other asset prices tend to be falling and an escape from the stock market may mean no more than an entry to another declining market. This matter is also discussed more fully in Chapter 8.

Booms and bubbles

The 1990s boom is only the most recent manifestation of the repeated pattern of stock market fever bringing in irrational players to dominate the markets. This irrationality often extends to market participants who, at other times, manifest healthy signs of rationality. As we shall see in Chapter 7, investors are easily borne along by waves of enthusiasm and fear of drowning as the optimistic mood is replaced by equally exaggerated gloom. At times like these understanding the psychology of markets is more important than understanding economic fundamentals.

However, psychology alone will not explain the extreme volatility in stock markets. To understand the wild swings from optimism to pessimism requires an appreciation of why markets rise so rapidly and form bubbles.

Economists usually define bubbles as situations in which the price of an asset does not match its underlying value. This description is rather inadequate because disparity between share prices and underlying value is so frequent as to suggest that bubbles are a perpetual feature of stock markets. The more generally understood definition of a bubble relates to situations in which markets bestow exceptionally high valuations on assets. They become so high as to defy the possibility of sufficient profits ever being generated to pay dividends in any way commensurate with the share price. In other words, during bubble periods, when share prices stand at something like 100 times the earnings of a company, it is highly unlikely that dividend payments will match the share price in any period of time during which the shares are held. The only way that profits can be made from the shares is by selling them and thus fuelling the bubble, which has taken on a life of its own almost regardless of the underlying assets.

Eugene White has contributed to this debate by suggesting that 'bubbles arise when the underlying fundamentals become more diffuse and more difficult to predict'.[4]

This is a helpful contribution to the discussion but seems not fully to take on board the simple fact that underlying fundamentals are not that difficult to predict in bubble periods. This is because when the market gets into a frenzy it is easy to see the consequences as valuations are so self-evidently out of line with reality.

The following is a quick checklist of characteristics of market booms and their causes. It may not be comprehensive enough for some students of boom-ology because I have tried to strip it down to elements found in most situations. What is notable about this list is its applicability across time and across continents. In other words, these elements are found more or less everywhere in the world and have remained more or less unchanged since stock markets were formed.

Causes of stock market booms

▶ Fads, trends or new developments emerge encouraging new investment.

▶ Rising share prices encourage optimism and expectations of yet higher prices.

▶ A benign background of economic growth supports corporate profitability.

▶ Deregulation and liberalisation create new opportunities, particularly in emerging markets.

▶ Buying sprees are fuelled by plentiful credit supply.

▶ More equity issues are made to satisfy investor demand.

▶ New types of derivatives make an appearance and margin trading increases.

▶ Share price rises rapidly overtake bond price increases.

▶ A common interest in talking up the market is created, stretching from governments to small investors.

▶ Buoyed by strong performance, fund managers grow more bold, feel more omnipotent.

▶ News of spectacular profits draws in gullible novice share buyers in great numbers.

▶ Fund managers and professional investors try to replicate high level of gains by taking bigger and bigger risks.

Speculative bubbles form easily and collapse with equal ease. 'Any serious shock to confidence can cause sales by those speculators who have always hoped to get out before the final collapse but after all possible gains from rising prices have been reaped,' wrote Galbraith. 'Their pessimism will infect those simpler souls who had thought the market might go up forever but who now change their minds and sell. Soon there will be margin calls, and still others will be forced to sell. So the bubble breaks.'[5]

Identifying crashes and panics

At this point a market crash is highly likely. It may not be a dramatic one-day price fall but it will almost certainly involve a sharp marking down of share prices over a period of time. What then is a stock market panic? In some ways it is like an elephant – easy to see but hard to describe. A definition might be found by applying a degree of statistical precision. Daily market movements of between 0 and 3 per cent rarely cause alarm, although in most markets movements are typically at the lower end of this scale rather than at the higher end. When daily movements gain momentum, causing share price falls exceeding 3–4 per cent, they can usually be taken as a sign of panic. More serious panics are generally denoted by price falls exceeding 5 per cent. The crisis of 2008 distinguished itself by registering daily share price movements exceeding 5 per cent far more frequently than in other crises. There are always aberrations in market trading and it is possible that a large one-day movement will not be a result of panic (particularly on the exchanges of more volatile emerging markets) and will soon pass. Even if these falls are not followed by subsequent declines they can still be viewed as panicky moments.

Most of the small panics, triggered by political events rather than economic or financial reasons, tend to be short lived, although they seem ominous at the time. For example Wall Street fell 6.62 per cent on 26 September 1955 when news of President Eisenhower's heart attack caused alarm and on 29 October 1987 the same market, already jittery, was unnerved by an Iranian attack on a Kuwaiti oil terminal, causing prices to fall by 3.92 per cent. However, like the President's heart attack, which changed nothing in terms of the economy, the Iranian attack did not presage the start of a war in the Middle East.

Panics of this and other kinds are discussed in the following chapter, where an attempt is made to classify panic types. For the time being, though, let's focus on panics of a more substantial nature and identify the elements that tend to bring them about. There is a large amount of literature on the causes of booms and crashes. It seems that the salient points can be boiled down in the following way:

Causes of crashes and panics

▶ First signs of doubt over rising markets emerge.
▶ News arrives to cast doubt on profit potential of the fads etc. which fuelled the investment boom.
▶ Corporate failures start to emerge.
▶ Prices start falling.
▶ Pressure builds on margin traders and other leveraged share buyers as banks call in loans, forcing more selling pressure.
▶ Market looks for leadership from government, gurus or anyone who can suggest what participants should do; this is rarely forthcoming, so prices fall further.
▶ News of scandals and scams comes to the fore, causing even more jitters.
▶ Negative news about the economy, corporate profits etc. multiplies.
▶ Panic sets in and feeds on itself, causing a rapid plunge in prices.

This pattern of events is repeated with monotonous regularity, sometimes one or two elements are missing but usually they are all in place. A fuller discussion of this matter is to be found in Chapter 4.

Particularly striking, almost to the point of being hard to believe, is the almost identical movement of share prices in the years leading up to and following the biggest market crashes of all time – the 1929, 1987 and 2008 crashes. As Mark Twain said, history does not repeat itself but, sometimes, it rhymes.

Figure 2.2 was produced by Gary Santoni and Gerald Dwyer, who point out that 'both bull markets began about the second quarter of the year, each lasted 21 quarters, each hit its peak in the third quarter with the timing of the peaks separated by only a few days. Fifty-four days elapsed before the peak and the crash; and each crash slashed more than 20 per cent from the stock market averages.'[6] The similarities stretch coincidence rather too far for comfort.

Figure 2.2 **Markets rhyme in 1929 and 1987**

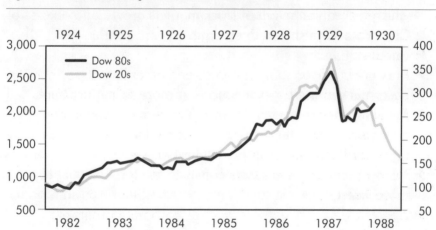

Source: Gary Santoni and Gerald Dwyer, 'Bubbles or Fundamentals: New Evidence from the Great Bull Markets'.

Telling signs

Because there is a certain consistency in the boom and bust cycle it is also possible to identify a number of typical telltale signs which help to forecast the imminence of coming disaster. Among the more typical indicators which should be alerting investors are:

▶ high levels of corporate debt,
▶ high interest rates,
▶ sharp rises in bank lending,
▶ heady price–earnings ratios,
▶ sharp increases in merger and acquisition activity,
▶ big rush of new stock issues,
▶ stock price news is elevated from the depths of the business
  pages to the front of newspapers and newscasts,
▶ too much talk of new eras or new paradigms,
▶ stockbroking firms and investment banks go on recruitment
  sprees,
▶ conspicuous spending and lavish behaviour by financial
  institutions,
▶ the gross capitalisation of stock markets grows far in excess of
  the gross domestic product of the countries within which they
  are located.

These matters will be examined in greater detail in Chapters 4
and 5, but for the time being it is sufficient to observe that there is no
excuse for suggesting that crashes are some kind of force of nature
lacking in predictability. The predictability does not mean that it is
possible to pinpoint when a crash will occur, but it should be possible to forecast the likely conditions indicating that a crash is on the
way.

Learning from history

Although history has a remarkable record of repeating itself in stock
markets it is reasonable to ask who learns from history. Charles
Kindleberger's classic study of financial crises, *Manias, Panics and
Crashes,* quotes a marvellous comment on the fate of the firm Overend, Gurney, which collapsed during the Black Friday crash of May
1866. The company was said to consist of 'salient nincompoops'.
Talking of their losses, Walter Bagehot said they 'were made in a

manner so reckless and so foolish that one would think a child who lent money in the City of London would have lent better'.[7]

Were it the case that salient nincompoops disappeared from the financial scene after the nineteenth century we might be able to laugh more freely at the idea of big financial institutions being run by people so easily caught up in a share-buying frenzy. However, scarcely a new market boom has passed without scandals, spectacular stupidity and a solid determination to learn nothing from history. Some more recent events underline the need for historical perspective.

After the 9/11 terrorist attack on America in 2001, the market reopened on 17 September and trading soared to a new record with 2.37 billion shares changing hands. The Dow registered a 684.8 point fall, a decline of 7.13 per cent. Despite all the fuss this represented no more than the fourteenth biggest single-day decline on Wall Street in percentage terms.

In 2001 investors had before them all the information they required about what happens in situations like this yet, and despite official exhortations not to give the terrorists the pleasure of seeing prices fall, sell orders piled up as the starting bell was struck. The usual suspects were wheeled out to warn of worse to come. True, other voices suggested that selling was not wise at this time. Only a few were brave enough to suggest aggressive buying, a strategy that would have yielded quick and profitable results.

The so-called cautious investment advisers recommended a focus on defensive stocks. Those who followed this advice should note that in the two months it took for the DJIA to register a 10 per cent gain from the fall on 17 September, the utilities index, traditionally the bastion of defensive stocks, had suffered a 12 per cent decline. (Chapter 8 contains a fuller discussion of defensive strategies in the face of panics.)

The panic seizing American investors, which quickly rippled around the world, seemed to demonstrate that past experience had taught them little. However, there does seem to be evidence that something was learned from history following the 1987 crash. In the United States and among central banks elsewhere there was a realisation that the crash would be a lot worse if 1929 was repeated and liquidity dried up. Therefore the central banks deliberately set out to increase money supply, a move widely credited for making the fallout far less damaging than it would otherwise have been. If this is so, it shows that central bankers, if not others, are learning about how to deal with panics once they have taken hold but it remains an open question as to whether any lessons are being learned about preventing the onset of panics in the first place.

It is hard to imagine that future panics will be that much different from those we have seen in the past. If there was the smallest indication that investors are learning more from history, it would be tempting to be more qualified in this assertion, but such evidence is hard to come by. History is never a definitive guide to the future, but it is ignored only by the foolhardy.

In May 1932, after Wall Street stocks had seen 85 per cent wiped off their value from the high point reached in 1929, the stockbroker Dean Witter issued the following note to clients: 'There are only two premises which are tenable as the future. Either we are going to have chaos or else recovery. The former theory is foolish. If chaos ensues nothing will maintain value; neither bonds nor stocks nor bank deposits nor gold will remain valuable.' Dean Witter was confident that recovery would come and stated 'emphatically that in a few years present prices will appear as ridiculously low as 1929 values appear fantastically high'.[8] The broker was fundamentally right but a little misleading on the matter of time scale.

Time matters a lot in markets because as a group investors seem to be rather impatient. They want results and they want them yesterday. However, markets need time to sort themselves out.

Sometimes the tables are turned and investors are overinfluenced by history, assuming that what has happened before will replicate itself. This is almost as dangerous as learning nothing from history because, although markets exhibit both cyclical and repetitive behaviour, they do not always do so in exactly the same way. History should be used as a general guide, not a detailed road map.

Professionalism, Oscar Wilde and the conducting of orchestras

It might be thought that the increasing 'professionalisation' of the stock market would produce a more rational market. Fifty years ago individuals owned over 90 per cent of shares on Wall Street. Today they directly own less than half and this represents a recovery from much lower levels of individual ownership in the 1970s and 80s. Chapter 5 examines the question of whether the concentration of share buying power by big institutional investors is making the market a more or less rational place. In summary, the conclusion seems to be that what might be called the growing institutionalisation of the market is not to be equated with growing rationality. There is no evidence that institutions are less panicky than individuals. On the contrary, most evidence points to the fact that at times of crisis institutions and individuals behave in much the same way.

If this is so it brings us back to the idea that, despite the different routes through which investment decisions are taken, they keep manifesting a tendency to be irrational, especially at times when the market comes under pressure.

Besides being prone to panic, the Achilles heel of all stock markets is temptation. Like Oscar Wilde, investors seem to be able to resist everything else. If temptation were removed from the equation markets would be considerably less volatile, bubbles and panics would be rarities and fundamentals would rule the day. However, stock markets are a heady mixture of places to raise capital, centres of sophisticated financial manipulation, homes for the investment of hard-earned money and casino-like organisations. This is why it is unrealistic to endow markets with a blind belief that they are perfect instruments for the rational conduct of business. Equally, it is wrong to see them as wild, unpredictable places where fortunes are made and lost. They are a mixture of both. Stock markets contain many different elements and play host to participants with vastly differing and often conflicting motives. For this reason they cannot fail to be exciting, nor can they fail to be places of great opportunity for those able to find their way through the conflicting interests and understand how these markets really work. Once such understanding is achieved, investors can proceed to make money from stocks.

This usually means that the smart investor needs to be doing what the rest of the crowd has decided not to do. Another way of looking at this idea was rather more graphically put to me on a visit to the trading room of Deutsche Securities Asia, in Hong Kong. One of the traders, Simon Sadler, said, 'If you want to conduct the orchestra, you must turn your back to the crowd.'

3

Types of panics

O NE OF THE BEST ways of understanding stock market panics is to devise a method of classifying them. Once the nature of panics is better understood, the means of averting damage or gaining advantage are easier to find. This chapter outlines four main categories of panics which serve not only to classify panics that have occurred but can be used as a model to help understand new panics as they emerge.

The purpose of this categorisation is to identify the main characteristic of a panic; however, most panics are not of a single type and so there is considerable overlap between the categories.

The four categories are:

▶ *Phoney panics* – panics caused by events that have nothing to do with the intrinsic operation of stock markets or the performance of the companies which underlie them.
▶ *Self-induced or end-of-cycle panics* – these panics could also be described as bubble-bursting panics.
▶ *Contagious panics* – all panics are contagious to some extent, but this type of panic is driven by the contagion itself rather than by the incident or cause which provoked it in the first place.
▶ *Real panics* – these panics are triggered by real events such as economic recession or sharply falling corporate profitability that give investors sound reasons for concern.

Phoney panics

Let us start with the least logical form of panic because panics of this kind are most easily described and most easy to deal with. It is well known that stock markets are filled with edgy people who tend to overreact to new pieces of information; they also overreact to information that really has nothing to do with the fundamentals of investment.

A phoney panic is almost always short lived and is provoked by an ill-judged response to some piece of news that is most unlikely to have any impact on corporate performance. There are many examples of this kind of panic; one of my favourites is the 9.9 per cent fall on Wall Street back in October 1957 when Americans learned that the Soviet Union had beaten them into space with the launch of the Sputnik rocket. Certainly this event was damaging for American morale and also a stark reminder of the weakness of US intelligence that had no idea of the advanced state of the Soviet space programme. However, the launch of Sputnik was hardly likely to make General Motors produce fewer automobiles or reduce the sales of Coca-Cola. As ever, it did not take long for even the dimmest investor to grasp this simple notion and so the sharp lowering of prices was soon reversed.

Tragedy is no cause for levity, but the stock market sometimes seems determined to turn tragic events into farce. It does so by ludicrous reaction to tragic events which have nothing to do with the business of business. When a German U-boat sank the Lusitania, a Cunard passenger liner, in 1915, New York shares fell by 4.54 per cent. There was some logic in investors marking down shipping company shares but this was not what happened; there was a sharp fall in the share prices of all manner of companies with absolutely no connection to the shipping industry.

Equally illogical, but on the other side of the equation, was the sharp rise in stock prices that greeted news of the American air strikes on Iraq during Operation Desert Storm in January 1991. The day after the air strikes began Wall Street rallied by 4.6 per cent and within ten days was up just over 8 per cent. No doubt Americans, including those who move stock markets, felt good about giving Iraqi President Saddam Hussein a kick in the teeth, but there was no logical reason why a strike on Baghdad should lead to increased corporate profits. As it happened, however, this boost to share prices came during a period when profits were rising, but that had absolutely nothing to do with Iraq.

If the market's response to the bombing of Iraq could be considered as illogical, consider an even more obtuse reaction to the October 1983 US invasion of the West Indian island of Grenada (population 101,000). Wall Street fell 2.7 per cent. Unlike the government in Baghdad, the administration of this tiny Caribbean state quickly succumbed to the will of the Americans and, from the point of view of Washington, the alleged Marxist threat was quickly dealt with. In other words, the invasion could be described as a success. Whether this was the case or not, it is hard to see why investors should have paid it the slightest heed.

The assassination of President Kennedy in November 1963 produced an immediate knee-jerk reaction as the nation was immersed in a state of shock. Wall Street prices tumbled by almost 3 per cent on the news but recovered 4.5 per cent the following day and were up by over 7 per cent after three weeks. This makes the Kennedy assassination one of the shortest panics on record and rightly so, because the death of the President did little to change economic policy and had no impact on corporate activity.

President Eisenhower neither was assassinated nor died in office, but in September 1955 he suffered a heart attack which provoked a much sharper fall on Wall Street than the death of President Kennedy. This is so even though the Kennedy assassination made a far greater impact on the American national psyche. Shares on Wall

Street fell 6.5 per cent on concern about the heart attack, but prices recovered with far greater speed than the health of the President, even though the market was going through a period of doldrums at the time.

American investors also reacted with unease to Britain's tiny little war in the Falkland Islands in April–May 1982, when prices fell by 2.9 per cent. Even in retrospect it is very hard to see how this could have had the smallest effect on the value of American shares, or British shares for that matter, but if this war had somehow escalated the repercussions in Britain could have been more serious.

Over on the other side of the world, the invasion of South Korea by the North in 1950 triggered an immediate 5 per cent fall in share prices and a subsequent 12 per cent fall within a month. This was a major event marking the warming of the Cold War, which commanded considerable media attention and was a source of genuine concern to Americans. However, Korea is a distant land and all but the most alarmist observers realised that it was a confrontation most likely to be confined to Asia. As this reality sunk in investors regained confidence. Within three months Wall Street had registered a gain of almost 20 per cent.

The response to the Japanese attack on Pearl Harbor is more complex. Wall Street shares lost 6.5 per cent in value in the two days that followed the attack but stocks were up 4 per cent within three weeks. We now know that the attack provoked America's entry into World War II and therefore provided grounds for investor concern. However, on a purely economic level, the outbreak of hostilities was a godsend; an event that finally broke the grip of recession which had lasted for over a decade. Although it has been claimed that President Roosevelt's New Deal policies ended the 1930s recession, they had far less impact than the outbreak of hostilities with Japan and Germany. By the end of the war the American economy had doubled in size and corporate profits were two and a half times higher than in 1929. Yet it took almost a decade following the end of the war for share prices to regain the levels achieved in the post-1929 crash period. Logically shares should have risen to reflect the economic stimulus likely to be produced by war. This happened for a short while, but justified fears of war also led to a subsequent fall in prices.

The cases cited above are picked from a clutch of examples of illogical stock market responses to events that could not possibly affect the fundamental value of companies or were likely to do so in a way contrary to the manner in which the market was moving. Other cases are not quite so clear cut. A classic example here is the response to the 9/11 terrorist attacks on the United States in 2001. Not only did the terrorists strike at the heart of the US administration by hitting the Pentagon but they also literally destroyed a part of New York's financial heartland by demolishing the twin towers of the World Trade Center. It is hard to imagine circumstances in which there would be a more traumatic impact on the people who work in the world's biggest financial market. Moreover, the attacks destroyed vital parts of the infrastructure which supported the operation of this market. That is why the New York Stock Exchange had to close for six days in order to ensure that all the systems were functioning when the market reopened. As we have seen, as soon as the starting bell was struck share prices began to plummet and the market ended over 7 per cent down on the day. Markets across the world mirrored the fall on Wall Street which, in terms of logic, is even harder to understand because they did not suffer any of the damage seen in New York.

This sharp fall was followed by a very rapid rebound, suggesting that a lot of the selling pressure was generated by sentiment, but it was also a consequence of a bearish mood which began building well before the attacks and is more accurately associated with an end-of-cycle panic. In this instance it was the cycle of dotcom madness that was coming to an end. The combination of a growing mood of unease about inflated share valuations and the trauma of the terrorist attacks cannot be lightly dismissed as illogical, but it can be said with confidence that it led to greater volatility. Ironically, it could also be argued that infusing the more irrational elements of the response (the terrorist effect) with more rational concerns about overblown valuations of hi-tech stocks succeeded in actually slowing the decline of the bear market. This is because, as the overreaction to the terrorist attack became clear, investors who might otherwise have decided to sell came back into the market and bought heavily. The fact that the response to the attack was so short lived may even indicate that investors are starting to learn something from history. However, excessive optimism about learning should be guarded because we cannot ignore the fact that there was overreaction both in the share price slump and in the very quick recovery of prices.

In a famous piece of research David Cutler, James Poterba and Lawrence Summers (one of America's most cerebral Treasury Secretaries, who became President of Harvard) examined non-economic events that have moved the American stock market in the period between 1941 and 1987. They found that, taken on average, the impact of the forty-nine crises they surveyed was to effect a 1.46 per cent change on the Standard & Poor's 500 Index on the day following news of the outbreak of the crisis. This compares with an average daily movement of 0.56 per cent for the period.[1]

One problem here is identifying whether a piece of news was the actual cause of the panic or coincidental with it. For example in this study the authors note that Wall Street registered a 3.67 per cent fall on 18 November 1974 because of an announcement of an increase in the unemployment rate, a delay in gaining approval for a new coal contract and fears of a new Middle East war. The latter fear was clearly misplaced, the other circumstances were matters of fact; however, whether all or any of these factors were the real cause of this sharp downward movement in prices (the thirty-fourth biggest fall in the period under review) is open to question.

The authors argue that non-economic events do not add that much to the volatility of stock markets, certainly not as much as may be suggested by the amount of media coverage they receive. In any event the volatility is short lived and the impact on share prices ephemeral. But even though the impact is no more than transitory it is reasonable to ask why, after all the experience of phoney panics, it happens at all.

The people who shape stock prices are perpetually hungry for new information. There is much debate in academic circles about the kind of information that moves markets and whether a lack of information or a surplus of conflicting information plays an important role in determining prices. It is easy to avoid the temptation of joining this debate because what passes for empirical evidence is far from conclusive. Nevertheless, what is clear is that new information, whether or not it is relevant to the intrinsic value of shares, has the effect of moving share prices.

I first became vividly aware of this when working on the business section of a Sunday newspaper in London. We were forever being given all sorts of titbits by public relations people and others who were anxious for publication on a Sunday rather than a weekday. The reason for this was that they knew that when the market opened on Monday morning market makers would be desperate for some kind of news to stimulate trading. Much of the information we were given was dubious but, had it appeared, was very likely to influence prices at a time when there was no other information in circulation. The movement in share prices might well have been short lived but this is not the important point. What matters is that movement occurred, and as long as that happens someone can make money.

The business of market makers is to trade shares. The option of doing nothing is rarely perceived as viable. However, action needs to be prompted by reason to act, and new information is always a good reason. So the fact that share prices can be moved by, for example, a big news event which has no real connection with the value of shares, is no surprise. Markets and market players crave action, they get restive when things are quiet and so they will take action on all sorts of pretexts.

All experience points to the simple fact that panics triggered by events that have no relationship with the fundamental value of shares quickly fizzle out. You might expect that they should not arise in the first place because investors would simply shrug off these irrelevant pieces of news, but this is not how stock markets work. The only sure-fire consequence of major non-economic events is to create wonderful opportunities for investing in shares because any market decline that results from this kind of news is almost certain to be reversed in the very near future. In other words, phoney panics are great 'buy' signals.

Self-induced or end-of-cycle panics

In a sense all stock market panics are self-induced inasmuch as they feed on themselves and become self-perpetuating until good sense sets in. Self-induced panics are classed here with end-of-cycle panics because these panics are most likely to arise out of the very operation of the market itself when it comes to the end of a cycle. This is different from panics created by external circumstances that are reflected by the market. In other words, it is overenthusiasm followed by the excessive pessimism of markets that provokes a panic. The fact that the enthusiasm may well be for an industry or an idea that is of lasting value matters little because the market is destroying its utility by betting too heavily on its success and gambling with equal fervour on its downside. Yet the idea or product may well survive the excesses of market response to it. Thus it can be said with confidence that the end of the dotcom boom does not mean the end of the Internet. On the contrary, use of the Internet will accelerate but many of the companies that were seen as likely to gain most from this growth have already disappeared or will do so soon. Some deserve to go but others, with sound ideas, became hapless victims of market excess. The end-of-cycle panics are brutal, often sweeping away some of the good with the bad. Because bubble bursts cause market crashes they tend to be rather indiscriminate in their effect.

The word 'bubble' has taken on something of a pejorative meaning in the context of stock market analysis. It carries suggestions of irrationality and recklessness. However, in most instances there has been a rational basis for the creation of enthusiasm for certain classes of investment.

Perhaps the most famous example of excessive enthusiasm comes from a period that predates stock markets but directly relates to the operation of what these days would be called a commodity market. This famous bubble was the period of Dutch tulip mania, which spanned 1634 to 1637. It might, however, be more accurate to describe this as an early form of a futures market mania because what really pushed up tulip prices was speculation on individual bulbs before they started flowering. There was also spot trading on the flowers once they had bloomed, but trading in flowers as opposed to bulbs was responsible for fewer of the heady price rises. At its height the tulip mania resulted in individual bulbs being sold for sums in excess of $50,000 in current-day prices.

The tulip frenzy is widely cited as a prime example of irrational markets running away with themselves. However, Peter Garber has presented a compelling case for suggesting that there were market fundamentals which justified the rapid growth of the tulip market but that they became distorted by market players.[2] The rational element of the tulip market was contained in the laws of supply and demand. Rare and beautiful tulips were much treasured and in short supply. Therefore it made sense to try and secure the rights to buy certain types of tulip bulbs before they flowered, as there was certain to be a market for them once they were in bloom. However, the speculation soon became an end in itself as futures contracts changed hands with a vengeance and profits were made by exchanging contracts rather than by taking possession of the underlying asset they represented. In this case it would have meant taking delivery of tulips. That the mania came to an abrupt end in February 1637 was no surprise. Like all bubbles, the trick of this bubble was to have got out of the market before it burst.

Equally famous, or possibly equally notorious, was the South Sea Bubble that collapsed in October 1720. It is mainly remembered as a giant piece of swindling but Larry Neal has suggested that this is a distorted way of viewing this event. He sees it as being 'less a tale about the perpetual folly of mankind and more one about financial markets' difficulties in adjusting to an array of innovations'.[3]

The South Sea Company was founded in London by George Caswall and John Blunt, both ex-stockbrokers with experience of various aspects of financial markets. They presented a plan to the British government which involved turning £9.47 million of short-term war debts into equity, funded by a new joint stock company. In return the company would gain profits from obtaining a monopoly on trade with the Spanish Empire and, rather surprisingly, an annual payment in perpetuity of £576,534 from the government. The terms of this arrangement appear from a distance to be surprisingly advantageous to the new company and must have appeared so to the investors who rushed to subscribe for South Sea shares. In the space of just six months after the company's flotation the share price increased almost tenfold.

If ever there were a sure-fire way of getting rich, this was it. As Viscount Erleigh observed in his contemporary account of the affair: 'Statesmen forgot their Politics, Lawyers the Bar, Tradesmen their Shops, Debtors of Quality their Creditors, Divines the Pulpit, and even Women themselves, their Pride and Vanity!' The madness quickly spread as a host of companies in both Britain and continental Europe shot up and attracted funds on the basis of all manner of dubious schemes, such as one for making pirate-proof ships. Further examples of these schemes can be gleaned by examining a list of companies deemed to be 'public nuisances' that were banned in June 1720. Among them are companies promising to extract silver from lead, companies dedicated to improving the art of making soap and schemes for the transmutation of quicksilver (mercury) into a malleable fine metal.

The rise and fall of dubious companies might fit more neatly into the category of contagious panics that will be discussed next. However, as already stated, these categories are not mutually exclusive. There are elements of each type lurking in every niche. Bubbles, of course, are contagious but the element which distinguishes self-induced panics is that they are rooted in the very structure of stock markets.

This is not to say that the structure is basically unsound, merely vulnerable to erratic behaviour. Nor can it be said that a bubble cannot emerge from a perfectly rational set of economic circumstances. This was so in the case of the South Sea Bubble, which presented an idea attractive to investors and was appealing to a British government faced with a sharply increased debt problem arising from the costs of the War of Spanish Succession (1702–13). The government had good reason to favour a scheme under which debt would be transferred into equity and over £9 million could be wiped off government borrowings. The scheme appeared to be feasible because it followed a successful government debt elimination scheme involving the New East India Company just twelve years before Caswall and Blunt proposed their idea. The problem was not the scheme but the purposes for which the directors of the new company used the funds which flowed into their coffers. In the end the South Sea Company had to be rescued by the Bank of England, but not before investors lost a great deal of money. The interest in this event for our current purpose is simply to provide an example of a logical scheme that attracted enthusiastic investor support. This in turn led to a dizzying rise in the share price. The purpose of the scheme was eventually lost in the frenzy of speculation as investors gambled on the ability of the South Sea Company's directors to maintain the share price as an end in itself. When the company collapsed it swept along with it all the other dubious schemes hatched in the bubble it created.

Travelling down the history of stock markets we keep encountering variants of this phenomenon. The mania for railway shares in the 1840s, the 1920s boom fuelled by new inventions such as television, talking pictures and colour films, all of which have turned out to be cornerstones of the economy, were also responsible for overenthusiasm on stock markets that resulted in crashes. Two of the hottest stocks of the 1920s were General Motors and Radio Corporation of America (RCA). Both crashed during the 1929 melt-down, RCA at one point losing 98 per cent of its value. However, both companies survived the long depression triggered by the 1929 crash and arguably did better when they came to be seen as boring old shares, way out of the mainstream of fashionable investments.

Moving closer to the end of the twentieth century we have wit-nessed yet another classic boom and crash with the end of dotcom and Internet frenzy. It was this boom that fuelled the biggest and most consistent stock market growth seen in any decade, which took the Dow up from over 2,000 points in 1990 to almost 12,000 by the end of the 1990s.

Most of the growth came in the second half of the decade when the fortunes of individual companies far outstripped the growth of the DJIA as a whole. The stock of Microsoft Corporation, for ex-ample, rose sixteenfold in the second half of the decade. The Dell Computer Corporation's share price rise was even more spectacular, multiplying by a factor of 93. Intel Corporation, like Microsoft, was seen as having cornered a vital part of the hi-tech market, and saw its shares rise by 1,900 per cent in this same period. Smaller compa-nies, with far less substantial businesses, enjoyed even bigger gains.

They did so because this was a time when vulgar terms such as earnings were shunned in favour of 'concepts'. The companies of tomorrow were said to have great concepts that would generate truly spectacular profits. Henry Blodget of Merrill Lynch, one of Wall Street's star analysts, was riding the crest of a wave in the late 1990s when he endorsed investment in Internet leaders such as Yahoo! Inc.: 'It is a mistake to be too conservative in projecting future per-formance,' he said. Yahoo! at that time was trading at 500 times projected profits for 2000. 'The real "risk" is not losing money ... it is missing major upside.'[4] Blodget became a central figure in an investigation over alleged misleading of investors, which will be discussed later.

When it became clear that these profits were not actually going to arrive any time soon new ways were found of dressing up the meagre profits that were actually being generated. Thus when companies reported they no longer simply detailed their pre- and post-tax profits but instead came up with something called EBITDA, an acronym which stands for earnings before interest, tax, depreciation and amortisation. This was very helpful because these so called 'new economy' companies typically had high levels of gearing, which ate considerably into the bottom line. So by taking interest payments out of the equation it appeared as though profitability was higher. Even more ingenious was the idea of pushing amortisation out of the picture so that these companies could simply write off all the mistaken investments made during the dotcom frenzy.

Despite the heavy mist of fantasy that enveloped stock markets at the time, obscuring real corporate performance, there was reason to invest in the new economy. Clearly, computer-based technology was growing during the 1990s, just as railways were growing in the nineteenth century and just as there was good reason for governments to look for ways of refinancing their debts, as they tried to do in the early part of the eighteenth century.

History truly repeated itself as expectations of the profits to be realised by the hi-tech boom far outstripped the pricing levels that prevailed on the world's stock exchanges. Expectation rose even higher in the second half of the 1990s when the earnings growth of hi-tech companies far outstripped that of all other sectors.

Inevitably the market came to realise that there needed to be a serious downward adjustment of hi-tech stock prices and of all the other companies that had ridden on the tail of the dotcom boom. This was already well in place before the 9/11 attack but, as we have seen, this event both accentuated the downward pressure in the short term and probably slowed down an even more severe reassessment in the longer term.

Every cycle has to end. The trick is to know when this is likely to happen. A dedicated band of analysts known as chartists believe that movements in the market can be broadly determined by looking at individual share prices and volume charts and at charts of the whole market to determine when to buy and sell. In summary, chartists believe that all market trends can be forecast in the light of past stock market movements. Chartists say that you can ignore the motives for movements in the market; in other words, they are not interested whether they are the product of psychology or fundamental matters such as interest rates, what matters is the pattern of past history. Some believe this is the closest you can get to an exact science of market movements but few seriously argue that trigger points on charts are a form of absolute guidance. At best it is probably a good way of identifying trends.

Investors are really left to exercise common sense in deciding when they think a cycle is coming to an end and taking appropriate action. If they have made good money while a bull cycle was in play, they might simply consider that the time to take profits comes while the market is still rising. To do so they need enough will power not to be concerned by the possibility that even more money could have been made by sticking in the market until its very peak.

One certainty is that high levels of increase in markets are always met with high levels of decrease. Everyone knows this, yet every time the downturn comes a large number of investors stare into the falling market like rabbits trapped by the headlights of a car and wonder why they did not move.

Contagious panics

Almost by definition all stock market panics are contagious. The purpose of this category is to talk about types of panics that are primarily the product of contagion; in other words, panics that have occurred in stock markets or in sectors of markets directly as a result of a contagion as opposed to intrinsic reasons relating to events in a single market or an individual market sector. Contagious panics spread from market to market, sweeping up the good with the bad.

Most major stock market panics contain an element of contagion which accounts for the speed with which they take hold and spread. This is certainly true of the three biggest stock market panics in history, the 1929, 1987 and 2008 panics, which spread like wildfire affecting markets throughout the world.

Although the 1987 panic is commonly seen as a panic essentially emanating in the United States and then spreading to the rest of the world, there is an important sense in which this panic was a product of contagion from Japan spreading to the United States. Most observers attribute little importance to this factor but not George Soros, the famous hedge fund manager. He points out that the collapse of the Japanese bond market led to a minor rally in the Japanese stock market in October 1987, as investors moved from bonds to stocks in an attempt to recoup their losses. This accentuated the disparity between bond and stock prices. In addition there was a considerable outflow of Japanese money from the New York market putting further pressure on American stock prices.

While other markets went into free fall the Japanese market dipped for just one day and then just to the level of one-day falls allowed by law in Japan. The following day Tokyo started recovering, mainly because of government pressure on big corporations urging them to buy. Writing in 1987 Soros concluded that the crash marked 'the transfer of economic and financial power from the United States to Japan'.[5] It may have looked that way to Soros, writing as the great Japanese boom was underway, but subsequent events have shown that Japanese world domination is as much an illusion as the currently popular idea that America will dominate the world for ever. Nevertheless, the point he makes about how events in Japan had a direct impact on America and then on the rest of the world provides an interesting perspective on the impact of contagion in the 1987 crisis. It is both interesting and unusual because nowadays it is usually the American market that sets the agenda for other markets and it is events on Wall Street that trigger a line of contagion overseas. Indeed, it is no exaggeration to say that other world markets spend most of their time following Wall Street.

The British market has followed movements on Wall Street very closely. This was most noticeable in 2001 when the sharp decline on Wall Street, following the 9/11 attack, was exactly mirrored in Europe.

However, the previously very close relationship between the Asian and US markets has been broken by the decade-long stock market recession in Japan and the onset of the Asian financial crisis in 1997. This caused Hong Kong's stock market to become far more erratic, although at times of great pressure, such as the 9/11 attack, Hong Kong dutifully mirrored events on Wall Street. The Japanese market was far too bombed-out in 2001 to register much of a response, although it did indeed dip along with the rest of the world. Generally, however, the Japanese market stands out by resolutely remaining flat for almost two decades from the late 1980s though it fell back in line just before the crash of 2008. This issue is revisited in Chapter 8, when we look at a longer-term comparison of how markets have moved in tandem and the implications of this for portfolio diversification. The purpose here is to stress that most contagion emanates from Wall Street.

Such is the power of Wall Street that it is almost always the leader in global stock market movements. However, there have been moments, always short lived, when this has not been so. A rare break in the upward spiral of the Dow occurred in 1998 when the Asian financial crisis was at its height and a particularly sharp fall on Hong Kong's Hang Seng Index triggered a downward movement on the DJIA. Hong Kong, which has a currency tied to a fixed link with the

US dollar, is generally particularly sensitive to movements on Wall Street. It was therefore highly unusual to see the tail wagging the dog in 1998.

Whereas good news on Wall Street can raise share prices throughout the world, it is rare indeed for good news in other markets to be reflected by a surge in New York prices. Even big exchanges such as London have only a minimal influence on Wall Street when they are affected by an outbreak of good news. The opposite is more likely: really bad news overseas can cause a tremor on Wall Street, but it is unlikely to be more than a tremor. Conversely, a panic on Wall Street is almost certain to be quickly reflected in other markets, even when the fundamentals of those markets are far more sound than those of Wall Street. The panic of September 2001 is a good illustration of this point because European markets were not nearly as overvalued as Wall Street and projected corporate profitability was holding up far better. Yet European markets tumbled alongside America's and recovered at more or less the same rate.

The reason why stock markets tend to move in tandem is well known and comes under the heading of globalisation. Stock market funds are becoming increasingly international and the allocation of funds therefore often involves plucking money out of one market to put in another. Not only is it technically easier to move funds from one market to another but ready access to information about markets overseas facilitates quick responses to developments wherever they take place. However, we should not get carried away here because cross-market contagion has been a feature of stock markets more or less since their creation. The 1846 potato blight and failure of the wheat crop in Europe, for example, led to the 1848 crash that quickly affected markets across Europe and spread to the United States, where speculation in railway stocks was running out of control. When the Crimean War ended in 1856 this too sparked a Europe-wide stock market panic, triggered again by the collapse of railway stocks. In 1890 the London stock market suffered an outbreak of panic because of the collapse of speculative activity in South America, principally Argentina.

Throughout the 1950s and 1960s markets tumbled in succession as a consequence of sharp currency declines while in the mid-1970s, following the sharp rise in oil prices engineered by OPEC and the collapse of the Bretton Woods currency agreement, markets plunged almost in unison. They fed each other's concern over further price falls, as well as real concerns over the impact of rising fuel prices on economic growth.

Yet again, it worth stressing that these market panics were not fundamentally caused by contagion alone but fuelled by the effect of one market responding to the other. Nowadays some people talk loosely about how globalisation impacts on more or less all economic developments. What is really meant by this is that rich countries and powerful corporations are increasingly responsible for determining the fate of the less powerful. In essence this is true, but for our present purposes caution needs to be exercised in the context of stock markets because it is unrealistic to paint a picture of a small cabal of fund managers sitting in New York or London manipulating world markets. The most prominent proponent of this viewpoint is Mahathir Mohamad, the former Prime Minister of Malaysia, who blamed the 1990s Asian financial crisis on shadowy figures in the West. 'There may be no conspiracy as such,' he told a World Bank seminar in 1997, 'but it is quite obvious that a few at least, media, as well as fund managers, have their own agenda, which they are determined to carry out.'[6] The irony is that a study of the Malaysian market during the Asian crisis found that foreign hedge funds, widely blamed for triggering the crisis, barely changed their portfolios before its outset and therefore had a neutral impact on the outflow of funds.[7] Moreover, World Bank figures for the region as a whole show that during the Asian crisis period domestically generated fund out-flows played a far bigger role in bringing down Asian currencies and decimating Asian markets than the activities of foreign players.[8]

A similar conclusion applies to the 1994–5 Mexican crisis which, like the Asian crisis, was widely blamed on foreign capital flight. However, a study by the International Monetary Fund found that the biggest flight of capital came from within Mexico itself.[9]

The experience of the Asian and Mexican crises demonstrates that it really is not so simple to point to globalisation as the source of all evil and all contagion, particularly in emerging markets, which tend to be more vulnerable to panics. There are practical reasons why this is so. Most fund managers cannot in fact shift funds so easily from one continent to another, not least because the charter governing their funds tends to limit their geographic scope. Secondly, most of the biggest funds remain concentrated in the biggest markets. Smaller markets simply lack the liquidity and depth to accommodate the requirements of large institutional fund managers. This explains why contagion is more prevalent within smaller geographical areas than on a worldwide scale because the big institutional players tend to move funds within defined areas rather than on a truly global basis. However, there are far fewer restraints on funds moving from smaller markets to bigger markets, which explains why Wall Street often shows strength at precisely the times when other markets are in trouble. The American market has become a sort of safe haven; anyway, this is how it is often perceived.

This leaves contagion to take its toll in smaller areas. In this sense the Asian financial crisis was a classic example of this phenomenon. When the Thai government decided to devalue its currency on 2 July 1997 it set in train a house-of-cards-type collapse which spread throughout South East Asia. Among the markets that collapsed were those of Singapore and Hong Kong, which were fundamentally much stronger than the markets of Thailand itself and places like Indonesia and Malaysia. Before the collapse all these markets had been growing at a heady pace and were achieving price levels that would be hard to sustain. Despite this, there was no objective justification for them all to collapse with the force that gathered as the Asian financial crisis reached its apex in 1998.

The fate of Asian markets was hardly new. Just three years previously Latin American markets suffered a domino collapse as a result of a crisis in Mexico which led investors to believe that all South American markets were vulnerable, a view that turned into a self-fulfilling prophecy.

What we are really talking about is the bad-neighbourhood effect. It matters little if you build a fine house in a bad neighbourhood; its value will still be depressed by the prices that prevail in the area. The same applies to good neighbourhoods and stock markets located in areas considered as hot for investment. This is why during the go-go years of the late 1980s and early 1990s shares listed on Asian stock exchanges did very well, almost regardless of quality. When they lost their lustre, the good was swept up with the bad.

Sometimes contagion occurs on an industry-wide rather than geographical basis. A bank failure, for example, quickly casts a shadow over other bank stocks, good or bad. This is despite the fact that the failure of one bank is good news for other banks that take over its customers. Industry-wide or sector-wide contagion is not always illogical but almost always exaggerated. Thus when investors marked down shares in the travel industry following the 9/11 attacks that involved the hijacking and blowing up of aircraft, they were reflecting the logical view that people would be far less likely to travel by air in the aftermath of this event. However, a major result of the attack was to promote consolidation in the airline industry, which has ultimately produced stronger companies. The wise and calm investor would have sought out the companies most likely to survive and bought their stocks at bargain prices.

The calm investor would follow exactly the same tactics in the face of a regional meltdown, probably focusing buying activity on blue chips most likely to emerge from the carnage as a number of competitors were knocked out of contention.

Real panics

The well-worn joke about paranoia goes on the lines of 'just because you are paranoid does not mean that everyone is not against you'. This train of thought can readily be applied to real panics – just because everyone else is panicking does not mean that there is no reason to do so. A real panic is a panic rooted in genuine fears over economic growth and thus corporate profitability. If profits really are going to fall because fundamentals have turned sour, investors have good reason to exit the market. Here, again, it is worth stating the relationship of real panics with other types of panic because in practically all panics there is an element of rationality. The bursting of stock market bubbles, for example, provides a good objective reason to get out of the market, but not for failing to get back in when prices are sufficiently low. Objective reasons for concern over stock valuations lie behind most panics, even if the panic itself has created these reasons. Most panics, however, are not based on fundamental concerns over corporate performance, so when these concerns do come to the fore they need to be taken seriously.

What is interesting is the extent to which changes in fundamental conditions have not had an impact on the stock market. For example, the recession of 1923–4 was accompanied by modest rises on Wall Street. The 1920–1 recession caused no more than modest falls, while the 1927 mini recession did absolutely nothing to halt the rise of the market. As we move closer to the present time the same pattern repeats itself. The recession of 1960 had little impact on Wall Street. There were no more than modest falls during the recession of 1981–2. On the other hand, the sharp recession which began in late 1973 and ended at the beginning of 1975 came in the middle of the period when markets worldwide declined between 60–75 per cent.

The decline was particularly sharp in Britain, which suffered its worst bear market from May 1972 to December 1973. During this period share prices declined by 73 per cent but, as elsewhere in the world, the British market slid gradually and in the absence of panic. This is particularly interesting because on one level it shows the stock market reflecting the state of the economy and on another level that it can do so without the extreme kind of reaction which would have sent the market into free fall.

The panic most thoroughly associated with the onset of economic recession is, of course, that of 1929, but history is likely to record many parallels with 2008, the panic more fully discussed in Chapter 1. Some argue that the collapse of the stock market itself triggered the recession. There must be something in this because a sharp decline in wealth as a result of the crash had a rapid effect on consumption and thus enhanced the cycle of depression. (This is examined in greater detail in Chapter 9.) However, this cannot be the whole story. It is certainly not a story believed by those who maintain that the crash was simply a reflection of worsening economic conditions. If this argument is to be sustained its proponents need to explain why the market did not fall sooner. The market collapsed in October but throughout the preceding summer industrial production was falling and other economic conditions were showing clear signs of deterioration.

This situation was exacerbated by the very nature of the speculation which preceded the crash. Funds badly needed for investment in production and the development of services were poured into the stock market, thus depriving the 'real' economy of its lifeblood to ensure continued expansion.

Naturally, when the market crashed it had an even greater impact on the real economy because the supply of credit suddenly froze. Companies were forced to repay loans and there were no funds for financing production. Understandably a traumatic event, such as a stock market collapse, cannot fail to have an impact on the wider economy, but it does not answer the chicken-and-the-egg question. History shows that in general stock markets are not the best reflectors of real economic conditions; if anything, stock market responses to changes in economic conditions come as lagging indicators. There is a discussion in Chapters 5 and 9 about the extent to which markets reflect the state of the real economy. For our current purposes it is enough to note that the most remarkable and prolonged stock market crash, the crash of 1929, was accompanied by many valid fundamental reasons for stock prices to collapse. Not only did it take stock prices a quarter of a century to recover to pre-crash levels but the crash also mirrored the period of the twentieth century's most profound recession. As we have seen, although the stock market spent most of this time in the doldrums, this did not prevent the emergence of periods when investors could make money in the equity markets even though the recession was retaining its tenacious grip.

While the 1929 crash coincided with the longest period of recession in the twentieth century, the crash of September 2001 marked the end of the twentieth century's most sustained period of economic growth. However, as we know, the crash was triggered by the 9/11 terrorist attacks, not by a sudden collapse of confidence in the economy. On the contrary, were that to have happened it should, objectively speaking, have occurred earlier. A report by the National Bureau of Economic Research, produced by some of America's most prominent economists, concluded that the end of the 1990s boom came in March 2001, almost six months before the plunge in the stock market. In March employment in the United States peaked, industrial production had been in decline since September 2000, sales were on a downward trajectory from the beginning of 2001 and all the other signs were showing that the boom was over. However, in the period prior to 9/11 the Dow did not really reflect this downward shift, trading (albeit erratically) in a range between 10,000 and 11,000 points. The hi-tech NASDAQ registered much bigger falls but this was less because of general fears over economic decline and more to do with the bursting of the dotcom bubble. The very rapid recovery on Wall Street following the plunge in September 2001 clearly demonstrated that, despite some dire warnings of recession and reduced profitability, investors were not convinced that the economy was in trouble; those fears came later. It seems reasonable to conclude, therefore, that the panic of 2001 was much more of a phoney panic than a real one even though there were real reasons to be concerned, if not about recession, at least about a severe slowdown in the level of economic growth. That is not to say that the bubble-type conditions still embedded in the post-2001 period will not produce another panic.

In the light of this and other panics, it is hard to find a single example of what might be called a real panic. Certainly it is not possible to draw a general correlation between recession and stock market panics. The biggest single-day stock market decline in history, that of October 1987, took place at a time of economic expansion. Moreover, there is a strong argument for suggesting that stocks were not overpriced at the time of the October crash. It is an argument most strongly made by using a method devised by James Tobin, the American Nobel laureate, who developed one of the most useful ratios for judging the value of stocks. It is known as the 'Q' ratio. Using this ratio the market capitalisation of companies is compared with the replacement costs of a company's fixed and other assets. Prior to the crash share prices stuck tenaciously towards the average trend line of this ratio. In other words, they were fairly valued on the rational basis of comparing prices with the underlying assets they represented.

While markets may well not reflect underlying economic reality, they are heavily influenced by the economic predictions of the very people who make markets. In his seminal work destroying the mysteries of investing Jeremy Siegel shrewdly observes that, when it comes to economic news, 'markets respond to the *difference* between what the participants in financial markets expect to be announced and what is announced'.[10] In other words, even if they have got their predictions spectacularly wrong, it matters not, because these predictions have been factored into what is known as market sentiment and reflected in share prices. When contrary information arises, adjustments are made accordingly. This all takes place within the cocoon of the market's own reality, which is internally generated and continues to feed of itself. Therefore the impact of economic decline or expansion really starts to have an effect on stock markets when information about these trends starts to contradict earlier held views on where the economy is heading. It does not matter whether there have been real shifts in the development of the economy, what matters is the perception of shifts.

If it is hard to find real evidence that economic developments have supplied the cause for panics it is even harder to find evidence of damaging non-economic developments that have caused panics. This is so despite the fact that some non-economic developments which are largely irrelevant to markets have produced sharp responses in them. Changing political conditions can give rise to rapid changes in the economic environment, yet some of the biggest political convulsions have taken place without producing stock market panics. When they have – a case in point being a sharp fall on Wall Street following the fall of France to Nazi Germany in 1940 – they are the exception rather than the rule.

Given the problematic nature of real panics and the fact that it is close to impossible to identify a single panic caused solely by fears which have a direct impact on corporate profitability, it might be more appropriate to conclude that there is no such thing as a 'real' panic. It is more usual to find that real reasons for market pessimism cause a longer term decline in share prices, rather than sudden and sharp price falls. Having said that, the eventuality of real (short-term) panics cannot be ruled out because there are many rational seeds of concern embedded in other forms of panic. And, of course, real panics might well occur in future.

Panics follow the market's own bizarre logic

It is safe to conclude only that most panics reflect the internal logic of the markets in which they occur. Thus it is rational for stock markets to fall when there is a credit squeeze or other measures are taken that reduce the ability of market players to raise the funds needed to play the market. It is equally part of the internal logic of markets for them to respond to specific issues such as changes in the value of the currency in which stocks are denominated. The very mechanisms of market trading may be the cause of panics. The crash of 1987, for example, is widely attributed to computer generated program selling, induced by the then fashionable business of portfolio insurance which triggered buying activity when stock prices were rising and did the reverse when they were falling.

None of this gives much comfort to the supporters of the efficient markets theory which maintains that markets faithfully reflect underlying reality. When markets get overexcited the players pay scant regard to whether share prices reflect the value of the companies they represent. Thus equally little attention is paid to changes in the level of earnings, which, according to efficient markets theory, is supposed to be the trigger for revaluation of share prices.

If the proponents of this argument were right and markets served as the best reflection of economic reality, they would then become a more reliable mirror of the economies they reflect. As matters stand this is not so.

Jeremy Grantham, a partner at the Boston-based firm of contrarian money managers, writes, 'I used to think financial markets were approximately efficient and getting more so. I was touchingly naïve... Today I believe that the markets for all asset classes are gloriously *inefficient*. Far from markets being approximately efficient and getting more so, the market is bloody inefficient and, if anything, getting less efficient every day.'[11]

4

The panic cycle

I T MAY HAVE BEEN less alarmist for this chapter to be called 'business cycles', because the propensity to panic tends to emerge from the great sweep of business cycles. However, not all business cycles produce panics, even though panics emerge in a cyclical fashion. The intention here is both to examine the nature of the cycles and to look at how they are changing, or maybe not changing as much as we imagine. Lastly, there is an attempt to identify the ways in which cycles descend into panic and are exacerbated by fraud and other forms of dubious behaviour.

Everyone knows more or less how the cycle works. Booms are always, always, followed by crashes; indeed, it could be said that crashes and panics are the ugly sisters of booms. Even though we have yet to see a really severe crash that was not preceded by a vigorous bull market, investors can be very determined to ignore the lessons of history. Students of the 1929 crash tend to be familiar with the famous statement by the Yale Professor Irving Fisher, whose dismal record of predictions at the time of the 1920s boom has already been discussed. Just before the crash he wrote, 'stock prices have reached what looks like a permanently high plateau'. In a sense he was right about the long term, but of course he was quite wrong about the short term. It is hard to believe that Fisher did not know enough about markets to realise that there are no examples of vigorous bull markets that have not been followed by a crash. There seems to be something deeply embedded in the psyche of investors that makes them believe that the good times will roll for ever.

History also reveals extraordinary similarity in the naïve beliefs of investors as each new market fad arrives. A vivid example of this can be seen by looking at an extract from *A Short and Sure Guide to Permanent Investments in Railways: A Few Plain Rules*. It was published in 1847, in the midst of the British railway investment boom, but could just as easily describe the dotcom phenomenon of the late 1990s, as my bracketed insertions demonstrate. The pseud-onymous author, 'A Successful Operator', writes:

> *Many were long prejudiced against Railways [The Internet] as an investment, because they regarded them [it] rather as an experimental novelty, than as an established system. They [it] must now, however, be considered as forming, for many generations, the only public means of intercommunication. Every previous mode of conveyance [communication] is giving place to the Engine and Train [Internet]; and the capital which has embarked in this extensive change, offers a security as ample as the most cautious can require ... The shares of lines [dotcom companies] which are not paying any dividend at all, or a very trifling one, may be a good investment in the hands of those who are acquainted with the causes of failure, and who know that there is a probability of their being removed.*[1]

Within three years of these words being written railway shares had lost around 85 per cent of their value, most railway companies had gone out of business and there was a messy period of clean-ing up the financial wreckage. The similarities between the railway boom of the mid-nineteenth century and the dotcom boom of the late twentieth are considerable.

Those who believe in new fads (even those like the railways and the Internet that prove to be enduring) would do well to recall the old adage that what goes up must come down. This law applies as much to stock markets as it does to gravity, though not always so predictably: markets can fall rapidly even when there are objective reasons for them not to do so. For example, as we have seen in the previous chapter, there is a case to be made that shares were fairly valued prior to the crash of 1987. Nevertheless there was nervousness about the rapid climb of share prices and not enough consideration given to whether valuations were reasonable when prices suddenly started to slip. Because serious consideration of this matter was suspended, there was a rush for the exit.

Panics get bigger, more unpredictable

In at least one respect, the nature of panics has changed. In the nineteenth century most stock market panics went hand in hand with banking panics. Although there continues to be a close association between the two, there is no longer an automatic connection. The major crashes of the twentieth century were not triggered by banking crises, although there were elements of banking crisis contained in them, particularly in the case of the 1990s Japanese crash and, of course, the crash of 2008. Stock market panics have become rather less predictable, and thus more dangerous, because they now have a greater variety of causes and affect a far larger part of the economy than in earlier days.

The jury is still out on what might happen to Wall Street following the events of 2008, but the lessons of the twentieth century show clearly that all crashes were preceded by some form of wild speculation, although not necessarily in equities.

The crash of October 1907, which was largely confined to the United States, followed a bout of excitement in the coffee market and a failed attempt to corner the market in the shares of the United

Copper Company. In the spring of 1921 the British and American markets signalled disillusion with the postwar boom that produced a sharp decline in the stock and commodity markets and in the then fashionable business of shipping investment. We know that the 1929 crash followed sharp rises in share prices, but it also followed high levels of land speculation that had come to an end four years previously. In the 1950s and early 1960s, with stock markets still depressed, speculation focused on the currency markets, resulting in a chain of crashes widely dispersed throughout the world and separated by at least a year. The chain began in France in 1958, spread to Canada in 1962, Italy in 1963 and Britain in 1964.

Taken as a whole, the twentieth century saw fewer dramatic market crashes but many more instances where there were significant movements in share prices. An analysis of the US market by Ned Davis Research shows that the period of greatest share turbulence occurred in the 1990s when there were 4,494 days in which the S&P 500 Index recorded gains or losses of over 20 per cent. This is more than double the level of the previous decade and appears to be an all-time record. The expansion of financial markets, especially in the last period of the twentieth century, ensured that sharp price fluctuations delivered higher degrees of damage and, yes, greater rewards for those on the right side of the market movements.

Volatility

Stock market turnover is much higher these days. This is explained mainly by the increasing size of markets and the way that inflation has placed a higher value on companies. In addition, turnover has increased because shares are now traded more actively. On Wall Street in 1960, for example, only 14 per cent of shares changed hands within the year. By 1987 84 per cent of shares were changing hands. There is also evidence of bigger one-day price movements accompanied by a greater level of instability in both long- and short-term interest rates.[2]

All this creates the impression of greater volatility in the market, an impression reinforced by improvements in communications that have made even those not particularly interested in stock markets more aware of the onset of financial crises, which appear to occur with alarming frequency. But this impression is false. The stock market today is no more volatile than it ever was, and financial crises are less frequent now than in the nineteenth century, particularly in the period 1816 to 1866, which saw a crisis per decade.

In *Stocks for the Long Run* Jeremy Siegel states that the greatest period of volatility on Wall Street was in 1932, during the Great Depression. In that year volatility reached over 65 per cent, which was seventeen times higher than in 1964, the least volatile year on record. His research shows that volatility is more pronounced during recessions and market declines than during periods of expansion. In recessions, annual average volatility is about 23 per cent, whereas it is less than 16 per cent in periods of expansion.[3]

The dubious distinction of achieving record levels of volatility in 1932 held good until 2008 when volatility levels soared to a new high, approaching 70 per cent. However, it remains to be seen whether in the first decade of the new millennium this record will end up exceeding the levels of volatility seen throughout the 1930s. Markets calmed down a lot after that time, only to see an upsurge in volatility in the 1970s. Yet, even October 1974, the most volatile month of this period, ranks only 46th in the table of the most volatile months on Wall Street. The 1980s do not figure at all in the volatility record highs despite this being the decade when the biggest ever crash in history occurred in 1987.[4]

Looking for causes of boom-and-bust cycles

The boom-and-bust cycle affects markets as a whole and can be attached to particular types of investment, but all these cycles share some characteristics. Examining these characteristics and identifying the causes of the cycles is the meat of academic research. Let us now look at some of these ideas.

Although everyone knows about cycles, no one has yet produced the golden key which opens the door to pinpointing when they are likely to occur. If there really was a perfect mechanism for predicting crises or stock market panic it would have made a lot of people very rich.

I tend towards the line of thought advanced by John Maynard Keynes, who eschewed predictions about where the economy was heading but concentrated on how people were likely to react to news that would move markets. Predicting reactions is arguably less scientific but more likely to succeed because human behaviour tends to follow patterns which can be readily identified. Investor behaviour seems to stick even more closely to an established pattern, making the job that much easier. When it comes to times of panic, investor behaviour becomes even more rigidly predictable. This issue is examined in greater detail in Chapter 7.

Among the most popular and most eloquently argued theses concerning the way cycles form is the monetarist theory. It states that cycles coincide with the availability of money circulating around the system. Milton Friedman, the leading advocate of monetarism, has consistently argued that the state of economies is directly linked with the level of money supply. Examining the three great bull markets of the last century, he found that they were all preceded by sharp rises in the quantity of money in circulation. There was an annual increase in the money supply of 3.9 per cent in the years 1919 to 1929, while the US stock market rose 333 per cent from 1923 to 1929. An even bigger rise was seen in the Japanese stock market from 1983 to 1989, taking prices up by 387 per cent, while money supply rose 9.1 per cent per year in the decade from 1980 to 1990. The US bull market stretching from 1994 to 2000 produced a share price rise of 320 per cent and was accompanied by an annual average increase in the money supply amounting to 4.1 per cent from 1980 to 1990.

According to Friedman, 'the evidence linking the behaviour of the stock of money with the behaviour of the economy goes well beyond these three episodes. Every great depression has been accompanied or preceded by a monetary collapse.'[5] Those who buy this argument will simply keep a careful eye on the money supply figures and draw conclusions about likely stock market booms and busts. Of course, money supply is not a force of nature; on the contrary, it is subject to the vagaries of government policy. Governments tend to use the tap of money supply as a means of controlling economic activity. In good times they may seek to turn the tap down and in bad times turn it full on.

Crises emerge when the supply of money suddenly dries up, as it did in 1929, 1987 and 2008. As money supply slows, interest rates rocket. This has an immediate impact on those who are already borrowing money to buy stocks or derivatives and has a considerable deterrent effect on anyone contemplating borrowing in order to play the markets. Indeed, there is almost always a knee-jerk response to interest rate rises in stock market prices, which tend to fall as soon as they are announced. The reverse is not so predictably the case. However, there is little doubt that market participants accept the close linkage between interest rates and stock prices.

Peter Spiro takes this assumption further and believes that short-term movements in stock markets are influenced by changes in interest rates above all else.[6] Besides the direct effect that changing borrowing rates has on market participants, interest rate changes also have an impact on company profits, particularly for highly geared companies which can do little in the short term to reduce their borrowing whereas they can take measures to reduce other fixed costs. The impact of the changes in the cost of borrowing will eventually work through into dividend payments and in this sense the market has good reason to keep a watchful eye on interest rates.

If interest rates start rising sharply at a time when corporate balance sheets are weak, the combination of the two produces a real reason to panic. This was the case of the panic in May 1940 when the markets were knocked sideways by the British evacuation of Dunkirk and the fear that the Nazis might triumph. Although the political implications of this development in the war were paramount, they were only part of the problem because in the background were companies with weak balance sheets who were very vulnerable to a sharp rise in interest rates. When interest rates rose a market panic ensued, triggering a decline that by the end of the month reduced Wall Street share prices by 22.6 per cent, a bigger decrease than that seen in the crash of October 1929.

High interest rates are not necessarily an immediate problem for markets, indeed at the peak of bull markets high interest rates are commonplace, but they should be taken as a warning signal. This is so because interest rates rise in proportion to perception of risk. If lenders regard the situation of individuals and corporations as risky and see the general environment as containing a high level of risk, it only makes sense for shareholders to appreciate these concerns and take them as a warning of possible problems in the equity market.

This is very much the case when high levels of interest rates are associated with high levels of lending, which typically occurs in over-heated markets. The Great Crash of 1929 was presaged by an enormous upsurge of brokers' loans – loans made by brokers to investors buying stocks on margin. In the early 1920s the average volume of loans stood at $0.5–1 billion, by 1926 the average rose to $2.5 billion and then rose by another $1 billion the following year. In 1928, the year before the crash, these loans rose to around $6 billion.[7] The same kind of loan explosion was seen before the 1987 crash and again in the 1990s. Although it is possible to establish a correlation between changing interest rates and changing stock prices, it is not possible to predict interest rate changes, and so the knowledge of this relationship has little use as a predictive tool. It is particularly unhelpful in predicting crashes because the sharpest movements in interest rates tend to come either immediately before a crash or immediately after, leaving little or no time to take defensive action.

When interest rates rise they make the dividend yield on shares look less attractive to investors. In theory, therefore, interest rate rises should cause a mass exit from the stock market. Before the 1950s it used to be an article of stock market faith that dividends on shares had to be higher than bond yields, otherwise no one would buy stocks. The higher dividend rates were supposed to compensate for the higher degree of risk entailed in share ownership. However, in 1958 US Treasury bond yields moved above stock yields and, with some significant exceptions, have more or less stayed there ever since. Although this development was novel in the 1950s it rapidly ceased to be regarded as important because stock investors were far less interested in income derived from dividends than they were about capital gains made as share prices rose. Indeed, as share prices started climbing steadily, the price rise in itself ensured that dividend yields would fall. This did not mean that companies were becoming less profitable, on the contrary, many became much more profitable, but because yields are expressed as a percentage of the share price they are likely to fall even while corporate profitability is rising. In the real world falling yields are not a cause of alarm to investors as long they are making healthy capital gains on the share price. With this in mind investors tend also to overlook the rapid rise in price–earnings ratios, which is another inevitable concomitant of a bull market.

As stock prices rise and profits of the businesses they represent rise, albeit at a slower pace, companies have more incentive to invest (although not necessarily, as we shall see, in capital goods) and investors become even more keen to borrow in order to pour more cash into the markets. The increased demand for loans leads to higher lending rates. This in turn has an impact on all forms of fixed income investments, but particularly on bonds which, like shares, see their yields fall as prices rise. This is the point at which the turn of the cycle moves towards panic. Because bond prices are, in large part, a reflection of the state of the lending market, they tend to peak before share prices. Share prices need a little time to catch up as more money, much of it supplied on credit, enters equity markets, taking them to a peak.

The main indicator of bond prices used to be the thirty-year US Treasury bond (the nearest British equivalent is probably the ten-year gilt). Although the US government announced in October 2001 that it would no longer auction this bond, it has to some extent remained a benchmark. In the last three decades of the twentieth century the yield on the thirty-year bond averaged 8 per cent. Many market watchers believed that when yields fell to around 6 per cent, this was a sure sign of an even bigger tumble in equity markets. Sure enough, when the bull market of the 1990s petered out, the thirty-year Treasury bond's yield started to drop sharply. Throughout 2000 it fell to around 5 per cent and just before the 9/11 crash it plunged further to around 4.5 per cent. But these modest yields bear little comparison to the slump in T-Bill yields seen in mid-September 2008 that fell to 0.3 per cent, the lowest level since 1954.

Bond yields, like other monetary instruments, are not in themselves the cause of a crisis but reflect changes in government policy, market demand and market sentiment, all of which contribute to creating a panic. This is why monetary policy makers have become more interventionist in setting interest rates and controlling money supply. Throughout the period of the 1990s boom and in its aftermath business on the world's stock markets was periodically interrupted by either anticipation or the digestion of the carefully worded remarks of Alan Greenspan, the chairman of the US Federal Reserve. In his wonderfully gnomic fashion he told the world his thoughts on the state of the economy, the state of the markets, and made cautious predictions as to where things were heading. Then came the thing markets were really waiting for; the news of the Fed's decision on whether interest rates were to rise or fall. Once the 1990s bubble had burst Greenspan did much to prevent a panic in 2001 by repeatedly announcing downward adjustments to the prime lending rate.

The marvellously dry and clear presentation of Greenspan's statements elevated him to guru status. However, he would be the last person to suggest that the Federal Reserve's adjustments to interest rates were the main cause of movements in share prices, even if some people came to believe that this was so, despite the fact that there have been a number of moments in history when big changes in interest rates had little impact on the markets. On the other hand, no one can deny that the constant tinkering had a beneficial impact on equity markets.

Stages of the cycle

Generally speaking, panics are not caused by investors taking a long hard look at movements in interest rates and judging their impact on corporate viability. Panics are much more likely to arise, as we have seen, from the way the markets themselves operate. Crudely stated, panics emerge as markets bump down to earth after they have risen beyond levels that are sustainable. A useful model for tracing the stages which lead to a panic is supplied by Charles Kindleberger in his book *Manias, Panics and Crashes*.[8] He builds on the model established by the monetary theorist Hyman Minsky. Minsky laid considerable stress on the consequences of mounting debts being incurred for the purchase of speculative assets that were intended for resale. In other words, high borrowings raised for speculation on stock markets. He saw this as marking the penultimate stage before the onset of a panic.

Outlined below are the stages of the panic cycle based on the work of Minsky and Kindleberger, with some modifications.

Stage I

The cycle starts with some kind of shock to the system that creates important opportunities for at least one sector of the economy. It could be an extraneous event such as a war, or some event more closely connected to economic development, such as the development of railways or, drawing on recent history, the rise of the Internet.

Stage II

This event starts a boom, which is then fuelled by the expansion of bank credit, enlarging money supply (the crucial point in the Friedman view of things).

Stage III

With more cash in hand euphoria takes hold, leading to what Adam Smith termed 'overtrading'. This term can mean a number of things, such as heavy speculation in anticipation of price rises or it could mean excessive gearing, caused by buying speculative assets on margin.

Stage IV

News soon spreads of the spectacular profits being made by those involved in this trading. Kindleberger says he always manages to raise a laugh from audiences by saying, 'there is nothing so disturbing to one's well being and judgement as to see a friend get rich'. So everyone else wants to get rich and a bubble forms. People who previously had never even thought about buying stocks suddenly start entering the market.

Stage V

The real danger signals appear when stock market news moves from the back to the front pages of non-financial newspapers. Illustrating this point was the alarming appearance of mutual funds as a Playboy magazine cover story at the height of the 1990s stock market boom. When stocks replace scantily clad young ladies with large mammaries in the most honoured position of a magazine such as this, logic has clearly taken a holiday.

Stage VI

Not only does the stock market suddenly become inundated with inexperienced players but their very presence increases demand and leads to the temptation for many new equity issues designed to capitalise on this window of opportunity for selling all manner of assets at inflated prices. There also tends to be a boom in derivatives issues, aimed at the allegedly more sophisticated investor. Because, by their very nature, derivatives are margin plays this increases the speculative nature of the market and, when the collapse comes, puts yet more pressure on institutions offering loans as investors try to raise cash to cover their positions. The result is that these institutions both hike interest rates and start calling in the loans.

Stage VII

As the bubble grows the markets become increasingly detached from the underlying assets they are supposed to represent.

Stage VIII

A number of scams and swindles and dubious investments come to the market. This is interesting as a symptom if not a cause of stock market panics, and will shortly be discussed in more detail.

Stage IX

By now the more savvy investors sense the time has come to head for the exit. Newer players are unsure what to do so they tend to stay put, but the fact that some players are getting out tends to put a brake on the rapid upward movement of prices. Once this happens there is an increasing movement away from assets into cash, further depressing prices and leading banks to call in more loans as the collateral falls in value.

Stage X

By now the market is in full retreat with even hardened speculators realising that the peak has passed and there is competition to get out before everyone has abandoned the field. This may be followed by a specific event, such as a dramatic bank failure or the revelation of a particular scam.

Stage XI

This accelerates the rush to the exit and leads to what Kindleberger calls revulsion against the very assets which were once so highly valued. Even those with the shortest memories will be able to recall the quick transition of the word 'dotcom' from a magic term denoting opportunity into a derisory one as companies were dismissed as being 'no more than dotcoms'.

With the panic in full swing a number of possibilities arise. Prices reach such a low that there is a temptation to buy again (this, in my view, tends to happen a bit later in the process). Secondly, there is a possibility of trading being cut off as regulators place a limit on the level to which markets are allowed to fall. On the other hand, a lender of last resort might succeed in convincing investors that there will be a sufficient amount of money in circulation to meet the demand for cash. If this happens it reduces pressure on the markets because players appreciate that there is no need to worry about liquidating assets over fear that there may be no cash to pay for them if everyone else does the same thing.

Government attempts to cope with panics

In Chapter 1 we saw the extent of government intervention in the wake of the 2008 panic and noted the argument that although this crash was more widespread and involved larger amounts of cash than at any previous time in history there was not a fundamental difference in official responses to the crisis. As panics take hold there is always demand for government action. However, governments tend to be rightly wary of too much intervention. The response of the authorities is crucial at this juncture and can do much to determine the next phase in the cycle. If government action works, as it is widely held to have worked in 1987 with money being poured into the system to avoid a credit squeeze, plaudits will be handed out for success. Where action is not taken, or is taken in a confused and piecemeal manner, as seen in Japan since the early 1990s, then governments tend to be blamed for more or less everything, letting the private sector off the hook.

Yet the pressure for government action becomes intense; even free market purists start calling for something to be done, using the slightly tautological argument that the market panic has been caused by distortions having entered into the marketplace that need to be eliminated. By and large, however, believers in the true faith of free markets argue that the market will right itself and that external intervention is damaging.

They have a good number of examples to flourish in support of the case against external intervention. As we have seen in the arguments of Milton Friedman, monetarists have long held that policies of the Federal Reserve were responsible for provoking the crash of 1929 by curbing money supply. Curiously, Friedman has also argued that the government acted in a timely manner by buying government bonds in the open market after the crash in order to put more money into the system. Kindleberger, on the other hand, thinks the government did too little, too late, and drove money out of other parts of the system, thereby unleashing the depression.[9]

More recent examples of dubious official intervention seem to be more clear cut. Possibly the most infamous examples come from the Asian region where, in the wake of the 1987 crash, the Hong Kong authorities closed down the stock market on the grounds that it would insulate the former British colony from selling pressure. It did nothing of the kind, the closure merely bottled up selling pressure that was released like a torrent once the market finally reopened, sending Hong Kong shares down much further than those on any other major market.

The officials who permitted this act of extreme folly appeared not to know that market closures had been tried elsewhere with a similar lack of success. The New York market was closed with disastrous results during the September 1873 panic and again in 1914 after the European exchanges shut following the outbreak of World War I. Closing markets as a deliberate act of policy is rare for the simple reason that bottling up selling pressure exacerbates rather than solves problems. The closure of the American market following the 9/11 attack on the World Trade Center, was not a result of deliberate policy, rather a consequence of the impossibility of conducting business after trading systems had suffered so much physical damage. Deliberate or not, the closure added considerably to the selling pressure that caused a price fall of over 7 per cent when the market reopened eight days later.

Back in Hong Kong, it seemed that the post-colonial government was determined to learn nothing from history as it sought to insulate the territory from the impact of the Asian financial crisis a decade later in 1998. It did so with an unprecedented one-day intervention in the stock market which ended with the government spending $15 billion buying up blue chip shares. As a result the market decline was indeed halted (even though this was not the stated aim of the exercise). However, since then the Hong Kong market has consistently performed well below other major regional markets, in part because of the overhang of the massive government portfolio.

Elsewhere in Asia it was the activities of the International Monetary Fund which did much to wreck markets as they tumbled during the 1997–8 Asian crisis.[10] Using the leverage of various rescue packages, the IMF insisted that governments needed to impose draconian belt tightening measures in order to qualify for rescue money. Not only did the IMF target the wrong issue, because corporate debt was more of a problem than sovereign debt, but the effect of these measures was to accelerate the crisis and cause more failures than might have otherwise occurred.

On the other hand, the IMF acted as lender of last resort to countries such as Indonesia and Thailand. Without this support the monetary systems of these countries would almost certainly have collapsed. The IMF was acting as any lender would by insisting on conditions for advancing loans. The power to impose these conditions is particularly strong in circumstances where the borrower is weak. Therefore its critics are wrong to quibble over the fact that conditions were imposed. Other critics believe that the IMF should not have been lender at all because its bailout prevented the markets from accepting the consequences of their actions and thus hindered the process of structural reform needed to prevent another crisis.

This argument does not apply just to Asia; it could well also be attached to the way that international institutions launched bailouts in Latin America and elsewhere. It could also, most certainly, be applied to the US government's bailout of Long Term Capital Management (LTCM), the famous hedge fund which stood on the verge of collapse in September 1998. It was saved when the Federal Reserve Bank of New York organised a consortium of investors to inject $3.4 billion in a rescue package. The government argued that it was not a party to the bailout because it had merely acted as organiser not an investor, yet it is hard to maintain that it had no role in saving a private company that might well have gone under without its help.

There was, however, no possibility of the US government pretending that it had not paid out vast sums of money to rescue the failing savings and loans associations in the 1980s. The reckless spending and borrowing of the people running these businesses was directly encouraged by the Reagan administration's bold policy of deregulation. By the time this policy had come to fruition the US taxpayer was left with a bill for some $200 billion. Few doubt that without the rescue America would have been plunged into a serious financial crisis, sweeping quickly into the equity markets and beyond. Although there was criticism of the bailout it is interesting to note that few of the critics who so glibly recommended that Asian and Latin American countries should be left to face the consequences of their actions, without help from governmental institutions, advocated allowing the US financial system to go into free fall.

Here is the nub of the problem. When crises and panics emerge quite a few people are prepared to advocate purely market driven solutions, but when it becomes apparent that the consequences of this approach might create real hardship in their own backyards, the number of enthusiasts for official inaction diminishes quickly.

The end point of most crises, therefore, is almost always some kind of official intervention. It may involve pouring money into the system, as in 2008 and 1987, or some form of government-inspired coordination to tackle the problem, as was the case in the rescue of LTCM. It is rare indeed for the market to tackle its problems without external intervention, and the idea that markets right themselves without help after periods of extreme downward pressure must remain little more than a theoretical possibility because it is hard to think of an example when such a laissez-faire approach has actually been tried.

The reverse is not true. The regulatory authorities rarely intervene when markets are rising, even if the rise of the markets is very rapid and possibly destabilising. Many people remember the famous remarks delivered by Alan Greenspan on 5 December 1996 when he described the state of the bull market as a product of 'irrational exuberance' by investors. His remarks caused a temporary fall in share prices from Tokyo to Hong Kong to London accompanying the 2.3 per cent fall in the DJIA on the day he made this comment. However, aside from fine tuning of interest rates, the Federal Reserve Board chairman's misgivings about the state of the market did not provoke any kind of full-scale intervention, let alone the establishment of a Presidential Task Force, such as that set up in the wake of the 1987 collapse. Market purists are right when they talk of the market righting itself when prices rise too high, but this is the only direction in which market forces are left to play out without official support.

This time, will it be different?

It makes sense that crises are less frequent as markets have become more developed, better regulated and more transparent. As we have seen, there is also some evidence that lessons are learned from crises, as was notably the case of the 1987 stock market crash when central bankers increased, rather than decreased, the amount of money supply. In so doing they avoided the fatal trap of the 1929 crash when liquidity dried up and the failure of the stock market helped fuel the recession. However, these improvements have not and will not prevent the onset of panics.

Every boom era nurtures a belief that this time it will be different and that somehow the boom can be prolonged. This absurd fantasy was especially prevalent during the boom years of the 1990s, when there was much talk about something called 'the new paradigm'. Credit, if that is the right word, for this concept probably goes to the Salomon Brothers analyst David Shulman, who produced a famous report entitled '1996: Stock Market Bubble or Paradigm Shift?' He argued that the pressures of inflation had created a fundamentally new form of stock market valuation that explained the logic for share values reaching an all-time high. His point was that previous forms of valuation should be discarded and that history was unhelpful in establishing comparative criteria for share valuation in the new hi-tech era.

Shulman's bullish views were just what the market wanted to hear. He was quickly followed by others who were delighted to be free of the old restraints under which valuations were made, creating the impression that the stock market was seriously overvalued. By 1997 the distribution of rose-tinted glasses had spread to the White House, where President Clinton blithely declared that the strong performance of the US economy suggested that old concepts of business cycles would need to be abandoned. The view took hold that growth could go on for ever.

Of course, this was muddle-headed. Despite the extraordinary resilience of not only the US economy but also of Britain and some other European countries, the new millennium was quickly shaken by the 2008 crash.

Meanwhile, the great dotcom share boom came conclusively to an end in 2000 but did so without causing a spectacular one-day market crash, although there were crashes in individual dotcom share prices and a very sharp decline on the NASDAQ, home to most of the dotcom shares. The performance of the NASDAQ gives the best idea of the severe hammering inflicted on investors who had put their faith in the dotcom new paradigm. The sharpest fall in the NASDAQ composite was from August 2000 to September 2000, when the index registered a decline of 534 points, or almost 13 per cent. However, the real damage was done over a longer time period. The NASDAQ slumped from a high of almost 4,700 points to a level hovering around 1,640 points in the middle of 2002. This knocked something like 65 per cent off the value of shares. It is estimated that the dotcoms collectively lost around $1 trillion in market capitalisation after 2000. However, the damage was contained in the sense that the virus of decline was not matched by share price falls on the main board. Indeed, there was a degree of orderly migration from NASDAQ stocks to main board stocks that helped keep the Dow trading at relatively high levels. The fact that an enormous boom evaporated without triggering a more widespread crash is remarkable

Indeed, it looked as though the absence of a more profound crash may mean that the greatest bull market of the twentieth century, that of the 1990s, would defy gravity (and logic, for that matter, because shares continued to trade on heady valuations after the 9/11 crash). By the end of 2001 Wall Street was trading on an historic average price–earnings ratio of close to 30. This is around double the average price–earnings ratio for the past seventy-five years. Other European markets which crashed in tandem with New York recovered at similar speed and continue to trade with high price–earnings ratios.

The real damage on stock markets started to emerge in 2002, some three years after economic growth slowed and the dotcom bubble had burst. However as the new millennium gathered pace it began to look as though these fears might be misplaced. Stock markets, particularly some of the newer emerging markets, once again surged forward. Although there were warnings that this rise in share prices was unlikely to be sustained, a mood of optimism swept through the markets and we again heard much from pundits who declared that a new era of sustainable growth had emerged. The events of 2008 provided a timely reminder of reality and the simple fact that the panic cycle never really changes.

New world – new crashes

In the final decades of the twentieth century, while markets in the United States and Europe were booming, the crash action moved to the newer markets. What we might be seeing is that the volatile and crash-prone nature of nineteenth-century markets in the fast-industrialising nations of the North and West is now becoming a characteristic of the industrialising nations of the East and South that are lumped into the general category of emerging markets. This suggests that the phenomenon of regular market crashes is partly explained by their stage of development, meaning that less mature markets are more crisis prone.

The Japanese market, however, is far too big to be described as emerging; in fact, during the height of the Japanese boom in the 1980s, the Tokyo market enjoyed a level of capitalisation far exceeding that of New York. Nevertheless, the stock markets of Japan (i.e. the markets in Tokyo and Osaka) are newer than those of Europe and the United States and had been relatively free of wild speculation before the 1980s. When speculative fever took hold it did so with a vengeance, drawing in, as in all speculative booms, many players who had no business being in the market, let alone borrowing to get there, and who were devoting far too high a proportion of their assets to equities and property.

When the boom came to an end at the beginning of 1990, the bust was devastating. The bubble that burst was of an extraordinary size. It took land prices up by 5,000 per cent in the three decades from 1956 to 1986. By 1990 the entire Japanese property market was valued four times higher than that of the entire United States. By 1986 the volume of trading on the Tokyo Stock Exchange had reached an average of 708.6 million shares per day. In the first four months of the following year daily turnover had soared to more than 1.2 billion shares. Tokyo was poised to become the world's biggest market. In the late 1980s share prices increased three times faster than earnings. The Nikkei recorded a fivefold increase during the decade. The average historic price–earnings ratio peaked at 90 x earnings in 1987 but enjoyed a heady average of around 65–70 x earnings for most of the decade, as against an average on Wall Street of no more than 25 x during the same period.

There was much talk about how the Japanese would soon be ruling the world. This view was encapsulated by Ezra Vogel's famous book *Japan as Number One*. Published in 1979, it was received with great enthusiasm in Japan and great dismay elsewhere. A consensus poll of 107 Japanese stock market experts conducted at the end of 1989, after the Nikkei had hit a peak of 38,900 points, predicted that the Nikkei Index would be standing at around 41,000 points by 1991. As Japan entered the new millennium the Nikkei stood at just above 12,200 points. The 'experts' appear to have seriously misunderstood what was happening.

When the bubble was finally pricked, not least by the deliberate actions of Yasushi Mieno, the new Governor of the Bank of Japan, the air came out in fits and spurts. There was no big one-day crash but a steady stream of deflation, so steady that at the beginning of 1990 many analysts still believed that the decline could be stemmed and that happy days would come again. By the end of the decade the Nikkei had seen some two-thirds wiped off the value of shares.

While Japan was sinking into recession, without having that much effect on other markets, the fashionable money switched to the emerging markets of Latin America and East and South-East Asia and later to Russia. The demise of the markets in Tokyo and Osaka impacted more on domestic Japanese investors than anyone else and was taken as a sign that the real money was to be made in smaller markets with plenty of upside. Mexico seemed a pretty good bet: not only was it ideally located as a low-cost supplier to the mighty US market but it had a government committed to a policy of deregulation. Money poured in, and poured out equally quickly in 1994 when the crash began. Other Latin American markets tumbled as the contagion from Mexico spread. It was a classic case of boom and bust.

Was anything learned from the Mexican experience? Not really, because the hot money simply moved on to the next set of emerging markets seen as having plenty of upside. Everyone started talking about the Asian tigers (Hong Kong, Singapore, South Korea and Taiwan) and then about the tiger cubs (Indonesia, Malaysia, the Philippines and Thailand). The claims made for the prospects of these markets were even more fantastic. Among the more silly and most popular at the time was a work published in 1996, at the height of the Asian bull market. This was John Naisbitt's book *Megatrends Asia*. In it he wrote, 'as we move to the year 2000, Asia will become the dominant region of the world: economically, politically and culturally'.

Like Vogel, Naisbitt was mesmerised by the dizzying climb of the stock market and the new notches on the economic growth ladder, which seemed to be stretching somewhere into infinity. Although there were many sound reasons for investing in Asia's so-called tiger markets, they were built on very weak foundations, so weak that it took little to blow them over. However, there was nothing unusual or unknown from history about the nature of the bubbles building in Japan and elsewhere in Asia. The symptoms associated with other crashes were all in place. To name but a few: high levels of corporate debt, in 1996 (at the height of the Asian boom) the average debt to equity ratio in South Korean companies was 3.5 to 1, in Thailand it was 2.3 to 1 and in Indonesia 1.9. to 1. Inflation was high and so were interest rates. Price–earnings ratios were historically high by the standards of the region, excluding Japan, standing at an average of around 25. And all the signs of conspicuous spending by financial institutions were there for everyone to see. The gross capitalisation of stock markets in the 1990s was growing far in excess of the gross domestic product (GDP) of the countries within which they were located. In Malaysia, for example, the capitalisation of the stock market was 2.5 times greater than the nation's GDP and the Hong Kong stock market was capitalised at more than double the level of GDP.

Given the familiarity of these overheating indications, why were there not more voices expressing caution about the rise of Asian stock markets? One explanation is that both domestic and overseas players saw the markets as casinos. Gambling on exceptionally high rewards, investors were prepared for high risk and, especially in the case of overseas players, they devoted only a small proportion of their portfolios to these markets. The proportion was so small in relation to investments on Wall Street that it mattered less if the gamble turned sour.

Secondly, and in a sense more worryingly, there were many people like Naisbitt who bought the Asia story and really believed that growth would continue with barely a falter. There is always an inclination to believe that something new, such as the emergence of the Asian economic powerhouse, would establish new ground rules and, in this instance, set new precedents for equity markets.

History has proved otherwise, although as the emerging markets become more developed it is probable that they will become less volatile and less prone to panics. If this is so it will give greater credence to the notion that the propensity to panic is related to the state of development of equity markets.

Dubious practices and crooks move in

When markets start to falter they have a tendency to reveal and encourage a host of crooked practices that were nurtured as the bubbles grew. After the bubbles have burst the revelation of these practices helps to accelerate the deflation. Kindleberger observes that 'the propensities to swindle and be swindled run parallel to the propensity to speculate during a boom'.[11]

To be kind, perhaps too kind, it can be argued that the propensity to swindle arises from desperation as markets fall and incautious investors face enormous debts. Looking at the 1929 crash Galbraith wrote about how booms and crashes lead to 'a traumatic exaggeration' of normal human relationships. 'To normal needs for money, for home, family and dissipation, was added, during the boom, the new and overwhelming requirement for funds to play the market or to meet margin calls.'[12] This leads to unscrupulous behaviour as those in trouble seek ever more desperate remedies for their cash problems.

A classic example comes from the end of the Asia boom before 1997, when the stock futures trader Nick Leeson turned to fraud to cover up his failed gamble on cornering the Japanese stock futures market. In so doing he caused the collapse of the British merchant bank Barings, but not before hiding his misdeeds from his bosses, mainly because they evidently did not want to see any evidence to suggest he was anything other than a great success.

Leeson's struggle to make good his losses was not that different from the desperate attempt of Clarence Hatry to keep his company alive in the wake of the 1929 crash. He did so by resorting to outright fraud, using phoney collateral in order try and secure bank loans of £8 million with which he attempted to buy United Steel.

The 1987 crash produced its crop of market bubble-fed fraud, none more spectacular than the arrest of the senior officials of the Hong Kong stock exchange, including its chairman Ronald Li, who was found guilty of accepting bribes from companies seeking a listing.

However, unscrupulous behaviour is a product not only of post-crash panic but also of pre-crash greed. Ray Dalio, president of the money management company Bridgewater Associates, believes that as bubbles develop conservative accounting practices and those responsible for this cautionary approach become discredited and the bending of rules becomes standard. 'You were in an environment where, since people didn't pay much attention to it, you were being rewarded for aggressive accounting,' he said.[13]

An article published in the *Wall Street Journal* went so far as to state that 'the scope and scale of corporate transgressions of the late 1990s ... exceed anything the US has witnessed since the years preceding the Great Depression'.[14] The less staid and rather more pithy *New York Daily News* summed up the popular perception of Wall Street in the summer of 2002 with a headline which simply read: 'Crook Street'.

In 2008 the US Securities and Exchange Commission (SEC) launched a record number of enforcement actions against market manipulation and investigated the biggest number of insider trading allegations in its history. Some of the highest profile scandals that were revealed after the crash of 2008, such as that which engulfed the blue-chip fund manager Bernard (Bernie) Madoff, involved billions of dollars invested by famous clients and household-name financial institutions who were drawn into a classic Ponzi scam (discussed in greater detail in the next chapter) where investments were not even made but older clients simply received dividends from funds supplied by newer clients.

As ever it took a severe market downturn to bring these corporate frauds to light as it had in 2001 when the SEC opened 570 investigations, a larger number than in any other single year of the previous decade, with the exception of 1994. Furthermore, 150 New York-listed companies had to restate their earnings for the end of the 1990s, a sure sign that their reporting to shareholders was, at best, incomplete. Such a high level of restated earnings figures has never been seen before.

The transgressions most famously include the fraud at WorldCom, which portrayed an image of growing profitability during the dot-com boom but was in fact overstating its profits and disguising costs to the extent of $3.8 billion. In July 2002 the company filed for protective bankruptcy. Then there was Tyco International, accused of tax evasion and secret pay deals to executives. The once high-flying cable company Adelphia Communications admitted cooking its books and making unauthorised loans to major shareholders. Even the well-established, previously rock-solid Xerox Corporation, was forced to pay a $10 million fine for overstating its revenues (it later admitted overstating profits by some $6.4 billion over five years). Most of those on the list of suspects came from the TMT (telecommunications, media and technology) sector, which flourished during the 1990s boom.

Even more notorious, because of the repercussions and allegations of criminal behaviour, was the collapse of the Enron Corporation and its firm of accountants, Arthur Andersen. The Texas-based Enron started life as a rather basic energy company. It enjoyed dizzying rises in its share price and turned to maintaining the momentum of the share price by boosting profits, at least on paper, by engaging in commodities trading and booking non-existent profits. Debts exceeding $1 billion were concealed from shareholders. Meanwhile its real energy business was left languishing on the sidelines.

Far removed from the scale of Enron's misdemeanours were the problems that engulfed America's most famous home-making television personality, Martha Stewart. On screen she was the embodiment of the American suburban dream, but this icon of the American Way was accused of using insider information to dump shares in ImClone, a biotech company that was about to face problems over the failure of its star drug product to gain endorsement from the Food and Drug Administration. The amount of money involved in this affair, a mere $200,000, hardly bears comparison with the bigger scandals of the day, but the alleged involvement of someone like Martha Stewart in a share scam had the effect of bringing home the extent of financial shenanigans to the general public in a way that the bigger scandals, carrying almost unimaginable numbers, could not.

The end of the 1990s boom produced more than just corporate failures, some of which were the result of dubious or outright illegal business practices. As the euphoria of dotcom stocks and highly leveraged wheeling and dealing faded, attention switched to the role of the professional advisory companies that were supposed to be making sure all these bad things did not happen. The collapse of Enron, for example, effectively destroyed Arthur Andersen, one of the world's largest accountancy firms, which had acted as auditor to the company. In June 2002 the accountants were found guilty of obstructing justice as a result of trying to cover up malpractices within Enron, but by then such was the loss of confidence in Arthur Andersen that it had already been reduced to little more than a shell.

Earlier in the same year Merrill Lynch, then one of the world's biggest investment banks, was forced into a humiliating out-of-court settlement with New York's Attorney General after facing charges that its analysts had knowingly misled investors over recommendations on stocks that it had brought to the market. Issues raised by the Merrill probe are discussed in the following chapter.

In many ways the scandals involving these very large and previously well-respected professional financial companies were more damaging to the credibility and trust that investors placed in financial markets than the usual crop of corporate failures and scandals that accompany the end of all booms. An immediate effect of these calumnies was to cause many investors, particularly smaller investors, to shun equity markets. The longer term impact is harder to predict, though if the cynics have got it right, memories may prove to be short – there is little doubt that in the 1990s few investors seemed to be bothered by the scandals which emerged in the wake of the pre-1987 boom, assuming they even remembered them. This notwithstanding the magnitude of those scandals was impressive.

They included the savings and loans crisis, discussed above, along-side a host of insider-trading scandals and the usual ragbag of false trading scams and market manipulation ploys.

One of the most famous culprits of this period was Michael Milken, the king of the junk bond market, who headed Drexel Burnham Lambert's Beverly Hills bond department. He was joined by Ivan Boesky, who gave new meaning to the word arbitrage by putting together complicated and audacious deals which turned small sums of stake money into vast profits. The only problem with the wondrous activities of both men was that they were breaking the law. They morphed with amazing speed from Masters of the Universe to indicted criminals. Arthur Litman, Milken's lawyer, said that his client had been turned into a demon, saying that the case against him had 'the characteristics of a heresy trial'. Self-serving as these comments may have been, they were not without an element of truth; society did seem to need some scapegoats for the excesses which had robbed so many people of potential wealth.

So booms encourage skulduggery when they are in full swing. And standards fall as the scramble to become amazingly rich overcomes the scruples that normally prevent this kind of excessive behaviour. At this murky end of the panic cycle there has to be intervention both to bring the law breakers to justice and to close loopholes in the law to prevent market manipulation and other dubious practices that have helped create a crisis.

More a case of neglect than fraud

Outright fraud is, in a sense, easier to deal with than the situation typically produced in booms, where real business is neglected as financial and stock markets assume an importance far exceeding other parts of the economy.

In addition, otherwise quite sensible business managers switch the focus of their attention from running the actual business to boosting the share price of their companies, which in turn, because they have share options, boosts the level of their remuneration.

In recent years there have also been tremendous opportunities for companies at the centre of bubbles to use their inflated share market capitalisation to acquire assets which would otherwise have been well beyond their means. They are able to do so by offering shareholders of asset-rich companies their inflated shares in exchange for those assets. It often seems to be the case that those running these highly capitalised companies are far better at massaging share prices than operating real businesses and that once they have swapped their overvalued paper for real assets, the value of these assets starts to dwindle. (These will be explored further in Chapter 9.)

At the time of writing uncertainty in global markets remains at a very high level as the consequences of the 2008 panic are yet to be fully seen. This panic followed a very impressive, but nevertheless rather short-lived, boom which, in proportionate terms, was smaller than the boom which preceded the 1929 crash. It is being argued that investors have become smarter and better informed because of the plethora of instantly available information over the Internet. But better informed does not necessarily mean smarter. What we saw in 2008 was all too familiar to observers of past booms and busts and provides ample evidence that the familiar cycle of market panics has not been broken. History will really be made if lessons are learned from the events of 2008 but no one is advised not to hold their breath in this regard.

5

A new age of panics

I T COULD BE ARGUED that in the 'good old days' stock market panics were relatively straightforward affairs. Markets got overheated
and let out steam at an alarming rate. Some of the panics were
related to other types of financial crises, some were the results of
scams that had been exposed while others were caused by events
external to the stock market that had an impact on the perceived
value of shares. Some panics were even rooted in real fears about
economic recession.

All the old causes of panics remain in place but nowadays are
exacerbated by the very nature and structure of modern stock markets, which are becoming more and more detached from the economies in which they are located. In addition, as markets become more
sophisticated and new forms of trading emerge, pressure is building
to create bigger and more devastating panics.

Yet, as we have seen in the previous chapter, developed markets
have become less volatile, if not on a day-to-day basis, at least over
time. The problem is that when these markets crack they tend to do
so with explosive force. The intention here is not to supply some
kind of Armageddon prophecy but to suggest that there is a build-up
of combustible forces which are combining to make markets more
unstable.

This chapter examines some of these forces and tries to identify whether they make markets more prone to panic. It also looks

at some factors, often cited as being highly combustible, that turn out to be not quite as dangerous as they seem. In this category are derivatives trading, hedge funds and program trading, all of which have taken a place in modern day demonology but for reasons that are less than convincing.

Stock markets bigger than national economies

Let us start by examining the growing detachment of stock markets from the economies and companies that they are supposed to represent. The key indicator here is a comparison of total stock market capitalisation with the sum total of gross national product (GNP). (GNP is always larger than gross domestic product (GDP) because it includes dividends, interest payments and profits remitted from overseas.) When stock markets start to be capitalised at levels way above the size of national economies, there has to be something not quite right about the valuation ascribed to equities. Warren Buffett has argued that 'if the percentage relationship falls to the 70 or 80 per cent area, buying stocks is likely to work very well for you. If the ratio approaches 200 per cent – as it did in 1999 and a part of 2000 – you are playing with fire.'[1] As the United States 1990s bull market climbed to its peak in March 2000, the New York stock market's capitalisation rose to being equivalent to 190 per cent of GNP. Previously and right up until the mid-1990s the US market's level of capitalisation relative to GNP had kept below 100 per cent, with the notable exception of September 1929, just before the crash, when it peaked at 109 per cent of GNP. By 2006, the figure was back up to almost 148 per cent.

A small caveat needs to be added here because the New York exchange, like the London exchange, has a relatively large number of overseas companies listed on its board. This obviously increases the size of the market's total capitalisation, but not to an extent that explains how market cap could come to be equivalent to almost double America's GNP.

Figure 5.1 **Comparisons of stock market size and GDP**

	%GDP	
	2000	2006
China	79.7	119.7
India	32.2	89.8
Hong Kong	368.6	903.6
Japan	67.6	108.2
Netherlands	166.3	117.7
Russia	15.0	107.1
Singapore	164.8	209.1
South Africa	154.7	280.2
United Kingdom	178.7	159.6
United States	154.7	147.6

Source: World Bank, Development Indicators 2008.

These heady market capitalisations which value stock markets above the size of economies are not confined to Wall Street, as can be seen from Figure 5.1. Indeed, what is most striking about these figures is the way in which the emerging stock markets of China, India and Russia expanded in the remarkably brief time span of half a decade so that in the case Russia stock market capitalization had overtaken the size of the nation's GDP, although just five years previously the infant Russian market hardly registered. Even in China, now home to one of the world's biggest economies, market capitalization is larger than the size of the economy itself. Hong Kong, where many Chinese entities are listed, appears to have a stock market capitalization which is a staggering nine times bigger than the size of the economy but this is precisely because the local stock exchange has become a home for the listing of massive Chinese corporations and produces these anomalous figures. The same is true to some extent for Singapore which houses many other South East Asian listings and also applies to both London and New York whose exchanges have housed overseas listings for a longer period.

The classic view of the function of stock markets is that they have served as an efficient centre for raising risk capital for corporate growth. The earliest stock market, that established in London, traces its origin to the time when seafaring adventurers were searching for funding for overseas voyages. The early days of stock markets were most certainly speculative, but they were also fulfilling the classic role of equity markets in matching the demand for funds with investors prepared to supply money in return for equity. True believers in the efficacy of markets would argue that this is exactly what stock markets are still doing today. I disagree, and suggest that stock markets are increasingly moving away from their original purpose and entering an era where the game of investment is an end in itself, having less and less to do with capital raising, less to do with equity partnerships, and everything to do with speculation.

Mr Ponzi is alive and well

In a sense, all stock markets are becoming Ponzi-scheme markets. This admittedly pejorative description takes its name from Charles Ponzi, who made a fortune in 1920 by spreading the story that a great deal of money had been made in investment schemes which in reality invested in nothing at all. The gullible were persuaded to invest in these schemes by others who had, or allegedly had, made impressive gains from Ponzi's endeavours. He managed to pay off shareholders by using the funds from one set of investors coming into the scheme to pay those who had already invested, while skimming a good deal off the top. This worked as long as new investors were coming in. When they stopped, Ponzi and his many emulators made an exit. Charles Ponzi managed to lure 30,000 investors and raise $15 million in the space of seven months.

The scam bearing his name has made guest appearances throughout the world ever since. Its most spectacular recent incarnation was the Madoff scandal discussed in the previous chapter but there was a more bizarre manifestation in Albania in 1996 and 1997. At the time Albania was a dirt-poor country emerging from the ravages of an exquisitely awful form of Stalinist rule. Seven Ponzi schemes raised $2 billion, equivalent to 30 per cent of Albania's GDP. When the schemes collapsed in 1997 they brought down the government, which had foolishly associated itself with this get-rich-quick bonanza.

Other Ponzi-type schemes have been plentiful, if less dramatic. It is not suggested that all stock markets are based on little more than a scam, but the unpalatable truth is that the essential basis of Ponzi's scheme is the essential basis of much investment in today's markets. The title of this section refers not to what is widely regarded as fraudulent practice but to the mainstream of investment activity.

The unprecedented bull market of the 1990s was all about investors pouring into the markets in the belief that those who had gone before had got rich as a result of doing so. The way they made their money was by selling shares to new arrivals. Those caught up in the investment frenzy were paying scant attention to the businesses they were investing in, had no knowledge of the ability of companies to pay dividends and, often, no more than a hazy idea about what these companies actually did. Clearly the investors of the 1990s boom were buying something more substantial than the international postal reply coupons that Ponzi at one stage said were a fantastic form of speculation. However, they were buying shares in companies that had little hope of paying dividends in any way commensurate with the investments made in their equity. Therefore the only way to profit on these investments was to sell the shares on to other investors who believed that they could make even more profit by selling them on again. In this way a Ponzi-style mentality and mode of operation became the norm.

New markets = new capital?

This cynical view of the state of the markets is not generally well regarded in the investment community and most definitely is not shared by those founding new markets in practically every corner of the globe. The rapid growth of stock markets around the world is seen as an important component of modernisation and development. No self-respecting industrialising nation wants to be bereft of a stock market. This includes allegedly communist countries such as China, and countries where the state plays a major role in the economy, such as India, alongside the more self-avowed capitalist states of Asia and elsewhere.

Governments like to underline their commitment to capitalism by not only establishing stock markets but also pursuing policies of financial market liberalisation which receive lavish praise from development organisations such as the World Bank. A World Bank study published in 1995 outlined the case for developing equity markets. It said: 'encouraging and sustaining a vital stock exchange does more for a national economy than simply bring in new capital. A developed stock market is as important to national economic growth as banks.'

The study stated that equity financing marked a higher level of economic development. 'Stock market development', argued the authors, 'does not merely follow economic development, but provides the means to predict future rates of growth in capital, productivity, and per capita GDP.'[2]

This ideal view of how stock markets work is impressive but somewhat undermined by the reality of the market's singular inefficiency as a capital raising centre. In developing nations, where stock markets are growing at a faster pace than in the industrialised world, share issues raise far less money for fixed capital investment than other forms of capital financing. In 1991 share issues in the developing world raised $4.6 billion for companies; by 2000 the amount raised was $34.8 billion. In the same year total bank lending amounted to $124.4 billion and bond issues raised $77.2 billion.[3]

Whereas it is highly likely that the bulk of money raised by bond issues and bank loans actually goes into the development of businesses, there is no evidence that the same can be said for equity issues. On the contrary, circumstantial evidence suggests that a high proportion of these funds simply flow straight into the pockets of company owners who use it for personal purposes. A World Bank study conducted at the height of the Asian stock market boom in the mid-1990s found that 40 per cent of the money raised by East Asian companies for fixed capital investments came from internal sources, 40 per cent from bank loans, 10 per cent from equity issues and about the same amount from bond issues.[4] However, while bond issues were supplying as much capital to companies as equity markets, the total size of the bond market was $338 billion whereas the market capitalisation of Asian stock markets amounted to $1,073 billion.[5] So while the size of equity markets was fast expanding, the amount they raised for fixed capital investment remained unimpressive. In terms of efficiency it is hard to argue the case for stock markets when, despite being three times the size of bond markets, the stock markets raised no more capital for business than their much smaller counterpart.

A more recent World Bank study underlines the manner in which stock markets are providing a very poor source of finance to developing countries. From 1972 to 1998 portfolio or stock market investments provided a mere 8 per cent of capital flows to these countries, as compared with 20 per cent provided by bank loans, 55 per cent from private resources and 20 per cent from direct investments.[6] The capital flow from stock markets is likely to have increased since then but it is highly unlikely that the supply of capital to business even vaguely matches the increase in the size of equity markets.

I have talked about developing markets because this is where stock exchanges are growing fastest and where, so it is argued, the development of equity markets is having the most positive impact on economic growth. Developing countries should also be able to make more use of stock exchanges to fund corporate development because they are less likely to have recourse to bond markets, which tend to grow in the wake of equity markets. Moreover, precisely because they are new, these markets should be in the business of raising new capital rather than recycling old capital as is the case in more established markets.

New markets, new volatility

What most characterises these new or emerging markets is their extreme behaviour. Robert Shiller looked at the biggest one-year rises and falls in stock markets around the world and found that the most spectacular rise came from the Philippine stock market between December 1985 and December 1986, when it registered an astonishing gain of 683 per cent. Next up was the Taiwan market, which rose 400 per cent in the year leading up to the October 1987 crash. Unkind as it may be, it is hard to resist observing that the Philippine stock market is based on an economy and a corporate sector that is a stand-out in terms of dismal performance compared with other places in the region. Yet during its moment in the sun when investors thought that the cigar-chomping former army general Fidel Ramos would use his presidency to turn everything round, investors bought the story and piled into Philippine shares. As reality set in, the Philippines moved from being a star performer to earning seventh place in the world league table of biggest one-year declines. Elsewhere on the list of twenty-five biggest one-year gains, other new markets are most prominent. The list contains only a handful of developed markets, notably those of Italy, Austria and Finland.

On the flipside of the picture, recording the biggest one-year falls in global markets, Taiwan tops the list with a close to 75 per cent fall in the year to October 1990. Jamaica ranks a close second with a fall of almost 74 per cent in the year to January 1994. However, perhaps surprisingly, Britain makes an appearance in fourth place with a 63 per cent fall in the darkest patch of the stock market's demise in the year to November 1974. While the list of biggest market increases is dominated by developing markets, a higher number of mature markets make an appearance on the declines list.[7]

What does all this suggest? Surely it cannot be that stock exchanges in developing countries are engines of corporate growth. They must be something else. The high level of volatility in these markets and the extremes of rises and falls that characterise emerging markets suggest that what is happening in these markets would be familiar to anyone visiting a casino.

Where does all the money go?

Before drawing the conclusion that developed markets are somehow better at raising capital for corporate development it is worth asking how much of the money invested in dotcom companies during the 1990s boom was actually devoted to investment in their growth. It is not possible to provide a reliable figure, but since the collapse of many of these companies it has become clear that a high proportion of the funds raised on developed stock markets went nowhere near investing in business development.

It should have followed that the funds pouring into these companies, which were supposed to be at the forefront of new technological developments, would at least in part have been devoted to research and development. However, a look at the comparative research and development study produced annually by the Organisation for Economic Cooperation and Development (OECD) shows quite clearly that the upsurge in stock market investment was not matched by a similar increase in R&D budgets. In 1999 (at the peak of the stock market boom) the United States was spending 2.47 per cent of its GDP on research and development, placing it below the average of other industrialised countries. Sweden topped the league table, devoting 3.80 per cent of its GDP to R&D.[8] These figures include both private sector and public sector spending and so do not provide a sufficiently clear impression of how much of the money pouring into stock markets was deployed in investments that would increase productivity. Although R&D expenditure in the United States was growing, it was growing at nothing vaguely approaching the rate of growth of stock market capitalisation.

A lot of the money that poured into stock markets was spent on the acquisition of 'hot' dotcom companies by other dotcom companies that turned out to be as insubstantial as the companies which were acquiring them. (A fuller discussion of this subject can be found in Chapter 9.) However, those who believe that stock markets are places where capital is efficiently raised for the purpose of business investment can take comfort in the correlation between rising stock prices and private investment. Evidence from Britain, Japan and the United States suggests that this is the case, but a different picture emerges in France, Germany and the Netherlands, as Figure 5.2 shows.

The existence of the correlation might allow some observers to believe that as markets raise more money it goes into the development of businesses. However, the reasons why this is not so are suggested by the national differences displayed in the figure. While investment rises along with stock prices in the United States and Britain, the rise in share prices has little impact on investment in continental Europe. This is because in both the US and Britain rising stock markets spur high levels of merger and acquisition activity. The bulk of the increase in investment shown in these charts is in fact an increase on merger expenditure of a kind far less common in continental Europe. The European countries show some modest increases in investment expenditure as stock prices rise, but they are not spectacular.

What is happening in the countries where stock prices and investment rise in tandem is not that businesses acquire new funds for growth but that money is devoted to changing the ownership of corporations. It may be argued that mergers then produce greater efficiency and higher productivity but, as we shall see in Chapter 9, the history of most big mergers shows that they achieve nothing of the kind.

Fascinating research on asset pricing and investment has been conducted by International Monetary Fund (IMF) economists,[9] who point out that rising asset prices lower the cost of new capital. As asset prices rise the balance sheets of corporations borrowing money improve, as do the balance sheets of lending institutions, therefore the financing premium falls. This produces an increased flow of funds and more low-cost financing. Big corporations, particularly in Britain and the United States, tend to use these funds to make acquisitions. Moreover, as we have seen, they can use their growing capital value on stock exchanges to offer stock in part or in full settlement of takeover deals. These acquisitions are recorded as being fixed investments and thus do much to inflate the total fixed investment figures seen in Figure 5.2.

Figure 5.2 **Stock prices and fixed private investment**

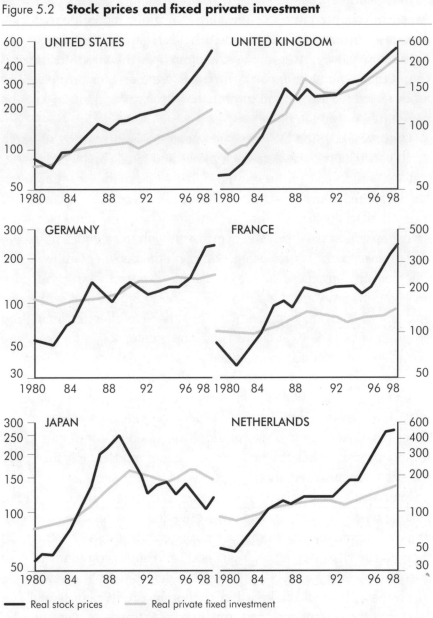

— Real stock prices   Real private fixed investment

Source: International Monetary Fund, 'Asset Prices and the Business Cycle', World Economic Outlook, May 2000.

European companies tend to be more highly geared than their American counterparts but they are not more highly geared than Japanese companies. In Japan, which has relatively little merger and acquisition activity, rises in investment are evident when stock prices rise. It may be that in Japan companies use a greater proportion of funds raised for investment in growth or it may be that they use the new funds to pay off loans.

Unfortunately, the IMF has not updated this interesting research on the correlation between stock prices and fixed capital formation. But the simple fact of the matter is that stock market capitalization has increased enormously since 2000. However, this expansion of investment in equities has not even vaguely been matched by a similar expansion in fixed private investment, with the significant exception of investment in real estate. Although the debate continues over whether stock markets actually facilitate or detract from productive investment in the economy, no one seriously argues that real estate investment is productive, even if it has the side effect of increasing corporate asset values and thus providing greater scope for acquiring financing or indeed raising capital by disposing of property assets.

New investment, of course, is not the only way to raise productivity and improve profitability. However, it tends to be the single most important driver in this direction, which is why it is necessary to discover whether roaring equity markets managed to contribute to the raising of new capital or whether the influx of funds simply increased the size of the markets themselves.

Hard evidence in this area is difficult to come by, but one way of judging whether bull markets have provided the basis for strengthening companies is to examine what happens after they have run their course. If the equity markets had been supplying funds to produce productivity gains or facilitated the development of new forms of business, it would follow that corporate profitability would rise following the end of a period in which stock markets were attracting vast amounts of funds. But in the aftermath of twentieth-century bull runs earnings dipped sharply. The evidence from the 1920s showed that the end of the bull run gave way not only to a collapse of profitability but to the onset of recession. In less dramatic form the end of the 1980s bull run led to a period of falling corporate profitability. In the aftermath of the 1990s bull market, corporate earnings started to dip while the market was still rising.

It seems likely that the rise in earnings during the 1990s, while share prices were still rising sharply, was largely a product of profits made in the financial markets themselves. Many listed companies are in the financial sector while others made good money during the boom years. They did so in part simply by playing the markets. It is far from clear how much of the money sloshing around the equity markets actually made its way back to boring old business development.

So, what role are stock markets actually performing?

Reading the literature relating to concepts of market efficiency it becomes clear that very little attention has been paid to the basic question of whether equity markets are actually performing the role of supplying capital to business. Instead more attention is paid to finding out how efficiently markets perform as price makers, as reflectors of value etc. It seems to be taken as read that stock markets have already performed a satisfactory role as capital markets, leaving questions of efficiency to be addressed solely in terms of the logic of the way the market itself operates.

An interesting study of the Japanese and American stock markets by Richard Pettway and Craig Tapley, for example, examines whether the Law of One Price (LOP) can be applied to both markets. The authors define LOP as stating that 'the same asset, valued in a common currency and trading in two different markets, cannot trade at different prices, except for differences in transportation and transaction costs'.[10] They found that the law can be applied to these two markets, even though there are significant economic and cultural differences. Both markets were found to deliver comparable returns.

This is the key point seized upon by many researchers. They examine returns and see if they make sense either in cross-market comparisons or in comparisons with various types of other assets. This is useful work but addresses only the issue of how markets perform as an end in themselves.

The point at which stock markets interact with the external economy is arguably of greater interest because it is here that we discover the extent to which stock markets are detached from the world of business and exist in a world of their own.

If stock markets are no longer performing a primary role of raising capital for business, what on earth are they doing and why do companies still queue up for listings? As we have seen, the longest queues for listings form during bull markets when investors are hungry for new investment ideas and more than ready to take a punt on new stocks. New issues that would have been marginal in less hectic times are taken up with enthusiasm and oversubscription becomes the order of the day. Investment bankers, stock brokers, legal advisers and accountants line up to persuade directors to obtain a stock market listing, not necessarily because they actually need more cash to make their companies grow but because there is plenty of money in circulation looking for a home. This is bonanza time for the advisers, who can earn fantastic fees by working on new listings, and it is an ideal time for company owners to think about realising a part of the capital tied up in their corporations.

While there is nothing wrong with entrepreneurs cashing in on their investments, it is more than likely that they are doing so at a time when the growth potential for their business has already passed its peak. In other words, shareholders often join the party only once a great deal of the excitement is over.

Stock market booms not only encourage new issues but also stimulate a large number of supplementary issues, or rights issues, of new equity in already listed companies. Characteristically the new money raised during bull markets is not ploughed back into the businesses of the company but used to play the markets and provide ever more lavish rewards for the company's directors. As long as markets are rising and investors are making healthy capital gains, at least on paper, no one complains. There is every incentive for directors to seek new ways of boosting the share price and increasing the number of shares on issue because nowadays it is commonplace for remuneration packages to be linked with stock options. This matter will be discussed in more detail later; for the time being it is sufficient to observe that when company managers have a bigger incentive to inflate share prices than to actually manage the businesses under their control, they often draw the logical conclusion. This means they pay more attention to the computer screens flickering with news of share price movements than to keeping an eye on what's happening back on the shop floor.

One of the outstanding characteristics of the 1990s dotcom boom was the way that the market capitalisation of 'concept stocks' was inflated out of all proportion to likely earnings. These inflated market capitalisations were then used to acquire real assets and take over companies with an infinitely more solid business than that of the predator.

The AOL–Time Warner merger, at the time record-breaking, is examined in Chapter 9 as an example of the way takeovers of this kind do more to destroy than to build companies, but there are plenty of examples from elsewhere in the world which illustrate the same point. In Europe there was the takeover of the German industrial conglomerate Mannesmann by the British telecoms upstart Vodafone AirTouch. In Asia there was an even more audacious deal in which a company called Pacific Century CyberWorks (PCCW) acquired Hong Kong Telecommunications (HKT), the then monopoly telephone network supplier controlled by Britain's Cable and Wireless. At the time of the takeover PCCW had assets amounting to some $48 million whereas HKT's assets totalled almost $7 billion. It was a classic example of the real assets of the predator company being minimal while its market capitalisation greatly exceeded that of the company in its sights. Because this was so, PCCW was able to offer its greatly inflated shares for real performing assets.

Can it be said that in these circumstances the market was performing its function as an efficient matcher of capital with investors? The reality is that the whole process of capital raising has been turned on its head and enabled companies without resources to acquire companies with resources. They do so by virtue of stock market valuations driven into a frenzy by exaggerated expectations of profits likely to be made by companies currently in vogue with stock market investors. Inevitably reality sets in following mergers of this type and the share price of the merged company promptly collapses while searching questions are asked about what possible benefits the victor of the merger deal is bringing to the new company.

Aside from the dubious transactions which take place at the height of bull markets, stock markets continue to raise capital for industry. Even in secondary exchanges, such as NASDAQ in the United States, where excitement often clouds judgement, there are solid examples of good ideas having found cash to create a better business. Going back further in history it is clear that the equity markets played an important role in transforming the American economy from an agrarian base to an industrial powerhouse in the 1890s. However, by and large stock markets have become something other than capital raising centres and have focused on their secondary function of trading capital once it has already been issued. This makes the markets more prone to panics. The growing detachment from real business and the real economy has yet to produce greater instability in equity markets but there is good reason to believe that it will do so, especially when some other relatively new market developments are taken into account.

Much has happened in the past few decades to transform how business on stock markets is conducted. Much has also changed in terms of how markets are influenced and in the types of equity instruments offered for investment. We shall now examine some of these factors.

Contributing to instability – derivatives trading

A good place to start is derivatives trading. As the name suggests, this refers to trading financial instruments based on an asset. In the case of an asset based on stocks, the derivative is valued against the expected movement of the stock price or, as is often the case, against an entire stock index. There are a host of equity derivatives in the form of futures contracts on individual stocks and market indices and there are warrants which provide an opportunity to buy stocks at a future date for, usually, a fixed price. Then there are a number of options which are much like warrants but do not oblige those holding them to buy or sell the underlying asset.

Bonds used to be simply a form of loan financing but nowadays convertible bonds are commonplace, enabling bondholders to convert their loans into equity. This has moved the bond market closer to the derivatives sector and produced new and exotic forms of bond trading that are essentially related to futures market concepts.

Derivative trading has become increasingly complex as new types of derivatives come to the market. Among these relatively new instruments are equity linked notes, principal guaranteed notes, covered calls and covered puts. These instruments, alongside other forms of investment, can be seen as either ways of hedging equity investments or ways of playing the stock market with relatively small sums of money paid up front attracting great rewards and great risks. The effect of all these instruments attached to share prices is to create sub-markets that inevitably have an impact on the main equity, commodity or money markets.

Although many people seem to think that derivative trading is a new form of investment, this is simply not the case. The great bubble of tulip mania in the seventeenth century was essentially a product

115

of futures trading. Buying stocks on margin, which is not quite the same as derivatives trading but follows the same principles because it is based on an investor's view of the future price of the stock, is also just about as old as stock markets. Margin trading ahead of the 1929 crash rose to unprecedented volumes and accounted for the extent of the agony in its aftermath. Investors were faced with a great deal more than capital losses on their investments; they had to find cash to fulfil pressing margin calls. When they could not do so they sold more and more of their assets to raise funds and this in turn exacerbated the downward pressure on share prices. In the 1920s margin trading was hardly novel; on the contrary, it was a mainstream form of stock market investment. What is new is the growth of new forms of financial instruments and the alarm that their growth has stimulated. A study published by the accountancy firm Price Waterhouse in 1996 estimated that derivates notionally valued at $19,000 billion had been issued on S&P 500 index stocks in 1994.[11] But this figure is dwarfed by the Basel-based Bank.for International Settlements (BIS) estimate that by December 2007 the total global size of the derivatives market was $1,444 trillion. This figure is of such magnitude it is very hard to grasp its enormity but, to put it in some perspective, it represents a sum of trading that is 22 times higher than the world's GDP and is equivalent to around $190,000 for every person on the planet.

The size of derivatives trading may well explain why Henry Kaufman, the former chief economist at Salomon Brothers, and in the 1980s one of the most quoted men on Wall Street, said that when he contemplated derivatives trading he could 'think of no other area that has the potential of creating greater havoc on a global basis if something goes wrong'. In 1994 Gerald Corrigan, the former head of the New York Reserve Bank at the time of the 1987 crash, expressed fears that 'the increasing complexity of financial markets could override the ability of the most sophisticated efforts to monitor and manage risk'.[12]

His views were not shared by Alan Greenspan, the former Federal Reserve chairman, who believes in the development of derivative markets and favours the removal of controls on their growth. He clearly agrees with the Nobel economics laureate Merton Miller, who states that 'contrary to the more widely held perception, derivatives have made the world a much safer place, not a dangerous one'.[13]

Investors engage in derivatives trading as a form of insurance or hedging, or so it is argued. To some extent this is true. In this context derivative trading is considered as an efficient mechanism for managing risk. Those advocating this point of view see derivatives trading as a form of judicious hedging that allows investors effectively to insure the trades they make in the markets on which derivatives are issued. (The role of derivatives as a form of diversification for investors is discussed in Chapter 8.)

It may even be that derivatives trading has a neutral impact on the stock market. Franklin Edwards has noted that in 1987, when derivatives trading and program trading were cited as a major exacerbating cause of the market crash, other markets around the world managed to fall by more or less the same level as the American market. Yet 'outside the United States there were no significant stock index futures markets, no portfolio insurance trading and virtually no stock index arbitrage trading'.[14]

Edwards' view is given support by another study of the 1987 Wall Street crash. It found that the cash and futures markets were behaving in tandem, i.e. the cash market was not being led by the futures market. 'The analysis of the statistical lead of futures prices over stock prices during the weeks of October 12 and 19, 1987, are significantly overstated if the non-trading effect is not removed from the S&P 500 Index,' say the report's authors.[15] Non-trading refers to periods when the market simply froze because the flood of orders could not be settled. This study challenges other research, which the authors believe to be distorted by including non-trading periods in the equation and thus making allowances for prices that are frozen during these periods.

They argue that if this is stripped out of the equation the cash market managed to fall without any assistance from the futures market.

Evidence in this matter is hotly contested. However, it remains hard to find proof that derivates trading is actually destabilising markets to the extent of causing them to come crashing down.

Contributing to instability – hedge funds

Among the most active derivatives players are the hedge fund managers who came to prominence in the 1980s, although the first hedge fund was established many years before in 1949. The number of hedge funds expanded considerably a couple of decades before they sprung into the headlines in the 1980s. What propelled them to prominence were the extraordinary profits said to have been made by these funds as they swept across markets taking shrewd bets on whether they would fall or rise and then adopting positions in the derivatives markets to capitalise on these bets. The beauty of hedge funds was that they were positioned to make good money from both market falls and market rises.

In origin, hedge funds were designed to do precisely what their name suggests, i.e. to hedge each position taken in one market with a long (for buying) or short (for selling) position in another market. This means that as the market moves the fund managers can shift funds into either long or short positions in anticipation of making a profit as the movement gathers pace. Hedge funds were blamed for causing the Asian financial crisis. The Hong Kong government even claimed that it had thwarted a concerted attack on the Hong Kong dollar in 1998. It did so by draining the currency market of liquidity and embarking on a blue chip share buying splurge in order to give a 'bloody nose' to those who were speculating against the local currency. The Hong Kong administration maintained that speculators were engaged in a double play on the market, selling short both stocks and the local currency. Evidence of this conspiracy was never produced but the government buying spree did indeed relieve the pressure on the market, and did indeed bloody the noses of those with short positions, even though it created new and more long-lasting pressures.[16]

Perhaps the most famous hedge fund manager is George Soros, who was said to have 'broken the Bank of England' by speculating against the pound in September 1992. Whether or not the collapse of sterling can be attributed solely to Soros, it is clear that his activities had a considerable impact on the currency.

Soros made a killing on sterling, but by his own admission made large losses in Asia during the late 1990s financial crisis. This reverse was overshadowed by the far more spectacular losses incurred by one of America's largest hedge funds, Long Term Capital Management (LTCM), which tottered on the verge of collapse in 1998 when it had borrowings of $125 billion, more than most small nations keep in their fiscal reserves.

The heart of LTCM's problems was its involvement in highly leveraged deals. Deals of this kind have helped hedge funds earn a lot of money when times were good. The fact they tend to be highly leveraged, taking positions in markets with relatively small amounts of money that can be transformed into much larger sums if their bets work out, explains why profits can be so high. (Another form of highly leveraged deal was also common at the time – leveraged buy outs or LBOs. The success of these deals stands in vivid contrast to some hedge fund plays because many involved company managers buying control of their companies. In other words buying real assets that they understood very well and could put to work to make more money.)

Heavily leveraged plays and an ability to operate across a range of asset markets, sometimes in highly complex deals, gave hedge funds the kind of muscular investment image so beloved of market players who see themselves as killer hunters prowling the financial markets. While this image attracted many high-worth investors, it also drew in a number of eager investment managers who were bored with the old markets and liked the challenge of complex market plays, usually involving derivatives. All fund managers like to think that the performance of their funds is based on their skill. Yet impressive results are produced by more traditional fund managers simply as a consequence of being in a bull market. Hedge fund managers cannot just ride on the back of a rising market; indeed, they often do best in a falling market and do so because of the way they manipulate the funds at their disposal, sometimes taking heavy bets on even further downward pressure.

Not only is the challenge of finding opportunities in moving markets intellectually rewarding to hedge fund managers but it can bring exceptional financial gains. Many fund managers work on the basis of an incentive fee equal to 15 to 25 per cent of the fund's annual profits. In good times this makes the standard annual fee of 1–2 per cent for fund management almost irrelevant.

The big money going into the funds, the atmosphere of muscular investment and the thrill of finding yet more ingenious derivative instruments for playing the market placed the activities of hedge fund managers on a different plateau. It was a plateau that removed these markets even further from the assets they were ultimately supposed to reflect.

However, it is one thing to argue that hedge fund managers are operating in a manner which is markedly detached from the underlying assets in which they are investing and another to suggest that they are responsible for market instability. It is possible that their activities exaggerate trends that are already underway, for example by taking short positions in falling markets. But there is little to suggest that the activities of hedge funds actually initiate these trends. It is therefore hard to find much of a factual basis for the hedge fund demonology which arises from time to time.

Contributing to instability – portfolio insurance

Every time markets crash the search for scapegoats gets underway. This was very much so in the wake of the 1987 crash, the biggest of all time. One of the most prominent scapegoats to emerge from this crash was something called portfolio insurance. The operations of portfolio insurance figure prominently in the report of a presidential commission, established by President Reagan, to inquire into the causes of the crash and identify what measures needed to be taken to avoid a repetition. The report of the Presidential Task Force on Market Mechanisms became known as the Brady Report, taking the name from its chairman, Nicholas Brady. The report, published in 1998, concluded that because 'the market break was intensified by the activities of a few institutions [it] illustrates the vulnerability of the market in which individuals own 60 percent of equities'.[17]

The report stated that the initial decline in the stock market 'ignited mechanical price-insensitive selling by a number of institutions employing portfolio insurance strategies and a small number of mutual fund groups reacting to redemptions'. These institutions were operating in both the stock or cash and futures markets. 'Selling pressure in the futures market was transmitted to the stock market by the mechanism of index arbitrage.'[18]

Portfolio insurance sounds as though it is something with an actuarial basis, but in reality it is nothing of the kind. The insurance element is provided by hedging investments in shares by buying a put option on the portfolio or acquiring futures contracts to 'cover' the portfolio. A put option, in this context, is purchased in anticipation of a fall in the share price. It gives the buyer the right, but not the obligation, to sell the share to the option writer at a fixed price within a fixed period of time.

In practice portfolio insurance, which comes in a number of forms, is little more than a method of selling stocks when the market falls. Of course it is not quite that simple, which is why it took the combined brains of two University of California professors, Hayne Leland and Mark Rubinstein, to come up with the idea. They devised a mathematical formula for telling investors when the time was right to sell stocks or derivatives in order to cut losses. The concept of loss cutting was hardly novel but the addition of some covering in the form of hedging on futures markets added to an old idea. The idea caught on with a number of large institutional investors who brought it into play in 1987. By the time of the crash shares valued at $60 billion were 'covered' by portfolio insurance plays.

The crash effectively killed off the notion of portfolio insurance. It did so in part because it showed that a market under pressure was not liquid enough to accommodate simultaneous trades on the cash and futures markets. Even more important was the fact that when push came to shove the big institutions lost their nerve and abandoned the double plays on the cash and futures markets and simply sold everything. However, before they did so it was clear that portfolio insurance plays had added to the force of the decline. This is not quite the same as saying that portfolio insurance was the cause of the 1987 crash. It is also interesting to note that research conducted in the aftermath of the crash found only a few (5.5 per cent) institutional investors would admit to having employed a portfolio insurance scheme.[19]

Contributing to instability – momentum investment

Although portfolio insurance has effectively died it could be said to be partially living on in the form of momentum investment, which became especially popular with day traders during the 1990s boom. In a nutshell this is a theory of going with the flow: it encourages buying when stocks are on an upward trajectory and selling them when they are on a downward swing. It is the antithesis of the views of those who believe that money can be made only by heading in the opposite direction to the herd. However, following trends in a bull market is not without its merits and, because momentum investment created a momentum of its own, the stratagem had many followers. Like their predecessors who believed in portfolio insurance, the momentum investors did much to accentuate market movements and added to the volatility of the market.

Contributing to instability – program trading

Momentum investment and portfolio insurance have much in common with program trading – trading dictated by computer programs that automatically generate buy or sell orders when stock prices reach a certain level. Program trading accounts for an extraordinarily high level of Wall Street's turnover. By 2000 it was accounting for around 27 per cent of all trades.[20] Progam trading has declined considerably since this time. According to figures from the New York Stock Exchange in 2008, the percentage of trades generated in this manner declined to around 20 per cent, still a significant figure but less alarming than levels previously seen. It is misleading to paint a picture of computers dominating markets through this form of trading, not least because computers are dumb machines that require human intelligence to make them work. Program trading, as the name implies, is based on programs developed by strategists who have taken a view on where the market reaches crucial buy and sell points. The programs do little more than execute these views in a mechanical fashion.

Contributing to instability – new technology

Advances in technology have always played an important role in the way that stock markets operate. In the 1920s the growing popularity of the telephone was quickly pressed into service by share salesmen using it to promote shares and take orders. In the 1990s the big revolution was the growth of the Internet, which made share trading easier and gave individuals access to the kind of information that had previously been the exclusive preserve of institutional investors. Data from the New York Stock Exchange show that the average number of daily trades from online brokerage accounts grew from 96,002 per day in March 1997 to over 1,371,000 in March 2000. The investment company Chase, Hambrecht, and Quest estimated that in the last three months of 1999 online trading accounted for 17.6 per cent of all trades on Wall Street and that in the first quarter of 2000 the volume had risen to 20.6 per cent.[21]

Easier access to the stock market has added to both the volume and volatility of trading, more particularly in shares listed on NASDAQ, which are mainly in the hi-tech sector. The average rate of annual turnover (the percentage of shares changing hands) for NASDAQ stocks was 91.8 per cent in the period from 1980 to 1989. In the period from 1995 to 1999 the average annual turnover rate rose to almost 252 per cent. On the main board turnover also rose from 51.5 per cent in the earlier period to just over 67 per cent in the later period. By the end of the 1990s bull run in 1999 turnover on the main board was running at 78 per cent. Markets elsewhere in the world were seeing share churn increasing at a fast rate. In London in 1998 turnover reached an average of 79 per cent, in Paris it was at 67 per cent but the Frankfurt market surpassed them all with a churn rate of 289 per cent.[22]

Bull markets always increase volumes of trading but not necessarily levels of volatility. Thanks to the Internet, however, a new factor has come into play in the form of day trading, which greatly expanded during the 1990s. The Securities and Exchange Commission found that the number of online stock trading accounts in the United States rose from 3.7 million in 1997 to 9.7 million two years later. Day traders, as the name suggests, are not long-term investors. They play the market by the day, or even by the minute, selling relatively small amounts of shares many times over. Their presence in such large numbers did much to increase the volatility of day-to-day movements on Wall Street (and to a much smaller extent in places like London). Day trading, however, is very much a phenomenon of a bull market. When the bulls departed, so did many of the day traders.

Concentration of power

Although day traders were much in the headlines, real power in markets was increasingly moving towards institutional investors. They got information ahead of the retail investors and had the market muscle to push their trades through ahead of others. The power of the big institutional players is daunting, as is all power concentrated in few hands. Fifty years ago over 90 per cent of the shares listed on Wall Street were owned by individuals. In 1998 individuals owned just 41 per cent of the market.[23] But the number of individual share owners has grown, especially as a result of the 1990s bull run. There were 27 million individual shareholders in America in 1989; by 1998 the number had risen to 33.8 million.[24] Meanwhile more and more money was pouring into mutual funds (or unit trusts as they are known in Britain) and more money was going into pension funds and more into life assurance schemes. Although this meant that individual investors were indirectly playing a much bigger role in the stock market, the power over their funds was delegated to a relatively small number of people who were every bit as fallible as the non-professional participants in the market.

The question then arises as to whether fund managers were and are any better at exercising stewardship over this ever growing cash mountain than individual players? If you were to believe the flood of advertisements extolling the virtues of fund management, you might conclude that stock market investment was a business best left in their hands. However, a classic study of mutual fund performance, based on 115 funds surveyed from 1955 to 1964, showed that on average fund managers not only failed to beat the market but, once their management fees had been taken into account, the return from investments in mutual funds was less than that found in the market overall. Another study, covering the period 1968 to 1977 and looking at a wider range of 1,200 professional portfolio managers, showed that at best they only managed to beat the overall market rate of return by around 1.5 per cent.[25] In 1985 *Business Week* published a survey by Funds Evaluation Services which showed that in every year from 1975 to 1984 the majority of American money managers had achieved returns below those of the index averages. In the worst year, 1984, 74 per cent of managers had managed to underperform the index. Overall in this period 56 per cent underperformed the blue chip indices.[26]

It may be unfair to be too hard on the fund managers because it is no mean feat to consistently outperform the index. As Burton Malkiel has observed in *A Random Walk Down Wall Street*, 'no scientific evidence has yet been assembled to indicate that the investment performance of professionally managed portfolios as a group has been any better than that of randomly selected portfolios'.[27] Having made this blunt statement in 1973, Malkiel was often asked whether it still held true two decades later. He was happy to respond that he had no need to change his view because in the period from 1974 to 1994 two-thirds of professionally managed portfolios failed to beat the unmanaged Standard & Poor's 500 Stock Index.

Of course, some individual fund managers beat the index averages and do so impressively (although even the very best find it hard to sustain this kind of performance), but this is not the point here. What is more important is the power they wield. The fact that they exercise this considerable power while only sporadically outperforming the market suggests that at times of pressure they probably react just like amateurs – they panic.

While there is some limited evidence to suggest that professional money managers react in a way that sets them apart from retail investors, what is more certain is their herd instinct. This will be examined more closely in Chapter 7, but for now let us just say that the influence of the herd has considerable impact in the relatively small world of fund management. This is not least because of client pressure: clients tend to be wary of managers with a strategy that bucks the trend. At times of panic, many holders of mutual funds want out, so fund managers are forced to sell stocks to make good the redemptions. Perhaps the relatively poor performance of fund managers is no more than a reflection of their client's expectations.

But even blaming the customer – a tendency not unknown in service industries and in this case possibly justified – cannot obviate the disturbing truth that fund managers tend to cluster together in an unhealthy manner. For a start, they often work in very close proximity to each other. They nervously eye the same benchmarks against which their performance is judged. Like all close-knit groups, they speak the same jargon-filled language and use the same verbal shorthand incomprehensible to outsiders.

The fact that everybody is behaving in the same way explains why markets move in the way they move, but the new element here is the concentration of power. Even if we ignore the 'power corrupts' axiom it seems reasonable to suggest that power in the hands of relatively few people leaves those outside this charmed circle that much more powerless.

Figure 5.3 **The growth of fund management on Wall Street**

Type of fund	Percentage ownership of all shares		
	1950	1970	1998
Mutual funds	2.0	4.1	11.3
State & local govt. retirement plans	0.0	1.2	11.4
Private pension funds	0.0	0.0	8.9
Bank personal trusts & estates	0.0	10.9	3.8
Defined benefit private pension plans	0.8	8.0	5.6
Mutual funds not owned by households	0.0	0.6	5.0
Life assurance funds	1.3	1.5	3.5
Total	4.1	26.3	49.5

Source : Adapted from Table 16 in New York Stock Exchange, *Shareownership 2000*.

Figure 5.3 shows how the enormous growth in funds under management in America has led to domination of the market by the people who manage these funds.

Although the New York Stock Exchange has not updated its share ownership survey in September 2008 the United States Conference Board conducted a survey of ownership in the stock of America's 1,000 leading companies in 2006 and found that individual shareholders owned just 24 per cent of these shares, compared with 34 per cent of all shares listed on the exchange. This left 76 per cent of the leading 1,000 companies, shares in the hands of institutional shareholders, up from a total of 61 per cent in 2000. Institutional holdings in the wider market totaled 66 per cent in 2006.

The fund manager's control of the market has almost doubled in the two decades since 1970 and has risen more than twelvefold since 1950. Those who control the market are the market makers. This is so not only for technical reasons, because they have the muscle to make their trades ahead of anyone else, but also because the execution of their trades sets the trend.

The rise of the investment banks

The spectacular collapse of America's leading investment banks in 2008, with similar collapses in Europe, has left the more traditional retail banks looking better than their counterparts who hogged the limelight in the last decades of the previous millennium. The strength of the investment banks in the late 1990s mirrored, and was part of, the growing power of fund managers. These banks originated in Britain where they were known as merchant banks. Although Britain may be able to claim some primacy in the establishment of this form of banking, catering to the needs of corporations, helping them raise capital, arranging mergers and loans etc., British merchant banking as an independent entity has practically disappeared. American investment banks have secured overwhelming domination of the global market.

Before the late 1980s they were not allowed to sell shares but when this restriction was removed, and similar restrictions disappeared in Britain, the investment banks became not only the issuers of new shares, the underwriters of share issues, the principal advisers to companies seeking access to capital markets, but also the main share traders and the main source of information on shares.

As the power of investment banks grew the public was solemnly assured that they had erected 'Chinese walls' to prevent conflicts of interest between the various divisions of the bank. These walls were supposed to be especially strong in dividing the stockbrokers from the capital raising parts of the banks because each of these sections was dealing with sellers and buyers of stocks who had potentially different interests. Even within the stockbroking side of the business there were supposed to be strict barriers between those conducting stock market analysis and the share salesmen and the people on the capital issues side of the fence.

During the 1990s bull market these walls came under increasing strain as the capital raising divisions in the banks were generating far greater sums of money from new share issues than the stockbrokers who were operating on tighter and tighter margins as competition increased. The real money makers in the big investment banks looked to share salesmen to push the shares they were issuing on behalf of clients and, so it is alleged, the analysts in the banks were asked to provide supportive reports which would increase demand for these shares. Even if they did not issue highly enthusiastic 'buy' recommendations they were most certainly not expected to issue 'sell' recommendations on the stocks of actual or potential clients.

Matters came to a head early in 2002 when Eliot Spitzer, the New York State Attorney General, launched an investigation into the research department of the investment bank Merrill Lynch. His ten-month investigation claimed to show that, in order to secure invest-ment banking business, Merrill's research department deliberately issued misleading reports to stimulate share buying in companies sponsored by the bank. He discovered e-mails in which analysts were pouring scorn on stocks they were recommending to clients. In a phrase that was to become famous Spitzer described this as 'a shock-ing betrayal of trust by one of Wall Street's most trusted names'. Merrill Lynch denied these charges but in May 2002 reached an out-of-court settlement involving the payment of $100 million and a statement of contrition. Merrill also agreed to separate analysts' remuneration from earnings arising from anything other than services to investment clients and introduced various other measures to monitor their work. The following month Merrill announced that the remuneration of its analysts would be tied to the accuracy of their forecasts, introducing a tantalising new element into the equation of how analysts perform.

Spitzer was also looking into the activities of other investment banks and has proposed splitting off the banks' stock research activities from the investment banking side of the business.

The irony of the action against Merrill was that Charles Merrill, one of the company's founders, was a pioneer of so-called 'people's capitalism' and established a business designed to attract the small investor into the stock market. He was also famously candid in furnishing investment advice that was good for clients even if not profitable for his company. Just over a year before the 1929 crash he wrote to his clients in these terms: 'We do not urge you to sell securities indiscriminately, but we do advise in no uncertain terms that you take advantage of the present high prices and put your own financial house in order.'[28] It is hard to imagine one of Merrill's analysts issuing this kind of advice in 1999. Some two decades after the 1929 crash Merrill wrote to the new partners in his greatly expanded company, saying: 'Disturbing is the large percentage of potential investors and speculators in securities who are suspicious of the motives and operations of the securities business and the people engaged therein.'[29]

It seems as though Charles Merrill was talking to Spitzer from beyond the grave. The law of unintended consequences seems to be in operation here, although it may be some small consolation that Merrill Lynch was not alone in attracting the suspicion the company's founder warned of in the 1940s.

The Merrill case provided a focus for concerns that were widely discussed well before Spitzer decided to prosecute. Nor were the concerns confined to the United States. A survey by the financial newswire *Bloomberg* conducted in Britain in 2001 found that some

78 per cent of house brokers (a unique British arrangement under which companies appoint stockbrokers to act as corporate finance advisers and ensure compliance with regulations) for the thirty largest UK companies had positive recommendations on their clients' shares. This was in contrast to recommendations by other brokers, only 47 per cent of whom, including house brokers, had placed a positive recommendation on these companies. No house broker placed a 'sell' recommendation on the shares of its clients.[30]

In general the inclination to place a 'sell' recommendation on a stock has fallen sharply over recent years. Zachs Investment Research studied analysts' recommendations on 6,000 stocks in 1999 and found that only 1 per cent were rated as 'sells', 69.5 per cent were given 'buy' recommendations and 29.5 per cent were seen as 'holds'. Ten years earlier there had been nine times as many 'sell' recommendations as there were at the end of the Wall Street bull run.[31]

It may be argued that it matters little what brokers' analysts recommend because the share buying public will make up its own mind. However, there is a body of evidence that suggests that these recommendations do have a significant effect on the market. A 1984 study of 4,000 stock return forecasts by 35 stockbrokers relating to some 200 heavily traded shares on the London Stock Exchange found that transactions based on these recommendations outperformed the market by 2.2 per cent. Interestingly, the authors of this study attribute the close similarity of brokers' forecasts not to collusion but to objective work on the basis of similar information.[32]

The 1984 study was conducted while the market was in a far less euphoric state than in the go-go years of the 1990s. Stock analysts, particularly those with bullish views such as Abby Joseph Cohen of Goldman Sachs & Co. and Henry Blodget of Merrill Lynch, the great promoter of dotcom stocks, were darlings of the media. They were often quoted and much in demand to reassure investors that buying stocks was the right thing to do. Analysts who produced bullish forecasts delighted the companies they were promoting and pleased investors who saw the value of their stock rise. Their forecasts almost became self-fulfilling prophecies because they were no longer confined to small circulation investment reports but featured large in the media, a media reinforced with television stations, such as CNBC, devoted to broadcasting financial news. Meanwhile newspapers enlarged their business coverage as they cut back on the tedious stuff, such as major famines in Africa.

Being bullish showed good team spirit and demonstrated that the new paradigm had been fully embraced by these forward-thinking individuals. The 'value' of their analysis was no longer judged by actual corporate performance. What mattered was not what the companies were doing but what other analysts thought they were doing. Therefore companies were applauded not for meeting analysts' predictions but for beating benchmarks based on what other analysts had predicted for share price performance. The stock markets of the 1990s were no place for wimps with old economy hangups. Too many people had an interest in talking up the market to have much patience with those expressing doubts. Talking up started from the very top. In the White House President Clinton seemed both delighted and slightly bemused to be presiding over a great economic boom making citizens much more wealthy and more likely to re-elect a president whose term of office coincided with the boom. Alan Greenspan at the Federal Reserve was seen as the godfather of the boom. Managers of listed companies, weighed down with increasingly valuable stock options, convinced themselves that their genius was making everyone rich. Meanwhile the investment banks were raking in cash from new issues, from handling mergers and from dealing in stocks.

Having previously been cautious about proprietary trading or trading for their own account, investment banks, stockbrokers and fund managers poured into the market making their own deals. Worse, a great many individual managers and other market professionals were busily dealing on their personal accounts. Because at the time this was banned in many organisations, and is much more widely prohibited now, it is hard to tell, aside from anecdotal evidence, how much of this kind of trading was going on. Personal trading was a problem because it diverted the attention of people who were supposed to be making money for others and in some cases did so at the expense of their clients as they pushed forward their orders ahead of the clients'. In extreme cases clients' funds were used for quick margin trades on their personal behalf.

Corporate proprietary trading was and remains perfectly acceptable in terms of law and regulations in most jurisdictions. However, it causes inevitable conflicts of interest when positions are taken that are at variance with those held by clients who may be given advice to bring their trading positions into line with those of the banks or stockbrokers. If even the so-called professional advisers could not be trusted to keep calm and stay away from business that threatened the interests of their clients, what hope was there for sanity to prevail in the markets?

Neil Barsky, a journalist turned fund manager, brought a jaundiced eye to this mess and questioned whether investors deserved any better than the fate which faces them when bubbles burst. He wrote:

> The reality is that Wall Street's research analysts such as Merrill Lynch's maligned Mr Blodget were merely the town criers for an American stock market frenzy with few heroes. Option-rich corporate CEOs fixed both eyes on their share prices and pushed numbers to please Wall Street. Accountants were all too willing to give companies all the rope they asked for. And investors? Pardon me if I sound unsympathetic, but I don't recall fund managers complaining about Wall Street's well known conflicts of interest while IPOs were routinely popping 100 per cent in a day.[33]

One of Barsky's recommended ways to stop this merry-go-round is to force investors to accept responsibility for their own mistakes. He thinks companies should cease issuing earnings guidance, analysts should stop making share recommendations and investors should make their own decisions based on the material to hand.

In the unlikely event that Barsky's recommendations are ever taken up, a lot of highly paid people would find themselves experiencing the dubious delights of enjoying more leisure time. Unsurprisingly they are not lining up to take them on board.

The stock option virus

Even less enthusiastic about share price declines are the growing mass of people holding stock options from the companies that employ them. The National Center for Employee Ownership estimated that by the end of the 1990s ten million American employees were holding stock options. It sounds like the dawn of a new share owning democracy but the reality is that the bulk of these options are in the hands of senior management who view them as a major component of their remuneration packages. Instead of spreading wealth and providing greater incentives to improve productivity, stock options, as Warren Buffett has observed, provided an enormous incentive to overstate earnings.

This is no small matter. A survey by Standard & Poor's of companies in the S&P 500 Stock Index found that their combined earnings in 2001 would have been 23 per cent lower if stock option grants were treated as expenses. This is not merely an American problem, a separate survey by the investment bank Dresdner Kleinwort Wasserstein found that in Europe the failure to count stock options as expenses allowed companies to overstate their earnings by 23 per cent in 2001 and 11 per cent in 2000.[34] In May 2002 Standard & Poor's was considering changing the way it calculates earnings for the purpose of stock market ratios so as to treat company options as an expense against earnings. This proposal is in line with a bill in the US Senate proposed by Carl Levin and John McCain, called the 'Ending the Double Standard for Stock Options' bill, which would force companies to account for stock options as an expense or give up the tax deductions available to stock option holders. This bill and similar legislation did not pass into law. Concern over stock options is not confined to the United States; in Britain the International Accounting Standards Board started developing new rules in 2002 that mirror the American moves to treat stock options as an expense chargeable against profits.

We shall return to this matter and a more general discussion of how earning figures are distorted in Chapter 9.

Infectious greed

With so much riding on the value of the company's stock, as opposed to the actual profits being generated, the focus fell squarely on massaging the stock price, even to the extent of massive fraud, as is alleged to be the cause of the downfall of the Enron Corporation. The contrarian fund manager Jeremy Grantham, speaking in July 2000, said, 'The great bull market conspiracy this time is far bigger than ever before because of stock options. Stock options don't threaten to make senior managers rich. They threaten to make them disgustingly rich. Hundreds of millions of dollars are transferred from the shareholders to the top management these days.'[35]

Even Alan Greenspan, the chairman of the Federal Reserve, who is a fervent believer in free markets and an opponent of what he sees as market overregulation, was sufficiently worried by the stock option virus and other forms of accounting irregularities to call for stiff penalties on cheating executives. In a July 2002 address to congressmen Greenspan, who had warned of 'irrational exuberance' in the stock market in 1996, talked of the dangers of 'infectious greed'. He said that the 1990s boom had engendered 'an outsize increase in opportunities for avarice'. He added, 'it is not that humans (became) any more greedy than in generations past. It is that the avenues to express greed have grown enormously.'

The end of the 1990s bull run looked as though it might be accelerated by the big market fall on 17 September 2001, when Wall Street reopened following the 9/11 terrorist attack, but the sharp plunge reversed itself with relative ease. The absence of large sustained movements has served to obscure a slower but perhaps more damaging drip, drip effect that by the middle of 2002 had brought the American market down by over 40 per cent from the high point it reached on 24 March 2000. This steady erosion of share prices has caused the second biggest decline since World War II. There are signs that disenchantment with equities is especially strong among small investors. In July 2002 American investors pulled what was then a record $50 billion out of US equity funds. The high level of withdrawals put additional pressure on the market as fund managers were forced to sell shares to make good the redemptions and is indicative of a trend which bodes ill for Wall Street, at least in the short term.

A gradual slide in share prices spreading from Wall Street to other markets presents complex challenges to shareholders that do not exist when markets take giant leaps in a downward direction. The big worry is that new forces of inherent instability are being built into the system, shaking its foundations and threatening to undermine the stock market's traditional resilience.

6

The trader and the fund manager

HOW DO THE PEOPLE at the sharp end of the stock market business actually respond to panics and what strategies do they have for avoiding the consequences of panic? These questions need addressing once theories have been laid to one side and the agonising debates over the causes of stock market crashes have been exhausted. In order to explore this matter I conducted in-depth interviews with two leading stock market professionals who had direct responsibility for managing large sums of money at times of market panic.

Obviously, no two people can be truly representative of such a diverse collection of individuals, and it is doubtful whether an attempt to homogenise experience would yield insightful information. My subjects are simply two men who have seen at first hand what happened and have sufficient market experience to be able to make some sense of it. Like other market professionals they also have firm views on how markets behave and what money managers should be doing to cope with this behaviour. This chapter is designed to convey their unique knowledge and experience.

The trader: Warren Primhak

Warren Primhak, is the head of cash trading for Asia Pacific (ex-Japan) for Deutsche Securities Asia, a subsidiary of Deutsche Bank. He is a trader to his very fingertips who learned about the equities business starting right at the bottom. He has worked his way up to a senior position by using his wit and experience to gain a prodigious knowledge of the markets.

There seems to be something of an officers-and-men distinction in the investment industry, which is reflected in the social backgrounds and education of those who trade equities and those who manage and analyse stock markets. This is epitomised in the background of the two interviewees in this chapter.

Primhak is a fast talking, fast thinking Londoner who retains a distinct cockney accent despite having lived most of his working life overseas. His speech is littered with expletives that barely raise an eyebrow on the trading floor but would not be quite so well received in more genteel areas of the investment banking community.

He started work as a messenger for Spencer Thornton, a British stockbroker specialising in US equities. One of the lasting impressions gained from this experience was to realise the importance of settlements. In other words, the nuts and bolts business of executing and completing trades with all the paperwork in place. As he has progressed up the ladder he has found this to be 'an area people take for granted and the area which is often the first casualty in cost cutting exercises, but this is where you really need people with long serving experience. It is an area where you can lose a great deal of money if you get it wrong.' There is considerable scope for error under the pressure of high volumes of business, Primhak notes. At times of pressure, he says, stockbrokers are most vulnerable to loss and most likely to get into trouble.

This experience was reinforced when, in 1983, he joined State Street Bank, one of the world's leading specialists in custodial services. A year later Primhak moved to Barings Securities Far East, where he started work on the operations side but moved to the trading desk in early 1985.

In those days there was a much more direct relationship between the buyers and sellers of shares and traders. Now, he says, there can be eight people in the chain, including fund managers, analysts, sales managers, central trading desks etc. Each party can bring a different view to the trade. At times of panic two things can happen: on the one hand, they may all be gripped by the same notion that it is time to throw in the towel and they reinforce each other's views. On the other hand, the fact that there are too many people involved in the buying and selling can slow down decision taking when decisive action is required. Primhak quite likes the moments when the collective wisdom of all these parties veers towards throwing in the towel. 'That's the time to buy,' he says.

However, back in 1985 he was not confident enough to make judgements of this kind. Fortunately he had a valuable mentor in the shape of Christopher Heath, under whose leadership Barings was making a name for itself in Asian markets, especially the Japanese market which Heath correctly identified as heading for a major bull run. Primhak's steady rise among the traders took him to Tokyo to head the trading desk just in time for the 1987 crash. The recovery was rapid, but Primhak then found himself in a new crisis, lamentably, from his point of view, confined to his own company. In 1995 Barings was brought to its knees by the rogue trading activities of Nick Leeson. By then Primhak was head of Asian trading, based in Hong Kong, and while many other executives fled the company he remained to help sort out the mess left by the collapse. Shortly after that debris was cleared up he was in the thick of another crisis sparked by the devaluation of the Thai baht in 1997 and the major fallout on Asian stock markets that followed.

Now employed at Deutsche Securities Asia, Primhak is head of cash trading in the Asia Pacific region outside of Japan. He is responsible for trading and execution of everything from blue chips to small cap stocks. Primhak sits with his staff in an open-plan office on the fifty-sixth floor of Hong Kong's Cheung Kong Centre. It has a stunning view over the harbour, a view rarely noticed by those in the office who, if they look up, are more likely to glance at the large hanging television screens tuned to CNN and CNBC.

Most of the time Primhak is clicking through two of the four screens on his desk, while shouting out buy and sell orders, speaking into a microphone with connections to trading rooms overseas, taking other phone calls and having snatched conversations with his colleagues. 'You've got to be able to listen to four or five conversations at one time,' says Primhak as he nods approvingly at the screen showing one of his trades going through. Every now and again he roars out a big order which he wants a number of people to fill, 'I've got a million of [he names a stock] to sell', he yells. Within seconds someone comes back with part of the order filled.

Money is made by plunging into the market to secure deals which turn on fractions of percentage points. Traders do not see themselves as sentimentalists. Primhak is no exception: 'I don't fall in love with anything for more than two seconds,' he jokes. The share that was a great buy a minute ago has suddenly become a great sell.

'I'm like a conductor in an orchestra. I shout, scream, yell and joke. I pull it all together because our job is to put transactions together.

'Timing is our job, we try to make a pipeline and we try to dominate the market in certain shares. To do that you need to be on top of the information and you need to know where to provide liquidity.' The name of the game is to be 'a dictator of pricing'. This is achieved by following a relatively small number of shares and then making sure 'that our volume in these shares is bigger than anyone else's. This means anyone dealing in the share has to come to you to do business.' Primhak sounds aggressive and watches his trading position like a hawk, making sure that the competition does not better the positions secured by his traders.

He is a veteran of three major market crashes and saw at first hand the disintegration of one of Britain's most famous financial institutions as a result of Leeson's reckless trading. This makes him far more conservative in attitude than initial impressions would suggest.

He says, not exactly approvingly, 'In general, people in our business are optimistic people. So what happens when things go wrong is you have a scenario in which they think that, because shares have fallen a lot, they can't fall much more. But the fact is they can fall, they can fall by 99 per cent.' This is why he is interested in fundamental share analysis and very aware of risks, particularly credit risk among clients.

The learning curve on risk accelerated to a terrifying degree in 1987 when all the world's markets crashed more or less at once and he had just arrived in Tokyo. Never having experienced a real crisis, he was far from being fully prepared. Primhak was not alone because he was sitting in an office filled with newly arrived people who were not sure what to do but basically believed that the crisis would blow over in a couple of days. 'I was inexperienced in that I had never seen anything like this, but I couldn't believe the response of my so-called experienced bosses.'

It did not take long for major disagreement to break out between the traders and the management of the company. There is no doubt it was a scary situation. 'I came into the office and was confronted with sell orders. There were no buy orders at all. The futures market had collapsed and there was no stop loss system [unlike in the physical market where the Japanese authorities imposed a cessation of trading once the market had fallen by a certain percentage]. There was nothing I could do'.

Even then, he recalls, 'there was no realisation of how bad it was and it got worse because we had no other instruments we could sell'. On the night of the first day of the crash he went out for a drink with a client. 'I have never seen such a nervous wreck in my life. He was literally shaking because he had everything invested in the market.' Primhak's bosses were not exactly shaking but 'they were gobsmacked. They spent their time rushing around in meetings and waiting for the people overseas to come in and create some strategies.' Because of the global time clock the Japanese market is the most important market to open every trading day; traders in Japan have to wait at least eight hours to get a signal from European markets and another five or so hours before New York kicks in. This leaves the subsidiaries of foreign companies, with a large overseas client base, at a particular disadvantage at times of crisis when they fear acting without reference to head office.

According to Primhak the traders were told that the last thing the management wanted them to do was to make prices (i.e. offer buying and selling prices for shares); 'If pushed, we were told to make a really silly price' that no one would accept. 'Management wanted the clamps to go on and they shat themselves at the idea that we would be seen as attempting to make a market.'

The traders, on the other hand, 'argued that this was the biggest money spinner in the world … if you really believed in what you were doing this was one of the great opportunities'.

While the traders were saying buy, buy, buy and get into warrants, 'the management were screaming sell, sell. We lost a lot of money and we did not get into warrants' (a low cost, high risk way of gambling on a sharp reversal of the market).

It took only a day for the traders' view to be vindicated because, after the initial shock, bottom fishing emerged. 'Everyone wanted to buy,' Primhak recalls. Then there was a witch hunt to find out 'which idiots had sold futures at such a stupid level'.

The main lesson Primhak learned from the 1987 crash was that there were opportunities and that they could have been realised by sitting down calmly and asking how bad things were and how long was the market likely to go down. Assuming that the answers were not discouraging, the company should have bought shares in its own right. Barings had the money and should have had the experience to seize the opportunity.

As we now know, the effects of the 1987 crash did not linger long. In Asia, particularly in East Asia, the crash soon gave way to an unprecedented boom that sent stocks soaring to new heights.

Primhak was moved back to London and then to Hong Kong to supervise the explosion of trading that accompanied this bull market. His experience of the 1987 crisis and living in Japan made him very aware that the markets were precarious. He was especially nervous of the possibility of earthquakes in Japan, and when the big one hit Kobe on 17 January 1995, he was ready. The Nikkei 225 Index dropped by nearly 6 per cent on 23 January and lost over 8 per cent in the next ten days. In Singapore Barings' wild gambles on the Nikkei futures market were shattered by these large declines. They were initiated by Nick Leeson, who was the head of stock futures trading in Singapore and acting without the knowledge of his bosses in London. Once the earthquake struck Primhak had a strategy of buying Japanese concrete and construction related shares and selling everything else. The subsequent continual decline of the Japanese market validated this approach, but more pressing for Primhak was the fact that Barings was rapidly sinking and he was among those left to sort out the mess during the takeover by the Dutch-controlled ING Groep NV.

Within two years of getting the stockbroking part of the business back on its feet in Asia, there were signs that the Asian boom was coming to an end. 'Having had experience of Japan, I always believed that we had a stupid market here. It was crazy, everyone was geared up to their eyebrows, the management were spending their days out on the golf course, Rolls-Royces were running all over town.' In these circumstances his strategy was always to be prepared to be short in the market, in other words, taking positions that assumed a downturn.

This strategy should have worked, but it did not in Hong Kong, which became the most active and liquid Asian market outside Japan. As the Asian financial crisis tightened its grip, with currencies seemingly going into free fall and equity markets tumbling, the Hong Kong government decided in the summer of 1998 to prevent further falls in the stock market and thwart attempts to weaken the local currency. It did so by launching a one-day unprecedented buying spree in the stock market that ended up with the government holding something like 10 per cent of all blue chip stocks. 'I was absolutely screwed,' says Primhak. Anyone taking short positions had to scramble to get shares. This was a costly business as the Hong Kong government had virtually sucked all the liquidity out of the market. It delivered another lesson. 'Never underestimate the power of liquidity.' Before then he had not quite appreciated what liquidity does to the market. This dramatic, albeit highly unusual, governmental response to a market crisis demonstrated the dangers of illiquidity at times of crisis.

By the time the third big panic came Primhak had enough experience under his belt. However, he happened to be on holiday when the 11 September terrorist attack hit America. He recalls his mobile telephone 'lighting up like a Christmas tree' as calls poured in from colleagues urging him to get back to the office. This was to be no rerun of the 1987 crisis; for a start, the delay between the attack and the reopening of the Wall Street market provided an opportunity to think carefully about what to do. This is precisely what Primhak did, being 'much more concerned about contingency plans'. And he started to think about opportunities. 'It was not so much a matter of taking advantage of individuals selling their shares as of thinking about what we should buy.'

Like many people employed by big international finance companies, Primhak was preoccupied by the terrifying images of the attack on the World Trade Center. It made him wonder what would happen if the very physical infrastructure of the bank was destroyed in the way that the attacks had wiped out the premises of other companies. In the new circumstances created by these attacks finance houses had to start focusing a lot more on physical security while also busying themselves with matters of financial security.

While Wall Street was shut Deutsche Securities (in common with some other major stockbrokers) decided to establish a trading desk open twenty-four hours a day to provide cash and liquidity for clients who would otherwise have been immobilised by the closure of the New York market. This meant that they had to make their own market, prices were not established with other brokers. It was a risk but, as it turned out, it was probably not as risky as closing down the shop and allowing anxiety to build while clients could do nothing about it. 'Not many people used this service,' recalls Primhak, 'but they liked the fact that it was there. It helped stop the panic.' One of the fears that most affects investors is the fear that they will be caught in a position where they can do nothing. When Deutsche Securities offered this service they were, as he puts it, 'saying if you really want to sell, I will buy what customers offer. I am here to provide liquidity.'

In taking these actions Primhak drew on the experiences of 1998 and 1987. On the eve of the market reopening on Wall Street he worked all night to prepare for whatever might happen. But 'it was just an anti-climax', he recalls. There were both buyers and sellers filing orders, with quite a lot of buy orders from corporations wanting to buy their own shares.

The rapid market rebound after the sharp reopening plunge made the post-9/11 crash one of the briefest on record. However, Primhak is far from confident that the 2001 crash can be seen as the end of cycle rounding off the consequences of the 1990s boom. On the contrary, he believes 'we are going to see something worse than the '87 crash'.

The enemy for traders is complacency, 'I really do believe that complacency is the worst thing for our industry,' he says. 'There is always a tendency to think that everything will be all right in a couple of days and then there is a disaster. Things will not always be OK. You need to understand that.'

As a trader he insists that consequences of panics are avoidable by refusing to succumb to panic. He is a great believer in fundamental analysis. The problem at times of panic is that investors lose sight of fundamentals and ignore what is known about individual companies and their management. He pays a lot attention to research material and favours the old-fashioned approach of research based on company visits and hard analysis of what companies are actually doing, not what their financial reports say they are doing.

'If you've got to sell,' he says, 'don't try to be clever, just do it. Don't be afraid of getting rid of stocks that are not right; throw them out and move on.' Sometimes this means moving on by selling and buying back the same stocks on the same day. He firmly believes that the key to success is discipline. 'You have to be very strict in what you're looking at in terms of shares.' You have to know a lot about these companies and, as a trader, you have to try and create dominance in the market of these shares. 'If you've got dominance,' he says, 'then you should be able to predict where the market is going and catch the highs and lows and you should be able to achieve great opportunities.'

As he sees it there are panic attacks every day in the market. The job of a trader is to learn how to deal with them and not get caught up by the changing moods. 'We work in an industry that turns on a sixpence; people forget what happened yesterday.' The rewards, Primhak believes, come to those with a longer memory.

The fund manager: John Carey

It would be hard to accuse John Carey of knowing nothing about history. He originally thought of pursuing an academic career and gained a doctorate for a thesis on judicial reform in France before the 1789 revolution. A soberly dressed, quiet and low-key figure, Carey may well be the personification of what most people expect fund managers to look and sound like. In a word Carey is reassuring. He is the sort of person to whom people would feel safe about handing over their hard-earned savings. He fully understands that stewardship of these funds lies at the heart of his job and is not inclined to be too adventurous in executing this task.

Although he might well have become a college professor, the lure of the stock market drew him away from the academic life and he joined the Boston-based Pioneer Group, which is now controlled by UniCredito Italiano. In mid-2002 Pioneer had funds totalling some $110 billion under management. Carey is head of US portfolio management and also manages two of the company's biggest funds.

Carey arrived at Pioneer in 1979 as an analyst following a mixed bag of industries such as autos, publishers, broadcasting and machine tools. In 1985 he moved to the fund management side of the business, working on small stock funds. The following year he took over management of the Pioneer Fund, which he still runs. Four years later he was managing the Equity Income Fund, the other fund he still personally manages.

Asked why he moved from analysis to fund management, he replies, 'It's the difference between studying Bismarck and being Bismarck.' He saw it as a natural progression and a chance to move further away from his academic background.

Carey sees himself as a value investor. 'I tend to be a cautious kind of person staying on the conservative side of stock valuation, multiples and that sort of thing.' He very much reflects the value investor's creed: 'I think I understand companies better when I see tangible assets behind the share price. I don't relate to concept stocks; they seem like a mirage rather than a reality.'

He says that investing in real businesses with a track record 'is no guarantee that you won't lose money but, in the worst case, there is usually some liquidation value or a break-up value to provide a floor on losses'.

Carey feels vindicated in taking this approach when he contemplates the fate of the 'wonder' tech stocks that were popular when he started his fund management career. In those days the leading stocks were in companies such as Digital, Wang Laboratories, Prime Computer, Data General, none of which still exist as independent entities, whereas the allegedly boring and steady companies such as

US Steel, General Motors and AT&T are still there. 'They tend to be much more resilient, much harder to kill.' Reflecting on the 1990s Internet boom, he says, 'I'm sure most of the big Internet names will be footnotes in history, at best, a few years ahead.'

Carey remembers a conversation with an analyst at the height of the dotcom boom. 'He was trying to persuade me to buy some of these stocks. I said to him that they had interesting ideas but no earnings so I didn't know how to analyse them. He sat back and said that it was really unfortunate that I felt that way. He said he was sorry for me.' He adds wryly, 'I haven't heard much from him recently.'

The 1990s was a frustrating time to be a value investor. 'Our performance looked pretty anaemic,' he says. In 1999 the NASDAQ was up 75 per cent, the S&P registered a gain of just over 20 per cent, while Carey's Pioneer Fund only managed to rise some 16 per cent. The fund was down because it had a low weighting in high priced Internet stocks. The following year, after what Carey graphically describes as a 'picture of a punctured soufflé' emerged, his fund looked a lot better in relative terms.

Investment managers are under increasing pressure to improve their performance and are frequently accused of showing little imagination as they group in herd formation so as not to stray too far from benchmarks which seem to rule the lives of many in the business. Carey deals with the first criticism by saying that Pioneer has shown an average 2 to 2.5 per cent margin over the S&P 500 for a period stretching back seventy-four years.

Although he knows a number of fund managers socially and meets a great many more at industry gatherings, he 'almost never talks to other managers about stocks'. He might discuss the market in general terms but thinks it unprofessional to discuss individual positions taken in stocks. If there is some form of herding in managers' attitudes, it does not, in Carey's experience, come as a result of sharing views on stocks. However, he does not deny the growing pressure of benchmarking by which a manager's performance is judged against the performance of other fund managers. The proliferation of benchmark indices can mean that managers spend undue amounts of time studying how the competition is performing as opposed to examining the movements of the markets in which they are supposed to be investing.

Carey says that 'shareholders are interested in absolute returns more than relative concerns. The emphasis on benchmarks has caused some fund managers to lose sight of their job.' He concedes that benchmarking can be 'a useful discipline', even though it may be 'annoying and counter-productive'. When he started in the business the only index that he and his fellow managers watched was the S&P 500; now they pay attention to other indices because their clients expect them to do so.

While customers understandably want good performance from funds they are also showing signs of being more aware of risk and demanding better risk control. 'There's a great deal of attention to risk control,' Carey says. This means, for example, that he will not allow a newly listed share to account for more than 1 per cent of a portfolio even if the size of the issue suggests a higher weighting. And, to avoid the problems of overdependence on single counters, he will not allow the ten biggest holdings to account for more than 20–25 per cent of the total portfolio.

Carey is interested in stock manias and draws on history to conclude that it is most likely that the high values given to the tech, telecommunications and media stocks (the so-called TTM category) are unlikely to be revisited. When he entered the industry there was a mania for energy stocks, especially for oil service companies. 'It took about fifteen years for these companies to get back on their feet after the bust.'

Going further back in history he notes that after railroad investment mania abated by the end of the nineteenth century every single railway company in the United States had gone through some kind of bankruptcy. In the 1920s the great bubble stock of the day was

RCA, which never managed to get back to its bubble-period price. As if to remind himself of the history of corporate failures Carey has a fine collection of share certificates issued by failed 1920s companies. He gives a whole host of other examples of investment fads that have emerged and disappeared as one decade replaces the last. He keeps these lessons of history in mind as he avoids jumping on bandwagons, even when others are urging him to get aboard. His general approach is that 'investors should stick with their long-term programme'. In the short term, says Carey, 'the market is very emotional. That's why we have bulls and bears, they are volatile and violent animals who reflect market sentiment.'

With this determination not to be emotional and not to be pushed off course by a market panic Carey was thrown into the maelstrom of the 1987 crash with no previous experience of a similar event. 'That was an anxious day,' he recalls with studied understatement. 'I was fully invested, some 99.5 per cent invested in stocks.' Most of the money was in blue chips.

As news of the carnage wrought by Black Monday flowed in he waited for some response. 'I was sitting at my desk waiting for the phone to ring. I thought the shareholders service people would be telling me everyone was redeeming. But we didn't have any significant redemptions.' It seems that Pioneer had done a good job of explaining that it was in the business of creating value-oriented funds to be held for the long term. Most redemptions arose when people needed cash for reasons other than price falls.

He was under no pressure to sell shares in order to raise cash, so what did he do as share prices went into free fall? 'I did absolutely nothing that day. In fact, I didn't sell until November, and that was just for ordinary reasons ... I didn't consider selling because I thought the drop was unwarranted.' After the initial fall Carey did some modest buying, but as he was fully invested he lacked cash for a more impressive buying spree. Anyway, he was disinclined to do so because 'I didn't know where the bottom was. I just wanted to watch and wait.'

The other reason he did not buy was that he does not regard 'share price drops as some fine buying opportunity. Sometimes investors are right and the herd is correct ... Sometimes sharp corrections are the market's way of rearranging everything. It may mean that some stocks are permanently depressed.'

Carey does not rule out buying on price falls but insists that buying is wise only for fundamental reasons, not just because the price has dropped. 'If there is something that was interesting before the fall, then there is a case to buy.' He believes that investors have to separate the issues of price and value and 'resist knee-jerk responses to price movements'.

As he was deciding what to do in 1987 Carey's first thought was for his shareholders, 'I thought how they had worked to set this money aside and felt a little sick about the whole thing. But they stuck with it.'

In his Boston office the atmosphere was quiet and restrained. There was, says Carey, 'no drama or melodrama'. Some of his colleagues were more puzzled than anything else. He too was puzzled, wondering who was doing the selling while he and his colleagues were sitting on their hands.

The company's president came down to talk to his executives and get their views on what was happening but they held no formal meetings and there were no big attempts to draw up a strategy for dealing with the market crash. Pioneer had previously established some borrowing capacity designed precisely to deal with a flood of redemptions at a time like this. The lines of credit remained untouched but Carey was acutely aware that things may have gone another way and therefore decided that in future he would keep a higher proportion of his portfolios in highly liquid stock, just in case. When Carey spoke to the brokers who acted for his fund they said things like, 'My goodness, can you believe how far these prices are falling?' but they were not urging a particular course of action on him. 'It was a bit like watching a ship sinking but being too far away to do anything about it. It was really something we watched from a distance; there wasn't much we could do.'

At the end of the day after the market had closed, he simply went home. In fact, Carey had other things on his mind because his father was dying of cancer. 'It kind of put things in perspective,' he says.

Even with the benefit of hindsight he does not believe that he should have done anything differently. 'We didn't have to sell at distress prices.' He saw the crash as a consequence of investors being disappointed as a result of false expectations. They were expecting earnings to continue improving but by October such an improvement had not come through and this, he believes, caused a momentary panic as there were fears that falling earnings would not be able to support share prices. When the third-quarter earnings figures for 1987 finally came through and showed a sharp recovery, the panic was seen as overdone.

And so Carey opted for inaction. For the record, his fund ended the year with a 5.5 per cent gain in 1987, despite the crash. As far as Pioneer was concerned, the real damage came three years later. 'The worst year from my point of view was 1990; it was a brutal year,' he says. 'It was a year in which share price decline piled on decline and it was justified because it reflected the poor state of the economy.'

Carey deliberately missed out on the dotcom bubble and felt vindicated 'when it came screeching to a halt' some two years before the 9/11 crash in 2001. 'This was clearly an extraneous event, clearly nothing to do with the market or even the economy,' he says, 'more a general panic that affected the stock market and a whole host of other things like air travel. People stopped going to the movies, they stopped spending money. There was a general paralysis until people figured out what happened and put it into some kind of perspective.'

Nevertheless, as a fund manager he had to consider what to do while others were figuring things out. When the terrorists struck he was in Dallas giving a presentation and realised he needed to get back to the office. With planes out of action he began the long, gruelling drive back to Boston in a rented car. It gave him plenty of time to think. He mainly thought about the events themselves but he also did some mental calculations, running through the list of stocks in his portfolios and considering which would be most affected. On balance, he decided that the portfolio's stocks would offset each other. On the one hand were shares in Southwest Airlines and Boeing that looked set for a tumble, but on the other were some defence industry and oil and gas stocks. His only concern was the insurance stocks. In the end he decided to lighten up a bit on stocks in the reinsurance area, but he ended up buying a few more Boeing shares because he believed that losses on the commercial arm of its business would be made up by the defence side.

Again in 2001 there was no pressure from redemptions, although there were a few more than there had been in 1987, but not enough to cause any kind of cash flow problem. 'I didn't worry about the stock market drop,' says Carey, 'I saw it as part of the general lack of confidence.'

Basically, Carey adopted the same strategy in 2001 as in 1987, which was to stick with the programme and not sell at distress prices, nor make any significant purchases. In other words, he sat out the panic. 'The market will bounce back and in the long run the market will reflect the economy. Stocks in the long run will reflect the earnings of individual companies. So if you take a long-term view there is no reason to panic. In fact, if you have some money you should take the opportunity to buy, but never do so just because the price is low.'

One of the big differences between 1987 and 2001, he notes, was the greater proliferation of media noise. In Pioneer's dealing room a television set is permanently tuned to CNBC, everyone has the powerful Bloomberg monitors on their desks pumping out everything from charts to data to opinions and hard news. Back in 1987 Carey and his colleagues saw the *Wall Street Journal* as their primary source of information but, like all newspapers, it was mainly delivering yesterday's news. Now there was instant news and volumes of it. 'I find it amusing, sometimes nerve wracking, sometimes aggravating,' he says, 'but I can't say that it has affected my behaviour as a fund manager.' Nevertheless, he worries that the flood of financial news may 'create the illusion among investors that they know more and that they are more up to date.' This can be dangerous because it may lead to some kind of rash action.

Interviewed in mid-2002 Carey was in an upbeat mood about the American market. 'From a textbook point of view this is the time to be in the market, when pessimism is rampant and there is some sense of capitulation.' As a value investor he was not too bothered by the high price–earning ratios still prevailing in 2002 as he believes that there is a strong case for investing at peak multiple periods because these ratios are historic and can end up trailing earnings rather than predicting improvements.

While Carey is not anticipating a crash he does not rule out a stronger economic performance being derailed by political influences or renewed terrorist attacks. When the new millennium arrived many market commentators had views about how the bursting of the dot-com bubble would pan out. Understandably they were focusing on the economy and corporate profitability; now, however, the external environment needs careful consideration, especially when the threat of terrorism looms large. Both Primhak and Carey had this very much in mind as they contemplated the state of the market. If they in any way reflect the views of their colleagues in the industry, it is likely that this consideration will increasingly be factored into the list of conditions that create stock market panics.

There is no standard formula for responding to stock market panics, nor indeed for avoiding the consequences, but as Primhak and Carey have demonstrated there is no reason for wild gyrations of the market to cause great losses for investors. Primhak, more than Carey, sees these periods of panic as a time of opportunity.

7

The psychology of panics

I APPROACH THIS PART of the book with some trepidation because
there is an overwhelming tendency to describe stock market panics as an outbreak of madness. Indeed, on the infamous Black Monday of the 1987 crash the splash headline in the *New York Post*
read 'WALL ST. GOES MAD!' Similar headlines are not hard to
find during other times of panic, but they are notably less prevalent
during periods of massive stock market gains. However fast markets
are rising it is rarely seen as a manifestation of insanity; on the contrary, bull markets are viewed as reflections of strength, optimism
and prosperity.

So fast-falling markets are allegedly mad while fast-rising markets are perfectly logical. No wonder the search for understanding
quickly moves into the realms of psychology. The problem is that
psychological explanations of market behaviour are often supplied
by people like myself deficient in knowledge of this discipline and
ready to jump to conclusions based on vague theories about crowd
behaviour. Cynics might argue that ignorance is no disqualification
for explaining movements of the stock market, but cynics are not
always right.

If the explanation of stock market behaviour lay purely in a study
of mass psychology, we would be talking about little more than a
medical or social phenomenon somewhat devoid of financial or

economic explanation. This is taking things too far. Advancing purely psychological reasons to explain panic behaviour in stock markets strongly suggests an absence of rationality. However, excluding the possibility of rational explanations for market behaviour means, as we have seen Chapter 3, excluding a whole host of perfectly sound reasons for entering or exiting markets. It seems more sensible to view the psychology of markets as one among a number of tools that contribute to the understanding of how they operate.

Rational explanations for the seemingly irrational

Peter Garber, who has persuasively argued for a reassessment of irrationality explanations for such outbreaks of excessive investor enthusiasm as the Dutch tulip mania and the British South Sea Bubble disaster, urges caution on psychological explanations. He writes, 'Before we relegate a speculative event to the fundamentally inexplicable or bubble category driven by crowd psychology ... we should exhaust the reasonable economic explanations. Such explanations are often not easily generated due to the inherent complexity of economic phenomena, but bubble explanations are often clutched as a first and not a last resort.'[1]

Garber is arguing that explanations couched in terms of crowd psychology can be little more than a lazy person's way of avoiding understanding the real causes of large speculative moments in market history. As we have seen, he has made a strong case that, for example, the South Sea Bubble was in fact the product of an innovative and sophisticated attempt to alter the basis of government financing and that investors had been rational in taking a position in anticipation of its success.

It's people, not markets, who panic

Looking for single reasons to explain the onset of panics has not proved to be a productive exercise. All this notwithstanding, there is evidence to suggest that herd behaviour and psychological forces have an impact on market panics. As Adam Smith observed, well before anyone had even thought of the term herd behaviour, emulation is the most persuasive of human drives.

The reason for this is simple, and simply explained by Bernard Baruch, a famous financier and adviser to presidents, who made a number of shrewd observations about the 1929 crash. Baruch said, 'What registers in the stock market's fluctuation are not the events themselves but the human reaction to these events, how millions of individual men and women feel about how these happenings may affect the future. Above all else, in other words, the stock market is people.'

George Soros, the legendary hedge fund manager who seems to have made enough money to take a rather more sceptical view of financial markets than some of his colleagues, has some interesting observations on why the way people think influences markets. 'Thinking plays a dual role,' he writes. 'On the one hand participants seek to understand the situation in which they participate; on the other, their understanding serves as a basis of decisions which influence the course of events. The roles interfere with each other. Neither role is performed as well as it could be if it were performed separately.' He adds that 'participants act on the basis of imperfect understanding and the course of events bears the imprint of this imperfection'.[2]

Soros then applies this generalisation to the situation in stock markets. He believes that 'there is bound to be a flaw in the participant's perception of the fundamentals. The flaw may not be apparent in the early stages but it is likely to manifest itself later on. When it does, it sets the stage for a reversal in the prevailing bias. If the change in bias reverses the underlying trend a self-reinforcing process is set in motion in the opposite direction. What the flaw is and how and when it is likely to manifest itself are the keys to understanding boom/bust sequences.'[3]

Soros is describing the circular process through which market perceptions are formed and in which the very business of forming perceptions changes them. These changed perceptions then form the basis upon which action is taken because, as a new perception takes hold, a new course of action recommends itself.

This process is more sharply defined in the uncertain environment of a stock market where investors are confronted with a particular set of pressures. Peter Bernstein, the investment manager and author of a classic work on risk, explains the issue in this way:

> *Capital markets have always been volatile, because they trade in nothing more than bets on the future, which is full of surprises. Buying shares of stock, which carry no maturity date, is a risky business ... Such an environment provides a perfect setting for nonrational behaviour: uncertainty is scary. If the nonrational actors in the drama overwhelm the rational actors in numbers and in wealth, asset prices are likely to depart far from equilibrium levels and to remain there for extended periods of time.*[4]

This is the point at which considerable market volatility kicks in. And it is often the point at which the irrational behaviour of the crowd has more impact on stock markets than the activities of so-called rational investors. For this reason many people seeking an explanation for the extreme volatility of stock markets turn to a study of mass psychology.

One of the most influential books attributing the vagaries of investment to the product of mass psychology is Charles Mackay's *Extraordinary Popular Delusions and the Madness of Crowds*. Although it was first published in 1841, Mackay's work continues to be widely cited in stock market literature, suggesting that what held good in the mid-nineteenth century has not changed that much. In the preface to the 1852 edition Mackay wrote, 'Money ... has often been the cause of the delusion of multitudes. Sober nations have all at once become desperate gamblers, and risked their existence upon the turn of a piece of paper.'[5]

The impression of irrationality is much enhanced when the value of items of speculation is compared with more mundane items. In his essay on the seventeenth-century tulip mania that swept Holland, Mackay compares the price of one single root of a rare bulb called 'Viceroy' with a list of other items that could be purchased for the extraordinary price of 2,500 florins:[6]

Two lasts of wheat
Four lasts of rye
Eight fat swine
Twelve fat sheep
Two Hogsheads of wine
Four tuns of beer
Two tuns of butter
1000 pounds of cheese
A bed
A suit of clothes
A silver drinking cup

At least it could be argued that the 'Viceroy' bulb would spawn new plants and therefore new opportunities to sell bulbs. It is hard to make the same argument for shares in Yahoo! Inc., whose share price peaked at over $464 in 2000. A single share in Yahoo! was the same price as, for example, a cheap computer. The price of just four Yahoo! shares would have been more than sufficient to purchase a very good computer system with all the peripherals. There was absolutely no hope of regaining this investment in Yahoo! by way of dividends; only by selling the stock to another hapless buyer could an investor hope to make a profit. As the price of Yahoo! slid to a fraction of its heady 1999 value, anyone who bought its shares at $464 did not have even the consolation of a flowering bulb to call his own.

However, this was not the point of the exercise. When prices reached the levels achieved by shares in Yahoo!, the name of the game was pure speculation borne along by a wave of euphoria. There is overwhelming evidence of the way that investors get caught up in both the euphoria and depression of markets and allow the attitudes of the crowd to sway investment decisions. At times like these the spreadsheet is rapidly abandoned and other sophisticated forms of market assessment count for little.

It is often assumed that the markets have become infinitely more sophisticated and, so we are told, infinitely more professional, suggesting that logic and superior trading systems have replaced the irrational behaviour of unsophisticated investors. However, as we have seen in Chapter 5, the most sophisticated trading systems seem to rapidly disintegrate at times when markets come under pressure. The portfolio insurance method of preventing stock losses quickly fell apart in 1987 when sophisticated formulae for determining when to sell and when to hedge trades collapsed as those using portfolio insurance simply decided that they wanted to sell and wanted to do so at more or less any price. At the end of the day humans decide what happens in the market, their computers do not make that decision.

Herd behaviour

Human beings have a tendency to lose their capacity for individual thought when engaged in buying stocks. At the very least their ability to make individual decisions is diminished by the pressure of collective opinion. 'Men, it has been well said, think in herds,' wrote Mackay. 'It will be seen that they go mad in herds, while they only recover their senses slowly, and one by one.'[7]

Mackay, like most other observers, assumes that there is something automatically negative about herd or crowd behaviour, but is this fair? Gustave Le Bon, writing a century after Mackay, thinks it is. Identifying the characteristics of crowds he notes the following:

The turning in a fixed direction of the ideas and sentiments of individuals composing such a crowd, and the disappearance of their personality. The crowd is always dominated by considerations of which it is unconscious. The disappearance of brain activity and the predominance of medullar activity. The lowering of intelligence and the complete transformation of sentiments – the transformed sentiments may be better or worse than those of the individuals of which the crowd is composed. A crowd is as easily heroic as criminal.[8]

No one is suggesting that crowd behaviour in stock markets turns investors into criminals although, as we have seen, it is common-place during periods of market euphoria and depression to find a sharp rise in criminal activity that attaches itself to the workings of the markets. However, this is something of a side issue; what matters in this context is whether crowd behaviour introduces a greater element of irrationality into the operation of markets and either sparks or deepens the impact of market panics.

Le Bon clearly sees crowds as dangerous. He writes,

the most striking peculiarity presented by a psychological crowd is the following: Whoever be the individuals that compose it, however like or unalike be their mode of life, their occupations, their character, or their intelligence, the fact that they have been transformed into a crowd makes them feel, think, and act in a manner quite different from that in which individuals of them would feel, and act were he in a state of isolation.[9]

The voluminous literature on the subject seems to point clearly to a pronounced streak of irrationality in crowd or herd behaviour.

A famous experiment by Muzafer Sherif in 1937 records what happened when a group of people was asked to sit in a darkened room and observe a point of light through a small hole. They were told that the light would move and asked to estimate the extent of the movement. In fact the light did not move at all, but when the subjects were later placed in discussion groups they all agreed that movement had occurred and discussed only by how much. When subsequently questioned, none appeared to be aware of any group influence.

Aware or not, the influence of a group view seems to have been sufficiently strong to sway any doubters. Rational judgement apparently went out of the window under group pressure.

Investors are drawn from a wide variety of backgrounds, have differing levels of intelligence and in many ways have little in common. However, it is surprising how frequently they cluster together to take a view on the market and the degree to which this view changes, and changes collectively.

It is widely assumed that herd behaviour is a bad thing, but there may well be sensible reasons for such behaviour. As we shall see, following the herd can be seen as a means of attaching the investor to the market's momentum. As long as the momentum is heading in one direction and money can be made by following that direction, there is little reason to suggest irrationality. The problems arise over herding that can be deemed irrational. This is when the pressure of the herd causes prices to rise or fall way beyond any basis that reflects the underlying business of companies listed on stock exchanges.

Hostility to contrary opinions

The herd is also hostile to views and opinions that contradict prevailing wisdom. The Norwegian academic Lars Tvede describes what happens to those responsible for managing funds when they dare challenge the wisdom of the herd. He writes, 'Clients have a strong tendency to punish those [fund] managers who lose money unconventionally. If, on the other hand, the managers lose money simply by going down with the general market, they are forgiven.'[10] Or, as Keynes put it in his classic *General Theory*, 'worldly wisdom teaches that it is better to fail conventionally than to succeed unconventionally'. This leads to trend behaviour among money managers. It is not only money managers who need to beware of the wrath of the crowd. The stockbroker Roger Ward Babson became widely reviled for warning of the 1929 crash two years before it happened. Some even argue that his subsequent interventions actually caused the crash. Far more learned and famous people than himself were at one with the crowd in deciding that prices would keep rising and he was denounced by newspaper editorials and academics for talking nonsense. On 5 September 1929 he delivered a speech to the American National Business Conference, declaring that the market had peaked and that there would be a 60–80 point drop in the indices, followed by a decade-long recession. He was wrong about the extent of the drop but basically and overwhelmingly right in his general thesis. However, the speech attracted ridicule and, when the fall came, its most prominent prophet was seen not as a visionary but as being responsible for the damage.

John Kenneth Galbraith recalled a similar experience just before the 1987 crash when he was commissioned to write an article for the *New York Times* in which he argued that a crash was inevitable. The piece was rejected by the *Times'* editors on grounds of being too alarmist and was therefore submitted to the *Atlantic*. Galbraith's warnings were not received with much enthusiasm: 'Galbraith doesn't like to see people making money', was the terse response of one critic.[11] It was understandable; people do not like to be seen as foolish in making investment decisions, or any other decisions for that matter.

The fate of Galbraith and Babson demonstrates the extent to which collective opinion is impervious to contrary information until the contrary information becomes the accepted view of the crowd. This in turn explains the quite extreme reaction in the markets when the mood turns and collective wisdom dictates a new course of action.

Optimism overcomes fear

Time and again we have seen investors deciding that the stock market is a sound place to invest their money on one day and on another, possibly the next, deciding that the market has become a dangerous place and a rapid exit is required. Investors have to struggle between the conflicting forces of innate conservatism and a reluctance to accept new realities and the fear of not moving quickly enough to catch the movement of the crowd. The reluctance to change tends to diminish when there is overwhelming evidence that the crowd has adopted a new idea. The factual basis of the idea matters a great deal less than the comfort provided when an idea is adopted by a large group of people.

Research by Werner DeBondt and Richard Thaler shows that when new information arrives investors give greater weight to the information and are more likely to disregard previous information. They are describing something akin to a mood swing which focuses on the new mood to the exclusion of all that was learned and experienced while the old mood prevailed. This tendency helps to explain why prices of shares move so sharply.[12]

Another consequence of group behaviour is that members of groups seem to be less risk averse than they are as individuals. There is some research evidence that groups generally are not necessarily less cautious than individuals, but in investment situations this generalisation does not seem to apply. The comfort of acting along with a wider group of investors has been shown to provide the confidence to take risks that would otherwise be avoided. This confidence sweeps away doubt even when contrary information arises suggesting that the actions of the group are flawed and an alternative course is required. Panics arise when the consensus view suddenly changes and members of the crowd scramble to change their strategy to fit the new view.

Fear overcomes greed

It is not difficult to see how these observations may be applied to behaviour in stock markets, particularly at times of panic. Manmohan Kumar and Avinash Persaud have made the interesting suggestion that panics are essentially spread by a mass lowering of the appetite for risks. They write: 'When investors' appetite for risk falls, they immediately reduce their exposure to risky assets, which, consequently fall in value together. This type of contagion has been called "pure" contagion because it runs along the lines of risk, not shared fundamentals, trade or exchange rate arguments.'[13]

The stock market crowd tends to react more quickly to negative news than positive news. Fear, it appears, is a more powerful spur to action than greed. Amos Tversky, one of the inventors of prospect theory, a useful tool for understanding concepts of risks, says: 'Probably the most significant and pervasive characteristic of the human pleasure machine is that people are much more responsive to negative than positive stimuli.'[14] Investing is not necessarily an act of pleasure but Tversky's view holds good for explaining how investors react to pain or the fear of pain inflicted by losing money.

Benjamin Graham, a famous American investor, noted that when markets started to fall the behaviour of investors was akin to that of manic depressives. No glimmer of light was permitted to lift the gloom enveloping the crowd. Graham may well have been engaging in deliberate hyperbole by describing investors as manic depressives, but a post-1987 crash survey conducted among institutional and private investors by Robert Shiller indicates that stock market participants did in fact suffer unusual anxiety symptoms in the wake of the crash. These included difficulties in concentrating, sweaty palms, tightness in the chest and a rapid pulse rate. Such symptoms were most acute on Black Monday, the day of the crash, when they were experienced by 30 per cent of the professional investors interviewed and 20 per cent of individual investors.[15] So much, then, for the cool, calm and collected professionals in the stock market business!

The response to good news is slower to take effect because until euphoria really sets in, most investors are risk averse.

Risk aversion

Investors are perverse creatures who refuse to follow the logic of their own views. Even at the height of bull markets when investors pour disproportionate levels of cash into equities, mutual fund managers still find that most investors avoid funds labelled as being 'high risk', even though devoting high levels of personal wealth to an equity portfolio is inherently high risk, particularly in a rising market. In other words, investors have a high appetite for risk at times when the market is rising but remain nervous about investments carrying the label that most accurately reflects their mood.

Investors' attitudes to risk are somewhat explained by the work of two Israeli psychologists, Daniel Kahneman and Amos Tversky, who developed what they call prospect theory. Prospect theory explains why risk aversion in one set of circumstances turns to risk seeking in another.

Taking an example from the world of investment they asked some experiment participants whether they would prefer the certainty of gaining $100,000 rather than taking a 50–50 chance of gaining $200,000 or nothing. The majority opted for the former. In other words they are risk averse. They then lowered the stakes and asked whether their subjects would prefer an 80 per cent chance of gaining $4,000 and a 20 per cent chance of gaining nothing or a 100 per cent chance of gaining $3,000. The experiment subjects were again risk averse, opting for the $3,000. Now the choice was turned on its head and the subjects were offered an 80 per cent chance of losing $4,000 and a 20 per cent chance of breaking even. The alternative was a 100 per cent chance of losing $3,000. In response 92 per cent of those involved in the experiment opted for the bigger gamble of losing $4,000, with the small hope of breaking even, even though the losses they stood to bear were greater than the $3,000 they stood to lose if they have opted to risk all. The conclusion was that a choice involving losses turns the risk averse into risk seekers.

This experiment is helpful in explaining stock market behaviour because it shows how investors are likely to respond when faced with the prospect of losses. In real circumstances, however, the choices are usually not that clear cut because in a falling market investors do not know the extent of their losses until the point at which they sell their shares. Nor do they know the potential for gain in a rising market until they have actually sold their shares. So, leaving aside specifics, it is possible to say that the fear of loss is a more powerful sentiment than an inclination to take risks as a means of achieving gains. Indeed there is research evidence to suggest that rich investors, who make up the majority of the investment community, are even more risk averse than other investors.[16] In short this helps explain why markets go down a great deal faster than they go up when pressure is at its most intense.

It is also worth noting that risk aversion and the conservatism of experienced investors means that many of them, at times an overwhelming majority, never trade their shares at all. Trading is risky both on the upside and the downside. Trading shares involves taking a decision on whether the time has come to sell or buy, without having any idea if there is a better time to trade. Therefore those who hold portfolios, particularly blue chip portfolios, often opt to do nothing and hold their shares for a very long time. The people who move markets are a small minority of the total share-owning population. In normal times conservative investors are happy to let them move the market up and down but at times of panic even these placid investors question whether it is safe to do nothing. Once these people, arguably the backbone of the investing community, are influenced by the crowd busy selling shares, then panic truly takes hold.

Coping with new information

Investors need the assurance of sharing views with others before they act and this complicates their reaction to new information which generally provides the basis for action. Although most investors pride themselves on being ahead of the mob in identifying a new invention, a new trend or whatever, they are not really bold enough to head out too far in front of the crowd. Those brave enough to venture ahead of the herd are usually small groups of investors who tend to be adept as publicists and quickly generate support for their investment ideas.

And, of course, as long as the herd is heading in one direction and pushing prices up, they are, almost by definition, heading in the right direction because a consensus view of the market is what makes the market.

The mood turns on new information. Although market participants have far better access to information than at any other time in history, this may make things more difficult than it was in the days when information was sparse and hard to come by. The barrage of views coming from the new financial television channels, the avalanche of data and views on the Internet and the ease with which information is bounced from one side of the world to the other often combine to confuse rather than to elucidate.

Furthermore, it cannot be said that a greater *availability* of information is necessarily producing a better *quality* of information. Investors' Internet chat rooms are notorious as centres of disinformation, mixed in with often quite useful news. The problem comes when trying to distinguish between the two. The frenetic pace of financial broadcasting is also a problem, especially on television where the nature of the medium lends itself to hyperbole and generating excitement when there is really no cause for anything of the kind. Having spent most of my working life in the print media, I am all too aware of its imperfections. A leading analyst, who went on to form his own (unsuccessful, as it turned out) online financial analytical service disturbingly, but not unjustifiably, referred to financial journalism as a 'lagging indicator'. In other words, by the time information reaches newspapers it is not useful as a basis for action.

Joseph Granville, author of *A Strategy for Daily Stock Market Timing*, went further in writing, 'when it's obvious to the general public, it's obviously wrong'.

Granville overstates his case but it is not without merit. It is supported by the tendency of the media to make market judgements that are astonishingly unsound, yet have an impact on investors anxious for new information on which to act. Lars Tvede has rather cruelly examined the record of cover stories in *Business Week* magazine and compared their forecasts to outcomes.[17] On 8 October 1984 the magazine assured readers that the 'superdollar' was reshaping the world economy and would be gaining strength for a decade. Five months later the US currency started one of its longest and sharpest declines. In August 1979 readers were treated to a cover story on 'The Death of Equities'. Like Mark Twain's obituary this proved to be premature as the market began its spectacular 300 per cent climb in 1982. In July 1987 *Business Week* was among the stock market cheerleaders with a cover story entitled 'Stocks Are Still the Best Bet'. The events of just three months later told a very different story. It is, of course, unfair to pick on one magazine when examples are easy enough to draw from elsewhere, but *Business Week* is a generally sound and worthwhile publication that is far removed from the more unreliable types of news media. If publications of this kind get things so spectacularly wrong, little wonder that investors express serious concern over where to find reliable information that they can use.

Investors are constantly searching for new information as a basis for investment decision making but it is far from certain that published information is as influential as it is sometimes thought to be. Arguably, the information that has a greater impact is transmitted in a far more informal manner. Stock market folklore is littered with stories of how information passed from mouth to mouth has moved stock prices. Tvede cites the story of an English stockbroker wanting to get rid of South African shares before the crash of mining stocks in 1895. He did so by sending his mother a sealed package of gold mining stocks with an accompanying note telling her not to open the package and discover the name of the stock because it was a secret. He said it would rise tenfold in value. As he confidently expected, his mother could not resist the temptation to discover the name. Having done so she swore her friends to secrecy when passing it on. They, of course, went out and bought the shares and promptly told all their friends. The net result was a flurry of buying.

What this story shows is that everyone loves the idea of insider information. Such information is made even more piquant if it is supposedly confidential. Inside information gets you ahead of the game. Tellingly, in this instance, the broker implied only that he was party to a secret and allowed the mystery of supposed secrecy to work its magic. Friends of his mother, who presumably knew nothing about South African gold shares, were confident that they were party to some special information and acted accordingly. The facts of the matter were that there was no real information; on the contrary, the information was plainly misleading.[18]

Real insider trading is rightly illegal in many jurisdictions, but is practically impossible to stamp out. In the United States the Securities and Exchange Commission has a surveillance department established to detect trades based on insider knowledge. Looking through the records of this department's prosecutions, Robert Shiller found a court document that traced trading in Lotus Development Corporation shares ahead of an announcement of a takeover by IBM. Apparently a secretary employed by IBM discovered this information when photocopying some secret documents. She told her husband in confidence and the tip quickly passed to a total of twenty-five people who bought shares worth half a million dollars.[19]

In this instance they were dealing with real insider information, illicitly obtained. However there is every reason to believe that the response would have been the same to false information, for the recipients had no means of verifying what they had been told. All they knew was that they were in possession of a hot tip – one of the most valuable commodities in the stock market.

Hot tips, true or false, and word-of-mouth communication are, according to Shiller, one of the more important contributors to market fluctuations. In a 1986 study he conducted with John Pound, they discovered that a mere 6 per cent of respondents stated that their attention was drawn to a particular company's stock by reading about it in a publication. The overwhelming majority heard about the stock as a result of direct personal communication. A later study of the 1987 market crash, cited above, found that almost 82 per cent of respondents had learned the news before 5 p.m. on the day of the crash from sources other than newspapers or the evening television news.[20]

This tells us a great deal about market psychology because it shows that people are far more likely to believe what they hear from friends and colleagues than from third parties. Not only do they trust this information but they will act upon it. This may well be their way of dealing with the mass of information bombarding them from all sides: by ignoring it and making sense of the market by means of personal interaction.

This has been described as a 'trust your friend' philosophy. The problem lies in knowing where the information chain starts. Information from friends is generally drawn from a common pool, except in exceptional circumstances. Why do some elements from this common pool come to the surface while others remain submerged?

As we have seen in Chapter 5, the market is increasingly dominated by a small number of powerful institutional players whose actions account for a very large proportion of stock market trading. One theory is that their response to information determines what comes to the surface. The Presidential Task Force on Market Mechanisms, established to look into the causes and aftermath of the 1987 crash, found that on 19 October just fifteen sellers accounted for about 20 per cent of the market's total sales that day. In the futures market a mere ten sellers accounted for around half the total non-market-maker trading on the same day. This shows the way that a very small number of market players set the agenda. It also demonstrates that what matters is the information conveyed to this small circle of dominant players.

Momentum

Once the key players act they produce momentum in the form of increased buying or selling of shares. The momentum takes on a life of its own and snowballs, especially at times of panic when there is fear of being trapped as the herd stampedes out of the market. Shiller describes this as 'a feedback loop, with initial price declines influencing more investors to leave the market, thereby creating further price declines'.[21]

What is interesting is that the momentum explanation of accelerating movements in share prices applies not only to markets as a whole but to individual stocks. This was noted in 1901 by Charles Dow, the famous chartist and founder of the Dow Jones company. He found that individual share movements became credible only when broader movements in the market confirmed them. In a *Wall Street Journal* article on market manipulation he stated that large operators would buy two or three leading stocks and then keep buying small numbers of stocks if they found that the market mood was bullish. This encouraged more general buying of stocks and lifted the general value of entire portfolios. As markets have become larger influencing stock prices by this kind of buying has become a much bigger undertaking, but it is more feasible in smaller emerging markets where share price manipulation of this kind is very common and can be achieved by fairly modest levels of buying.

Although special circumstances might cause a rise in individual stock prices against a general trend, these prices can rarely be sustained if not validated by bigger movements in the market as a whole. As the momentum gathers investors lose interest in specific pieces of information and focus instead on the momentum itself. This is graphically illustrated by Shiller's post-1987 survey asking both individual and institutional share owners which news items were important to them in evaluating what would happen in the market. What is striking here is that there is relatively little difference in the responses of so-called market professionals and individual market players. Both were influenced above all else by the 200-point drop in the Dow on the morning of 19 October. They were also heavily influenced by the market decline from 14 to 16 October and the big falls in London and Tokyo prices before 19 October. In only one respect did the professionals respond significantly differently from individual market players. Unlike private investors they were heavily influenced by US Treasury bond yields hitting 10.5 per cent. High levels of yields on Treasury bonds, as we have seen, are generally taken as presaging declines in the equity markets. Other pieces of specific news, such as the trade deficit figures, the producer index figures and Chemical Bank raising its prime rate on 15 October, ranked as no more than of low or middling importance. What mattered to investors was what other investors were doing.[22]

Although not designed for this purpose a poll conducted by Harris Interactive the night after the 9/11 terrorist attack on America very much confirmed Shiller's earlier findings. The Harris poll recorded that a mere 1 per cent of those interviewed intended to sell their shares. The poll was taken after the news of the attacks had been digested but well before Wall Street reopened. No doubt respondents were being truthful when they said they had no intention of selling shares, but when the market finally reopened and prices plunged many investors quickly changed their minds and joined the rush to sell.

Sushil Bikhchandani and Eric Clifton have published an interesting study which flies in the face of most assumptions about herding and suggests that, in developed countries, 'investment managers do not exhibit significant herd behaviour and that the tendency to herd is highly correlated with a manager's tendency to pursue momentum investment strategies'.[23] Their thesis, based on a review of empirical literature studying herding among investment managers, is that there is no obvious intent for investors to copy each other's behaviour and that where behaviour is similar it reflects a common response to common circumstances. However, as they point out, momentum investment strategies are, almost by definition, strategies for following the herd. Because these strategies are so widespread in the market it is hard to conclude that herding is anything but a major force.

Illusions of control

There is another aspect which may help to explain the collective behaviour of fund managers and the analysts who are accused of herding. It was pointed out by Arnold Wood, the president and CEO of Martingale Asset Management. He argues that because investment professionals have direct contact with the companies in which they invest, certainly more contact than small shareholders would have, they are influenced by an illusion of control. 'History shows,' he says, 'that decision makers inevitably resort to cognitive instincts and neglect evidence that disconfirms their conclusions.'

To illustrate his point he gives the example of a card game involving a red and a blue deck of cards. The player pays $1 to withdraw a card from the blue deck. The card is shown to the player by the dealer but he does not touch it. Cards from the red deck also cost $1 but, crucially, the player gets to touch cards from this deck. If the card selected is pulled from the deck following reshuffling, the player wins $100. However, before the draw the dealer asks players whether they are prepared to sell their cards. In an experiment 37 per cent of those having bought red cards, i.e. cards they have touched, are unwilling to sell while only 19 per cent of those who have blue cards (that they have not touched) are unwilling to sell. To up the ante the dealer asks reluctant sellers what price they would be prepared to accept for their cards. The average asking price for blue cards was a mere $2 whereas the average for red cards was $9.

Why the difference? Wood believes that players thought they had conveyed some of their skill by touching the cards. 'Touching the cards created an illusion of control, increased their confidence they could win. Illusion of control is influential because most of us have been brought up to believe that decision making is based on rationality, that we can and do analyse circumstances objectively.'[24]

This theory can be applied to the behaviour of investors when it is realised that they gain an illusion of control by having contact with, or 'touching', companies in which they invest. And because they have contact they become confident that they are more in control of their investment. When this form of contact is multiplied, as it is, particularly, in the case of so called 'hot stocks', which rise in price as they are heavily promoted by eager people in investor relations departments, large groups of investment managers share a common experience and reach similar conclusions.

How the past becomes a distant country

Whatever the reasons for common behaviour among fund mangers and whether or not it is conscious matters little if it can be established that there is a pattern to their investing activity. Establishing such a pattern is the essence of chartism, which works on the basis of being able to identify past market behaviour and pinpoint when it is likely to repeat itself. Charts show normal trading ranges and then identify points at which they are likely to break out of these ranges. The fact that this can be done at all suggests more than repeated coincidence. In fact, chartists have quite a good record of finding the points of predictable movement in markets and, having done so, can essentially be seen as recording movements of the herd.

Their success lies in the fact that stock market history repeats itself with monotonous regularity. In the long term there is considerable certainty that good times will be followed by bad and vice versa. A famous piece of research by William Reichenstein and Dovalee Dorsett, published in 1995, demonstrates that this has been the case over a very long period of time.[25] Their findings and a mass of other evidence mean that investors need not feel they are in uncharted waters and that to enter the market is not to take a so-called 'random walk' in the dark. Yet market participants have a remarkable ability to forget what happened in the past. 'There can be few fields of human endeavour in which history counts for as little as in the world of finance,' writes Galbraith. 'Past experience, to the extent that it is part of memory at all, is dismissed as the primitive refuge of those who do not have the insight to appreciate the incredible wonders of the present.'[26]

Why do investors blot out the memory of things that have gone before, even though it may be more than useful in understanding the present? One explanation could be simple ignorance, suggesting that the memory is not being blotted out, it simply does not exist. This may be true for some investors but cannot hold for large numbers of others who remember the past but persuade themselves that this time around things will be different.

All booms are characterised by the emergence of one or more big ideas and the conviction that these ideas will change the course of history. The most recent boom, that of the 1990s, pivoted around the idea of the Internet transforming the way business was conducted and lives would be lived. The 1920s boom was very much associated with recent inventions such as the telephone, the motor car and a host of other new consumer products. Because these new ideas are genuinely innovative and exciting, investors like to feel they have caught the new wave and are riding along with it. To express scepticism is to be reactionary and against progress.

However, belief in whatever is the latest thing is probably weaker than the fear of being cast as a sceptic. As long as the idea of things being different prevails and share prices are rising and money is being made, looking over one's shoulder at past disasters might be seen as a way of contributing to their repetition. Non-believers are viewed as disloyal to the forces that are bringing about great profits.

There is strong pressure, not least on professional money managers, to be team players. If they warn of doom in the way that Charles Merrill warned investors of doom in Chapter 5, they are likely to be turning away funds and discouraging mergers and acquisitions, and they are highly likely to see their performance-related compensation packages slump. No one wants any of these things to happen.

This, at least, is a rational explanation of why there is a disincentive to recall history, but another explanation might simply be fear of memory. When optimism takes hold of the market investors do not want to be told that happy days will come to an end. There is every incentive to keep prices rising. Part of this incentive comes in the obvious shape of financial reward but it comes also in the form of self-reification. As Galbraith shrewdly observed, 'No one wishes to believe that this [rise in wealth] is fortuitous or undeserved; all wish to think that it is the result of their own superior insight or intuition.'[27] This view, he notes, is reinforced by the high regard in which those of modest means hold those possessing considerable wealth.

However, there comes a point when optimism can no longer be sustained and when pessimism exercises a grip on the market. When this happens investors pay little attention to the lessons of history that demonstrate the considerable opportunities provided by big market slumps.

The reverse side of the memory coin, which is equally unhelpful, is the tendency of investors to have their sights far too firmly fixed on the past when trying to assess current developments. This is particularly so when the past has offered unfortunate experiences. The memory of the 1929 crash and subsequent depression still hung heavy in the 1950s. It meant that investors shunned some interesting possibilities for making money in the stock market. They were reluctant to take the plunge because they still lived in fear of two and a half decades of depressed share prices. The economic recovery in the United States in the 1940s should have been sufficient to lure them back into the market but it was not until the 1950s that recovery eventually translated into rising stock prices. Following the price rises of the mid-1950s the market managed to record an average annual rise of 12 per cent per year from 1946 to 1969. The investors who were still busy drawing the wrong lessons from history in the late 1940s and early 1950s missed some fantastic opportunities.

Behaviour in emerging markets is different

There is some strong circumstantial evidence that investors in developed markets behave differently from those in emerging or very underdeveloped markets. Living as I do in Hong Kong, I am fascinated by the psychology of Chinese investors on the mainland. I have seen them literally besieging stockbrokers' offices waving wads of money in an attempt to buy shares. I have witnessed poor peasants taking out their very hard-earned savings and putting them in shares that they barely understand.

On the one hand, there is a perfectly rational explanation for what they are doing. They are taking money out of state-controlled banks that pay derisory rates of interest and putting this money into stock markets that have registered impressive gains. On the other hand, they are taking stupendous risks because many of these investors literally put all their saving into stocks. By any standards this is an unwise investment strategy. It turns from unwise to potentially fatal in the Chinese market, where share prices are high simply because the government places strict limits on the number of companies allowed to gain a listing. This causes the laws of supply and demand to work strongly in favour of those who possess a supply of shares. The companies represented by these shares are far from ideal investment vehicles, even assuming that the company accounts are sufficiently transparent for investors to make sense of the businesses they are supposed to be reporting on. If, as is quite possible, the supply of shares were to increase by a significant amount, the whole basis for inflated share valuations would rapidly crumble and prices would crash.

So, in China and in other developing markets, prices are effectively maintained at high levels by political control over the issuing of shares. In nations such as China, still officially a communist state, and other nations such as Russia where communism has ceased to be the ruling force, investors have a faith in stock markets which is almost directly inversely related to their lack of faith in the political system which bred considerable hardship. It is no coincidence that one of the biggest share scams in recent times emerged in Albania, where a particularly brutal form of Stalinist rule was replaced by something that was supposed to be a free market society. The lure of the free market and shares prompted enormous speculation and, as it turned out, speculation in fraudulent schemes. In these post-communist markets investors are registering a vote against a system that has failed and expressing a more or less blind faith in a capitalist future as represented by stock markets, although the reality of the situation is that the markets in these countries are far from being free.

Most of the bigger new markets are emerging from some form of authoritarian rule (as in Korea and all the east European states), or at least from a highly interventionist form of state control, as in the case of India. The process of establishing stock markets is seen as one of the most important symbols of a new, more liberal era. Investors in these countries may therefore be excused for wanting to invest in the idea of greater freedom. They enter the world of investing with more ambitious and more mixed motives than investors in developed markets.

This makes their concept of stock markets very different from that of investors in developed markets and helps to explain why volatility in these markets is so high. This makes them much more vulnerable to panics. The difference in risk perceptions between developed and developing markets seems to be worthy of more investigation. In the meantime it is reasonable to assume that the differences help to account for the different ways these markets behave.

It may be argued that in emerging markets the activities of local investors are mitigated by the participation of large institutional investors from overseas. The reality is that emerging markets remain dominated by local investors. Big overseas investors may dip in and out but, contrary to the impression given by some self-serving politicians, there is little evidence to demonstrate that these overseas investors call the shots. Exposure to emerging markets by major institutional investors represents a small proportion of their overall portfolios.

These big institutions behave in the same way as the investors they represent. They are basically risk averse and, while prepared to take a side bet on these exotic overseas markets, they make sure that the size of the bet is relatively modest.

Perception is all – defying the herd

During periods of market euphoria investors do not become less risk averse, rather their perception of risk changes. What was considered risky in more calm periods no longer appears to be high risk. In reality bigger risks are taken during raging bull markets, but they are seen as sensible ways of dealing with a new situation.

It seems reasonable to claim that most investors remain risk averse at all times. The only thing that really changes is risk perception. This explains why risk management has become such an important component of the investment business. Fund managers looking for new business rapidly came to understand that they were dealing with risk averse clients. Only a small minority have an appetite for high risk and will bet everything on investment gambles.

Investors, like everyone else, want the best of all worlds. They want to make a lot of money when markets are rising, they are prepared to take risks to do so, but they also want an assurance that what they are doing is not risky and will lead to ever rising profits. Little wonder that they get into a panic when the consequences of their risk taking turn sour. In these circumstances many investors feel cheated and want to remove themselves as quickly as possible from the source of what they regard as cheating. A rational group of investing folk quickly disintegrates into being a panicky herd. Precisely because the crowd is in a state of panic and prone to taking panicky decisions, there are great opportunities for those who do not join it. At times like these the true rewards go to those with the determination and sufficient confidence in their own judgement to take a view other than that shared by the majority.

It is not easy to take such an independent stance. Heading in a direction opposite to that of the herd always risks the danger of being trampled. However, in investment, as in battle, victory is often bestowed on those who go against conventional wisdom and can stand back from the rush of information seeming to point in one direction. This means the victors have an ability to see information that suggests an alternative course of action.

Tvede quotes Karl von Clausewitz, the German military strategist who has influenced many generations of military leaders. He wrote, 'Chance smiles on the receiver of contradictory information, who can reach decisions after due evaluation and criticism. But far worse it is when one message supports, confirms and reinforces the last – adding more colour to the picture, until finally forcing a decision. Such decisions soon turn out to be foolish, and all information lies and delusion. Most information is misleading and men's fears a fertile breeding ground for lies and untruths.' Clausewitz urges decision makers to trust their own judgement and let 'self assurance arm him against the pressure of the moment'.[28]

History delivers a mixed verdict on military leaders pursuing unconventional strategies but tells an altogether different story about the success of those who have been brave enough to entertain a contrary view of where the stock market is heading during moments of panic. That such moments will recur time and time again is without doubt. 'Recurrent speculative insanity and the associated financial deprivation and larger devastation is inherent in the system,' wrote Galbraith. 'Perhaps it is better that this be recognised and accepted.'[29]

8

Does diversification provide protection against stock market fluctuations?

I T IS NOW WIDELY ACCEPTED that one of the safest and most successful ways of investing is to diversify, or, to use the old cliché, to avoid having all your eggs in the same basket. However, there is considerable evidence to show that diversification is not as valuable as it is usually assumed to be and that at times of stock market panics, an attempt to diversify is filled with problems.

Peter Lynch, one of the most successful managers of all time when he ran Fidelity's Magellan Fund, summed up the sceptical view of diversification by coining an ingenious new word: 'di-worse-ification'. Nevertheless, investment advisers tend to insist that their clients should hold a portfolio that is as diversified as possible. This seems a pretty obvious notion, but before 1952 it was little more than a vague idea. It took a pioneering work by Harry Markowitz, *Portfolio Selection*, to elevate this concept into a disciplined approach to investing. He provided the tools that allowed money managers to quantify the efficiency of constructing diversified portfolios.

Peter Bernstein succinctly explains why diversification is so attractive. He writes: 'While the returns on a diversified portfolio will be equal to the average rates of return on individual holdings, the volatility will be less than the average volatility of its individual holdings.

This means that diversification is a kind of free lunch at which you can combine a group of risky securities with high expected returns into a relatively low-risk portfolio, so long as you minimise covariances, or correlations among the returns of the individual securities.'[1]

Decision regret

It would appear that the main reason for constructing a diversified portfolio is not so much to reduce the volatility of returns as to limit so-called decision regret. This takes us back to the subject of the previous chapter, where risk aversion and related matters were discussed. Bernstein sees this as the key motive for diversification. Investors, he observes, suffer regret over the success of stocks they failed to buy. 'Even though everyone knows that it is impossible to choose only top performers, many investors suffer decision regret over those forgone assets.'[2] In an attempt to avoid such regret investors choose to buy more stocks, even in small quantities, so that they have some chance of being on the winning side.

When to switch

This is all very well in good times, but what happens at moments of panic when investors find themselves in one asset class, such as stocks, that is fast dwindling in value? They then start wondering whether they ought to be in another asset class such as bonds or property or precious metals or more exotic types of investment such as antiques and other collectable items.

Switching out of one asset class and moving to another as the market falls is rarely a smart idea but, so we are told, the wise investor should have a stake in a number of asset classes at all times to hedge their risks. When markets start moving rapidly downwards the cry goes up for a safe haven. Before getting out of one asset class, particularly one that has produced good profits over time, investors need to consider carefully whether the replacement asset will be capable of generating a similar level of returns. As we shall see, most of the so-called safe havens such as gold and utility stocks in the field of equities have a far from convincing track record of rewarding those who make the switch.

Decisions about switching, and thus diversifying investment portfolios, are more generally motivated by negative rather than positive reasons. It is hard to argue that diversification is a sure-fire way of increasing returns; more generally it serves to minimise losses. The time to diversify is not when one market is falling and others look more attractive, but ahead of such turbulence. It is often the case that all types of markets fall and rise in tandem, in which event diversification is probably a waste of time. Even when there are differences in the performance of various asset classes, they may not be of significant magnitude to justify the forgone opportunities that could result from devoting most or all of the investment portfolio to just one asset class that has a history of outperforming the rest.

Returns for diversified portfolios

The subject of portfolio construction is much debated and has produced a voluminous literature, much of it self-serving as it comes from fund managers and salesmen who have constructed all sorts of diversified portfolios designed to provide investor confidence and claiming to offer high returns. The intention here is not to offer yet more general advice on portfolio diversification but to examine the benefits or otherwise of diversification at times of panic when it very much looks as though one asset class is doomed while others seem to be increasingly attractive.

Let us examine this question by taking a simple example of diversification covering the period from May 1995 to May 2001, the period which tracks the 1990s boom from its height to the beginning of the decline. This exercise demonstrates that diversification can produce significantly lower returns than are achieved by sticking with just one form of investment. The diversified portfolio examined here is about as simple as can be. It is made up of US bonds

Figure 8.1 **Diversified portfolio versus American and British stocks**

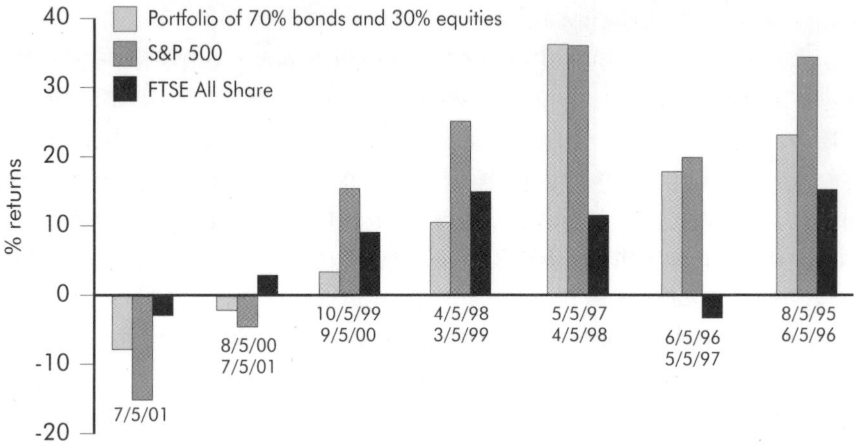

Legend:
- Portfolio of 70% bonds and 30% equities
- S&P 500
- FTSE All Share

Source: *FT Expat, June 2002.*

(accounting for 70 per cent of the total) and equities (30 per cent). This portfolio is compared with an investment entirely in stocks from the American S&P 500 Index and London's FTSE All Share Index. The diversified portfolio managed to achieve very slightly better returns in only one year (1997–8) and even when the S&P suffered a sharp decline in 2001 the diversified portfolio did not achieve a better result than would have been achieved by investing in London stocks (see Figure 8.1). Throughout this period by far the highest return on capital would have been achieved by sticking with American blue chips, although the diversified portfolio would have produced better returns than an investment in British blue chips before the S&P began its decline.

Even to raise the question of whether diversification is a wise strategy is something of a heresy within the community of investment advisers who, almost unanimously, recommend diversification of investment portfolios. A strong advocate of this view is Warren Bitters, whose studies in asset allocation have led him to conclude that 'diversification-maximised optimisation offers an attractive package in the overall level of portfolio diversification relative to standard Markowitz optimisation at a small cost to efficiency'.[3]

This rather complexly stated opinion is pretty much the standard view, but diversification was not always so much in investors' minds. For example, before the very sharp downturn of the American stock market between 1969 and 1975, few US investors were interested in overseas stock markets, although there was clearly scope for higher returns from overseas markets. Once it became generally acknowledged that it would be wise to diversify into overseas markets these markets started, by and large, to track the fluctuations on Wall Street. The Japanese market was the only major market not to follow US trends. This rather suggests that geographical diversification was a waste of time.

Diversification into property

The one asset class that appears to have consistently proved to be a good hedge against inflation and to have consistently held its own against other classes of investment is property. For this reason investment in property is usually high on the list of priorities for diversified portfolios. An extensive study of the literature relating to the history of real estate returns by two professors of finance, Stacy Sirmans and C. F. Sirmans, published in 1987, concluded that 'real estate served as a better inflation hedge over the time periods studied [mostly the middle period of the twentieth century] than common stocks and corporate or government bonds'.[4]

However, this is not the same as saying that real estate has provided the best opportunity for higher returns. An International Monetary Fund research paper traces the performance of property and stock prices from 1980 to 1998 in real terms, i.e. adjusted for inflation. It is fascinating to look at this comparison in three key markets. In the United States property prices remained more or less static while the stock market took off in the 1990s. Even the 1987 stock market crash did not succeed in allowing the property market to produce better returns than the stock market. In Britain there was a much closer relationship between the movement of property prices and the stock market, but as soon as the British stock market started to move out of its early 1980s doldrums stock prices accelerated at a faster rate than the property market. In the late 1980s when equity markets were still recovering from the 1987 crash, property prices overshot stock prices but soon after fell behind. In Japan the property and equity markets more or less mirror each other although, as Figure 8.2 shows, property prices started the 1980s at a much higher level of increase than stock prices but lagged during the subsequent Japanese stocks boom. When the equities boom turned to bust, stock prices became increasingly volatile as property prices went into a steady decline.

The better performance of stocks relative to property investments is arguably a more recent phenomenon because the research by Sirmans and Sirmans lists a number of studies that show a better performance for property assets during the 1970s, although other studies reach a different conclusion. Moreover, many of these studies are based on the performance of property funds, which may not accurately reflect movements in the property market itself. Overall there is no conclusive evidence that property consistently out performs stocks as an asset investment class.

The whole question of investment in property is greatly complicated by the fact that for many smaller investors buying a property is the biggest single investment they are ever likely to make. In most cases the purchase is viewed as acquiring not just an asset but rather a home. For this reason the investment tends to be motivated by a number of factors that may have little bearing on a strict return-on assets criterion. And because the asset also serves as a home it is highly unlikely to be traded with the speed and lack of sentiment that typifies trading in other asset classes.

Figure 8.2 **Property versus stocks in Britain, Japan and the United States**

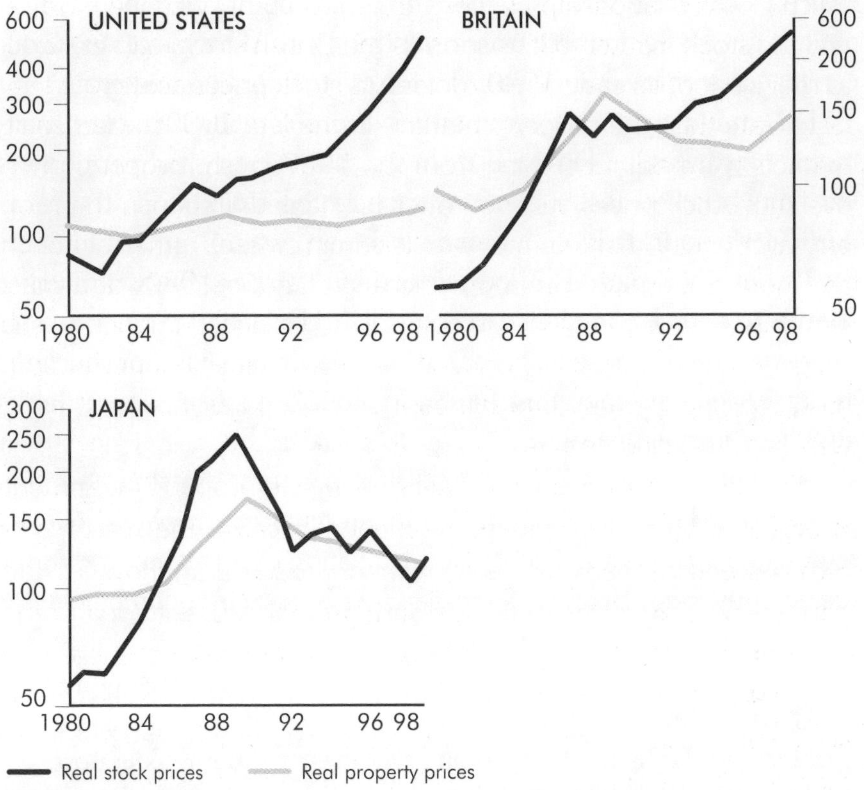

Source: International Monetary Fund, 'Asset Prices and the Business Cycle', *World Economic Outlook*, May 2000.

Nevertheless, in the real world of asset allocation, and bearing in mind the desire of investors both to preserve and increase their wealth, investment in property is seen as a major tool to achieve these ends. Property therefore serves as a significant competitor to other asset classes.

Unlike equities and fixed income investments, property investments carry a yield only if property is acquired for subsequent rental. Property ownership generally carries high levels of liabilities and costs that need to be deducted from the yield equation, which can seriously diminish returns. Less ambiguous is the purchase of property with the intent to make a quick sale. In these circumstances it should be easy to work out capital gains or losses incurred as a result of real estate trading.

This may explain why property is a problematic form of investment. Moreover, as Figure 8.2 shows, the value of the property is very much linked to the performance of the stock market. This is particularly so in Britain but even in Japan, where property investments have had periods of outperforming equities, the two markets show a remarkable tendency to coincide and broadly follow the same trend over time. Property purchase as a hedge against rapid declines in equity markets therefore hardly looks like a smart idea. It looks even less impressive as a strategy to avoid the consequences of a stock market collapse. The best case for property investment seems to be made during periods of high inflation when property holds its own against the corrosive forces of inflation. This is the finding of research by Peter Spiro.[5] His research is echoed in a number of the studies examined by Sirmans and Sirmans.

All this begs the question of what role property investments can realistically play in a diversification strategy. As we have seen, the property market is the least liquid form of investment. This poses its own problems in terms of shifting assets, but there are even more profound problems associated with property ownership for end users (there are end users in both the residential and commercial markets, of course, but as far as most individual investors are concerned, the residential market is of greater importance). Typically, the purchase of a home is the largest single investment a small investor will make in his or her lifetime, tying up a significant proportion of assets and incurring long-term debt. In effect, properties purchased for use as homes are not tradable assets: even when home buyers swap one property for another, any capital gain is usually invested in a new and better property.

Only in cases where property is held for purposes other than end use can it properly be regarded as a tradable asset, and thus considered to be an active part of a diversified portfolio. On the whole, property investment is better left out of the diversification equation, except in the most of unfortunate of circumstances where the failure of other investments or other pressing financial demands necessitate its sale to raise funds. At this point, property ownership provides a valuable if distressing means of balancing the books.

Property shares or indirect property holdings through trusts are better understood as simply being one form of equity investment. Whether or not it can be proved that property investment has out-performed equities over time, it matters little in terms of creating a diversified portfolio.

Diversification into gold

Enthusiasts for gold investment claim that it offers a good hedge against inflation but gold is better known as a safe haven investment at times when other markets are in turmoil. It is hard to find evidence supporting this assertion. Even though gold buffs loudly proclaimed they were vindicated by the sharp rise in the gold price in 2008, their enthusiasm for investment in this precious metal is distinctly belied by looking at the historical record. In September 1980, gold briefly achieved a price of some $670 per troy ounce. After almost three decades, it again briefly peaked at a price slightly exceeding $900, in September 2008, before falling back to a level somewhere in the mid-$700 range. This means that even when the gold price peaked it remained, in inflation-adjusted terms, significantly below the level achieved in 1980. Gold does, however, do well in the wake of stock market crises when a desperate search for alternatives to shares takes hold. But as the crisis of 1987 shows, and the crisis of 2008 confirms, the temporary surge in gold prices is hard to sustain and does nothing to prove the underlying case for investment in this glittering metal.

In the wake of the 1987 crash the average price of gold in the London market rose from $465.3 per ounce in October to $467.5 in November and then went to $486.3. The following year the average price of gold fell back to $436.94, lower than the average price of gold throughout 1987, which stood at $444.46. From then on the gold price moved more or less steadily downwards until it suddenly sprang back to life in 2002 when there was great excitement as the price rose to over $300.

In 2004 gold returned to 1987 prices but the price rise was exaggerated by the sharp decline in the value of the US dollar, in which gold prices are quoted. Gold buffs felt vindicated but their euphoria over returning to a price that prevailed almost two decades earlier seems dubious at best. Keynes famous view of gold being that 'barbarous relic' still seems a more appropriate way of viewing this metal as a viable investment alternative.

Not only is it a relic but gold is an investment that pays absolutely no dividend. On the contrary, those who keep gold as a physical entity usually incur quite high costs of storing it. As an asset class that carries no yield gold (and other precious metals, for that matter) needs to show a consistent history of extraordinary capital gain to justify consideration as a serious form of investment in a diversified portfolio. Aside from a relatively short period in the late 1970s and early 1980s and to some extent in the run up to the 2008 crisis, gold has generally delivered nothing other than miserable gains. On the contrary, as we shall shortly see, gold is by far the worst performing asset class over time.

Yet gold investment has a large band of impressively loyal followers. In some cultures, notably in India and China, gold is regularly dispensed on memorable occasions such as births and marriages and kept by the recipients over long periods of time, both as a store of wealth and as a contingency for dealing with hard times. Most of this gold is kept in the form of jewellery and is not actively traded.

However such demand for gold has helped maintain the price for those more interested in trading.

The advocates of gold investment make some strange claims for it, such as suggesting that it is one of the few investments with a true intrinsic value. Although this is not entirely untrue because there is a finite supply of gold and a consistent (albeit dwindling) demand for it, its real value is determined by much the same forces which determine the value of other assets. Its price shoots up when the perception of its value rises relative to other investments and falls when the reverse occurs. It is certainly not possible to argue that the gold price is a simple reflection of supply and demand. Indeed there are considerable distortions in the supply/demand equation for gold because a great deal of the mined supply of the metal is in the hands of governments who are motivated to buy and sell it for quite other reasons.

Another interesting claim made on behalf of gold is that it is the only asset which is nobody else's liability. This is indeed so, but this precise fact removes many of the pressures that work to keep the price of other assets up while gold drifts down.

Brave attempts have been made to manipulate the figures to put a better face on gold investment, but even the most committed gold fanatics cannot pretend that it is a superior form of investment, stating only that it should have a place in a diversified portfolio. This is the main rationale for gold investment offered in a study of the relative performance of gold to that of other assets prepared by Eugene Sherman, an economist and vice-president at the International Gold Corporation. He says that 'gold has an important diversification role in multi-currency portfolios. For the larger sample period (1968–83) gold continued to be independent of, and uncorrelated with, prices of stocks, bonds and money markets.'[6]

Sherman concludes that gold forms an essential part of a diversified portfolio. Fortunately, for his argument, he was working within the relatively small time frame when gold performance was at its best. As he concluded his study in 1984, just ahead of the sharp decline in the gold price, he is not guilty of sleight of hand, more the beneficiary of fortunate timing.

As Figure 8.3 shows, the picture of good returns from gold investment changes very rapidly after the early 1980s. The chart averages changes in the gold price and the movements of the Dow Jones Industrial Average Index over a period of four decades. While stocks have spent most of this period on a steady upwards march gold has proved to be more volatile. Moreover, unlike stock prices, which have consistently hit new peaks, dropped, recovered and shot higher, the gold price has remained unimpressive, despite some upward blips. What is most remarkable about this chart is that the price of gold has, as Sherman claims, continued to move without much reference to the performance of equities.

Figure 8.3 **US stocks versus gold 1968–2008**

If the gold enthusiasts were right we should have seen gold benefiting greatly from downturns in the stock markets. However, even the rise in the price of gold prior to the 2008 crisis proved hard to sustain and having reached around $900 per troy ounce at its peak, was still only a third higher than the price achieved three decades earlier. As a long term investment, gold certainly did not prove itself to be a viable alternative to other asset classes, although it clearly did provide some opportunities for profit making following the turn of the century. The increase in gold prices at this time was certainly greater than the blip in prices that followed the 1987 crash. There was also some excitement when gold finally broke through the $300 barrier in February 2002, but even at the level it remained half the price seen in the 1980s.

At best gold is attractive because, unlike other asset classes, its pricing does not always follow the equity market. It benefits only marginally, and seemingly rather briefly, from falls in stock markets. There is also some evidence that gold, like real estate, performs better during periods of inflation, although not as well as property investments. All in all it is hard to generate much enthusiasm for gold investment. It is even less attractive as an alternative to invest- ments in equities at times of sharp stock market declines when the gold price starts rising while highly attractive equities come on to the market at bargain prices.

Diversification into bonds

The other traditional safe havens in troubled times are the fixed income markets, particularly the bond market. Whereas gold carries no yield but offers the prospect of capital gain, bonds offer a steady yield but modest prospects of capital gain, although they can be traded for a profit before they reach maturity. The panic of 2008 appeared to give sustenance to the advocates of bond investment, not least because, in the case of corporate bonds, yields started look- ing very impressive. Yet, it should be noted that they remained well below the yields on most of the shares issued by companies who had also issued bonds. Of course these share yields were exaggerated by the price falls on the shares themselves but over time even the temporary bull market in bonds, seemingly attractive as investors fled for safety in the wake of the crisis, appears to be unsustainable.

Cautious investors like bonds because they pay a predictable dividend. The dividend or yield on bonds has often been higher than the yield obtained by investing in equities. As we saw in Chapter 4, this is a relatively new phenomenon because until the 1950s investors expected shares to pay a higher dividend commensurate with the higher risk of owning equities. Now shareholders understand that their reward comes principally in the form of capital gain and there is less pressure on companies to pay high dividends. This is particularly the case in Japan, where companies have a very conservative dividend policy and tend to plough profits back into investment for growth.

The result has been for bond yields to remain above equity yields over time. This has produced a strong band of bond followers who like both the stability of returns from sovereign and corporate bonds and the security of investing in these instruments. *The Barclays Capital Equity–Gilt Study*, an annual survey by the London-based bank comparing bonds and equity investments, consistently finds bonds more attractive than equities on the basis of the yield coming from bonds. The 2002 Barclays report recorded that in the British market corporate bonds achieved a record real 6.0 per cent return in 2001, outperforming equities, which showed a 13.8 per cent decline in yields. According to Barclays the average annual real return from corporate bonds over the previous ten years exceeded that for equities by 1.0 per cent. The American market, according to the study, provides even less comfort to shareholders in terms of comparing equity and bond yields. In 2001 equities underperformed bonds by 15.2 per cent and in the previous year the rate of underperformance was just over 30 per cent.[7]

Others share this view of the superiority of bond performance. For example Robert Shiller writes, 'the evidence that stocks will always outperform bonds over long time intervals simply does not exist'. Although his research examining market returns in twenty-year periods shows only one period, 1901–21, when stocks under-performed short-term interest rates, Shiller believes that in future shares will be delivering poorer returns. He points to the high valuations on shares and the changing investment patterns brought about by new technology.[8]

The problem with Shiller's analysis and the findings of the Barclays study is that they are focused on share yields rather than a combination of yields and capital gains. In the real world it is this combination that really matters. As we shall shortly see, the benefits of the relatively good yield on bonds are quickly obscured in the long run by the much more attractive returns on shares as a result of capital gains.

Every time there is a downturn in the stock market up pops the idea that investors would be better putting their money in bonds. The end of the 1990s boom produced a very large crop of so-called guaranteed funds which promised a return of the original capital invested and some additional gain. This is achieved by putting most of the invested funds, typically 70 per cent or more, into various bonds and leaving the rest with equities. In these circumstances it is easy to see how the 'guarantee' can be achieved. Less easy to see is why investors would not go straight into some fixed income instrument rather than suffer the consequences of handing their cash over to a fund manager who will take a hefty 5 per cent or so of the capital, plus residual charges, in return for looking after the money. Of course, the word 'guarantee' sounds good at a time when share prices are tumbling and the promise of a profit plus security seems like a splendid offer, but the concept of these funds, and the notion of switching from equities to bonds at times of trouble, suggests a great deal of woolly thinking. Returns from bonds look good when markets are booming but they are poor in real terms because market booms often coincide with high rates of inflation. This means that real returns (minus the effects of inflation) tend to be modest.

The problem with switching from equities to bonds at times of stock market decline is, as we have seen, that bond yields tend to move in tandem with stock prices. So when stock markets fall, bond yields fall. On the other hand, precisely because share prices are declining, yields on shares start to rise. This pattern is more pronounced at times of stock market panics provoked by reasons far removed from the state of the economy or the state of corporate earnings. The 1987 stock market crash provides a particularly good illustration of a situation in which corporate earnings were relatively good while share prices declined rapidly and the yield on shares rose sharply. Investors looking for better yields are therefore acting perversely if they switch from equities to fixed income instruments at times of sharp stock market declines.

The motivation for such switches is a desire for security. If times look really bad bond investors take comfort from the fact that they are higher up the line of creditors eligible for payment in the event of corporate failures. If they are holders of government bonds they may feel even more secure because governments are less prone to go bust and less likely to renege on their liabilities. However, as investors in Argentina found in 2002, governments suffering acute financial crises are likely to shift the goalposts for servicing and repaying debt. The simple fact of the matter is that there is no absolute security to be found by investing in any particular asset class. Some asset classes are riskier than others. Bonds remain comfortably low on the risk scale, which explains why they look attractive at times of financial turmoil.

The case for equities and only equities

Bonds, in common with property investments and investments in precious metals, have never managed to reproduce the returns earned on equities and, contrary to some widespread misconceptions, investments in equities have not only secured better returns but over time have proved to be less risky.

This may not be true in some of the emerging markets, where equities are indeed high risk, and in some smaller, better established markets that are not very liquid. However, it most certainly is true as far as investments in US equities are concerned and because Wall Street is now such an overwhelmingly dominant force in global equity markets, a good argument can be made for focusing almost entirely on American shares.

This is the crucial finding of Jeremy Siegel's influential research which concluded that 'over the past two centuries, the average real, or after inflation, compound return on US stocks has been 6.7 percent per year. This means that the purchasing power of investments in stocks doubles every 10 years and 6 months. After 21 years the stock market will produce a fourfold increase in one's wealth. After 42 years, a bit less than two generations, wealth accumulated in the stock market will have undergone a 16-fold increase in purchasing power.'[9]

The good news does not end there because if the increase in value of stocks is taken into consideration, as opposed to merely looking at the earnings they produce as a result of dividend payments, the value of owning shares rises even more dramatically and does so at the expense of all other asset classes. Siegel's research finds that $1 invested and reinvested in stocks since 1800 would have been worth $3,050,000 at the end of 1992. This figure includes both capital appreciation and dividend payments. The nearest competitor to stocks in this game would be bonds. By 1992 the value of a $1 investment in government bonds back in 1800 would have been worth $6,620. Treasury bills would have risen in value to $2,934, while $1 invested in gold would be worth a mere $13.40.[10]

These figures produce a very persuasive argument for focusing all investors' attention on stocks and largely ignoring other investment classes. Even Siegel concedes that in the short run investments in stocks can be riskier than investment in bonds but he has no doubt 'that over the long run the returns on stocks are so stable that stocks are actually safer than either government bonds or Treasury bills'.[11]

Even if a portfolio were to consist entirely of equities, the question of selection still remains and carries with it the notion of diversification either to achieve maximum gain or to provide some insurance against the risk of loss, but the basic standpoint of this book is much the same as that of Siegel; in my view, stocks have proved to be by far the most profitable form of investment over time. Indeed, I would go further and restate the view that equities look even more attractive when stock markets succumb to panic and prices start dipping to levels where buying makes a great deal of sense. Even those not tempted to buy when markets move into sharp decline should exercise extreme caution before selling into a falling market in the hope that funds raised from disposing of equities can be more productively deployed by investing in some other asset class. There is no evidence from history that diversifying out of stocks at times of panic is the right thing to do. On the contrary, it is usually the worst course of action.

Diversifying within the equity market

Although the case for a single-minded focus on the equity market is strong, even the most committed equities enthusiast might remain nervous about having everything invested in just one asset class, even though there is considerable scope for diversification of investment strategies even within a single class. At the most basic level this is why few experienced investors will allow their share portfolios to be dominated by either one particular share or even one share sector. Diversification among sectors and shares is so commonplace as to be hardly worth mentioning.

However, there is lively discussion among investors as to whether portfolios should be jiggled to take account of highly capitalised stocks that emerge from time to time in the investment cycle. For example there was great temptation in the 1990s for investors to clear so-called old economy stocks from their portfolios to make way for so-called new economy stocks from the telecom, media and tech sector. Precisely because they had flavour-of-the-month status these new stocks enjoyed high levels of market capitalisation which made portfolios look unbalanced if they were filled with stocks that accounted for a much smaller proportion of overall market capitalisation.

In Chapter 6 we saw the fund manager John Carey saying that he was very careful about allowing newly issued stocks to account for anything above a very small level of his portfolios, even if they enjoyed a high level of capitalisation. Others are less cautious and their lack of caution is reinforced by the impressive gains often recorded by these new wonder stocks. Investors who avoided these stocks tended to achieve lower rates of growth in their portfolios but in almost all cases avoided far higher levels of loss when those same stocks moved sharply into decline. A sensible compromise can be achieved by taking on a number of high-growth stocks while maintaining a sufficiently large holding in steadily performing stocks. Many investors use this compromise as the principal method of diversifying their portfolios.

The great defensive stock myth

This seems to work, but what happens when severe market downturns arise? At this point the diversification strategy preached by many financial advisers takes on the most odd manifestation. Investors are urged to protect themselves from the market's fall by rushing into so-called defensive stocks. This usually means buying the stocks of utility companies and other corporations that are seen as most likely to weather the storm. Boring old utility stocks lumber along without making many waves most of the time. At best they pay slightly higher dividends than other stocks but in general they sit for long periods of time in big investment portfolios doing very little.

The Dow Jones Utilities Index consistently underperforms the DJIA, often in a quite radical manner.

Figure 8.4 **A century of stock market recovery**

Date	Percentage DJIA fall	Time taken to regain 10%	Utilities index at time when Dow has regained 10%
19 Oct 1987	22.60	2 days	+14.5%
28 Oct 1929	12.80	5 months	+18.3%
29 Oct 1929	11.73	1 day	+18.1%
6 Nov 1929	9.90	3 months	+13.9%
12 Aug 1932	8.40	10 days	+14.6%
26 Oct 1987	8.04	4 days	+3.6%
15 Sept 2008	7.87	20 days	+13.4%
21 July 1933	7.80	20 days	+5.0%
18 Oct 1937	7.75	8 months	+7.8%
1 Dec 2008	7.70	7 days	unchanged

As a result, when stock prices in general start to slide there is a tendency for the prices of defensive stocks to rise. To put it another way, as other stocks start getting cheaper, defensive stocks start getting more expensive. This is certainly not the way the turnabout is described by the advocates of defensive strategy. To justify their view they need to be able to demonstrate that defensive stocks are worth the premium they command in times of market turmoil. The problem is that they cannot point to empirical evidence to support their claims. Figure 8.4 looks at how Wall Street's utilities sector has performed in the wake of major crises relative to the performance of the Dow Jones Industrial Average as a whole.

Figure 8.4 shows that in the aftermath of the biggest one-day percentage falls on Wall Street during the past hundred years a switch into utility stocks would have produced higher returns in the short run for the simple reason that at times of market panic there is a flight to safety which flows in the direction of defensive stocks.

Over longer recovery periods the performance of utility stocks lags far behind that of other equities. This was particularly so during the Great Depression, when it might have been expected that utilities would outperform other counters. In fairness it should be added that this period also saw some of the more impressive gains in the Utilities Index, particularly in the immediate aftermath of the 1929 crash, but once this was out of the way utilities severely underperformed the rest of the market.

All this notwithstanding, there might still be a case for switching into defensive stocks at a time of market panic, but only as a short-term gamble and assuming that investors are nimble enough to switch quickly out of utilities as the general index starts to rise. Over the longer term defensive stocks remain poor investments.

Switching between markets

If stock holders need not switch over to defensive stocks at times of panic they may wish to consider switching from one market to another, either to minimise losses or avoid them in the first place. This sounds like a good idea and, as we have seen, looked attractive to American investors when US stocks were stuck in the doldrums, particularly in the 1960s and 1970s. The Japanese market in particular seemed to offer a very attractive alternative to the depressed markets of the United States and Europe.

By and large, however, world markets have taken their lead from Wall Street, and as we saw in Figure 1.1 these markets have largely risen and fallen in tandem with the American market. The Japanese market, dominated by domestic investors, was a standout in this respect but it too fell back into line with world trends as the new millennium began. Hong Kong, which has one of the world's most open markets, also follows Wall Street trends but as Figure 1.1 shows, often does so in an exaggerated fashion. There have always been times when individual markets, or indeed whole regions, surged ahead of the general trend. In almost all cases these stellar advances, and indeed dramatic falls, have come from newly emerging markets attracting foreign investment for the first time and drawing in the capital of a relatively unsophisticated class of domestic investors entering the world of equities for the first time.

A case in point is the dramatic price gains in the markets of East Asia, particularly those located in the so-called 'tiger economies' of Hong Kong, Singapore, South Korea and Taiwan, followed by the 'tiger cubs' of Indonesia, Malaysia, the Philippines and Thailand. However, the Asian-tiger bubble burst dramatically and conclusively in 1997, since when these markets have retreated and once again started more or less to mirror developments on Wall Street.

If all markets are following Wall Street, this strongly suggests the folly of diversifying into other markets at times of crisis but raises the possibility of looking elsewhere for diversification at times of longer term decline in America.

Diversification through derivatives

Achieving diversification by moving from one market to another, or from one class of stocks to another, is a relatively straightforward form of diversification, albeit sometimes costly. Much more complex, but arguably more rewarding, is the attempt to achieve diversification by investing in financial derivatives. Although some students of finance see this as the ultimate means of diversification, others see derivatives markets as little more than wild speculative ventures carrying far higher levels of risk than would normally be acceptable to those seeking the security of a diversified portfolio.

As we have seen, derivatives markets are not as novel as some people seem to believe. Don Chance, a professor of financial risk management, somewhat with tongue-in-cheek suggests that their origin can be traced back to *The Bible*, in which Genesis records how Jacob secured an option, costing seven years' hard labour, on the right to marry Laban's daughter Rachel. Laban then insisted on Jacob marrying his eldest daughter Leah, so Jacob took out another seven-year option, paid by hard labour, to ensure the right to marry Rachel.[12]

This is all good knockabout stuff but makes the serious point that the concept of derivatives and options was a part of history long before they were adopted in the financial markets. Of course, financial markets transformed the derivatives business, making it infinitely bigger, more systematic, more transparent and a major method of controlling risk, otherwise known as hedging. The other effect of the derivatives business in financial markets was to permit speculation on an unprecedented level.

Speculation in derivatives markets is so vast that it has overshadowed the markets' other purposes. Greg Beir, a market participant rather than observer, makes the important point that those who see hedging in derivatives markets as a means of risk reduction may not be thinking straight. 'The intention may be risk reduction,' he writes, 'but in reality what happens is that the bet is shifted from the performance of the asset to the performance of the hedge [the underlying assets and the derivative instrument together]. When a hedge is entered, one is speculating on the risks of hedging, not on the direction of a price or a volatility.'[13]

However, many see hedging, especially in the stock market, as a form of insurance. In the words of the economist Alfred Marshall, a hedger 'does not speculate: he insures'. The person who accepts the risk passed on by the hedger may be described as a speculator. Strictly speaking, anyone who does not hold the underlying equity in a stock market futures trade may be considered to be a speculator.

Many traders in the futures market shy away from the slightly pejorative sense in which the word speculator is used. The people who run insurance companies certainly do not think of themselves as speculators, yet they are simply taking on the kind of risks assumed by those described as speculators in futures markets. In both circumstances the insurers and futures market investors are prepared to take on some risk and be paid for so doing. The only difference is that insurance companies are assured of some kind of return in the form of premiums (though they may still lose on their gamble with the insured) while futures market players are assured of nothing.

Derivatives markets could be seen as little more than hedging markets, although the fantastic profits and losses to be made there create an image which is far removed from the world of insurance. We have seen how trading in Japanese stock futures brought down the British merchant bank Barings. Equally famously, although not fatally, derivatives market trading in interest-rate swaps cost Procter and Gamble $150 million in 1994, meaning that it had to sell an awfully large amount of soap powder to make up the loss. Across the Atlantic in Germany the Metallgesellschaft conglomerate lost ten times that amount as a result of oil futures trades in 1993, and there are countless other examples of spectacular losses and gains on derivatives markets, all of which combine to suggest that these are places for wild speculation.

And so they are. This is the place where those prepared to take on impressive amounts of risk from hedgers are found. If Nick Leeson had pulled off his wild gamble on Japanese stock exchange futures he would have become known as Leeson the wonder kid who beat the Japanese market, much in the same way that George Soros gained a reputation as the man who beat the pound sterling through his gamble on the British currency falling. As it is, Leeson was the man who provided the insurance policies for all the many investors who correctly thought that the Nikkei 225 Index was heading for a fall. They, too, may well have been speculating rather than hedging, but their motives matter little: in the harsh world of financial markets there is only one measure of success – profits. Because derivatives markets provide the means to make bigger profits with less stake money and carry the potential for bigger losses they are seen as the place where an investor's skills are tested to the utmost.

This is not the view held by the Nobel laureate Merton Miller, one of the most articulate advocates of derivatives trading. He argues that 'financial futures markets not only provide price risk insurance but they do so in a way that is cheaper, that is more liquid and that is more reliable for the customers than the next best alternative'. He goes further and adds, 'a speculator is someone who isn't hedging.'[14]

A stock hedger can be seen as obtaining insurance by, for example, holding stocks in a company or group of companies and buying a short futures contract either in an individual stock or in a group by way of an index contract. In other words, taking positions in the futures market that anticipate the price falling. If the price rises, the profits made in the physical market will outweigh losses in the futures market and if the actual stocks fall in price the gain from a short position in the futures market should outweigh this loss. John Maynard Keynes viewed the cost of this kind of hedging as being a form of insurance premium which investors are prepared to pay to avoid risk. Even if hedging does not produce a profit, at least it minimises losses.

Miller gives a good example of how this works. He describes a situation in which a fund manager wishes to reduce his exposure to equities by $20 million. One way is to sell stocks and buy bonds. He points out that this can take time and involves two sets of transaction costs. An alternative method of securing the same degree of diversification is to take a short position worth $20 million in S&P 500 futures index contracts. In this simple transaction the $20 million worth of equities is fully hedged. In reality, Miller is saying that an investor can remain in the equities market, the market that has consistently outperformed all other asset classes, while being fully hedged against major losses. If there is a cost it is, as Keynes argued, akin to an insurance premium.

Doing nothing is best

Many people excel at doing little. In the world of investment they have the comfort of knowing that there is often a strong case to be made for doing nothing at all. This is because switching between various types of stocks in the physical market, and, more substantially, moving from one asset class to another, always carries significant cost implications. Effectively this means that investors need to consider paying a hefty premium for changing their investment strategy. They seem more willing to pay this price at times of panic when fear of losses overwhelms other considerations. However, at times of panic they are in fact more likely to make a loss by switching out of equities precisely because they are making a sale in a buyer's market. Diversification prior to a panic is supposed to obviate the need for panic selling but, as we have seen, this is not realistic because so many markets and parts of markets move in tandem. This makes the benefits of diversification more illusory than real.

Even if it is conclusively proved that equities are the unchallenged winning asset class, it is a brave investor who has sufficient confidence in equities to ignore other asset classes, so the futures market and other derivatives provide some hedging for those confident about equities while remaining risk averse.

There are always moments in time when equities are less attractive than other forms of investment, but this does not alter the basic fact that over the long term the equity market delivers the best returns. This must provide considerable comfort to investors who have neither the time nor the inclination to be constantly tinkering with their investment portfolios. The message is clear: once invested in a blue chip equity portfolio, doing nothing is often the best thing to do.

Although equities have shown consistent ability to outperform other asset classes, there will always be opportunities for switching from one asset class to another as markets move. Indeed, it is in the nature of markets for one to rise as others fall, if for no other reason than that cash coming out of one market has to find a home in another. Clearly there are significant opportunities for investors as the cash moves about. The fact that short-term opportunistic investment switching can yield significant returns should not be mistaken as a stratagem. At the strategic level, which involves longer term planning, finding windows of opportunity to make a profit certainly plays a part, but this is not the same thing as adopting diversification as a consistent investment policy.

The simple lesson of diversification is that it is very hard to achieve, rarely succeeds once panic sets in and is generally costly. As matters stand, the history of investment points to the solid message of sticking with equities through thick and thin. Nothing is for ever, so it is quite conceivable that the course of history will change. However, there is no indication that it will do so any time soon, nor is it at all certain what change will bring about if and when it occurs.

The short answer to the question posed in the title of this chapter is 'no'.

9

Is the market always right?

THE OLD SAYING that the market is always right is really a truism: a market price can never be wrong in the sense that it reflects whatever level the market happens to have reached at any given time. However, this statement is usually given a wider meaning, implying a greater wisdom for markets in general and the stock market in particular.

But there is mounting evidence that markets do not always reflect the true worth of the underlying businesses they represent. Indeed, company directors are spending far too much time making investors happy instead of focusing their energies on improving the performance of the businesses they are running. We have seen the extent to which the obsession with share performance has encouraged directors of even the biggest companies to embark on dubious manipulation of company accounts to present a better picture of their affairs and, in some cases, to resort to outright fraud in order to deceive investors.

Even the most avid market enthusiast would not deny that this is happening, but would argue that these events merely detract from an understanding of the market's role in providing a mechanism that can efficiently adjust financing requirements to changing circumstances. In addition, supporters would say that stock markets are a wonderful barometer of the way the economy is going and are a measure of its performance.

Back to basics

At this point it may be worthwhile to step back a little and return to basics to ask what function stock markets are supposed to perform. In pure theory the answer is simple: equity markets provide an opportunity for companies seeking risk capital to find investors willing to take on these risks in return for a share of the profits. In addition, the existence of an open market furnishes investors with an opportunity to trade their equity stakes and gives companies opportunities to return to the market for new capital should the need arise.

It is increasingly apparent that stock markets are not fully performing this function and, even if they are partially doing so, the perceptions of market participants are somewhat removed from the theoretical definition given above. Stock market investors are not supposed to dictate the way companies are run but nowadays they seem to want to do precisely that. Although holding shares implies ownership and entitles shareholders to a proportion of the company's profits, it is not supposed to bestow management rights on investors.

Nowadays listed company executives are constantly forced to look over their shoulders at the share markets. They resort to the advice of stock analysts, accountants, investment bankers and others who are supposed to be objective professionals but more often than not seem to have just one interest – to push up the share price. Yet once the capital has been issued, at least in theory, it should matter little to the companies whether the price rises or falls.

The origins of equity investment

Was it always so? Clearly, the answer is no, but looking at the origins of stock markets suggests that the seeds of the present day situation were planted early in their history.

Organised equity markets started rationally enough some four centuries ago when the sponsors of seafaring trading ventures in

Britain sought investors to back their schemes. They could not turn to the existing debt markets because these risky ventures lacked the kind of collateral which lenders typically required. So the sponsors offered a share in the profits of their ventures, potentially vastly exceeding the usual return on loans. The simple logic of this financial proposition caught on and soon moved from seafaring enterprises to other forms of capitalist endeavour. It was taken much further by the Dutch, who established an exchange in Amsterdam towards the beginning of the seventeenth century which dealt not only in company shares but also in government bonds and a variety of futures and options. This is a reminder that trading in derivatives, supposedly the more speculative and risky end of the equity market, is hardly something new, nor is it the preserve of a new breed of sharp traders who were much in the limelight in the later part of the twentieth century.

The formal London stock exchange, as opposed to informal gatherings of stock traders, began around 1670 when stock and merchandise dealers shared premises in Cornhill in the City of London. The stockbrokers established an exclusive exchange in 1698. The stock exchange which was to become the world's biggest, that in New York, started long after the European bourses when twenty-four men began gathering regularly under an old buttonwood tree to trade a handful of stocks in 1792. New York cannot, however, claim credit for the first American stock market because an exchange was already operating in Philadelphia before Wall Street came into being. It took until 1817 for New York's largely informal exchange to become a more substantial trading institution.

Only those with rose-tinted glasses believe that from their earliest days stock exchanges where anything but centres for speculation. True, they were also centres for capital raising, but it is arguable that from the very outset speculation was the bigger draw. In theory, equity markets exist primarily to channel funds for the development of businesses. While there is no question that many companies secure a great deal of capital from the public through these markets, it is questionable how much of it is really raised for investment as opposed to simply providing the majority shareholders with a means of extracting profits from their businesses.

Equity funding of business remains much smaller than loan funding to this day. One of the main reasons for this is that few business owners will give away equity if they believe that they can make more money by retaining ownership. However, as markets have developed many entrepreneurs have discovered that they can realise considerable gains by selling and trading equity, often more than can be made by being simply engaged in what might be called the business of business. This discovery was made very shortly after organised markets were established. It produced just one of the many distortions that have since multiplied in the world of equity markets.

As we saw in Chapter 5, equity markets are, if anything, a declining source of funds for investment. Nevertheless, stock markets are growing at a rapid rate and attracting more and more investors. In the United States the 1990s began with investors having some 22.5 per cent of their financial assets in stocks. By the end of the decade the average level of investment in equities had risen to over 50 per cent, according to research from the Investment Company Institute. It is reasonable to assume that these increased investment levels were encouraged by the lure of capital gain, not out of a desire to participate in the development of business.

This being so, the market has become increasingly detached from its original purpose and comes more and more to resemble a casino. The markets take on a life of their own, almost disregarding the underlying businesses they are supposed to represent. Once this happens their vulnerability to irrational and extreme behaviour becomes more pronounced. This tells us a lot about why stock markets can hardly be described as perfect markets or places where efficient markets theory can be proven.

The problem with efficient markets theory

This raises the whole question of how rational markets are and to what extent they efficiently perform the function of raising capital. The theory of efficient capital markets, much discussed in academic circles, pivots around the idea that share prices will reflect the value of expected dividends. Dividends are seen as important because they are the concrete expression of the link between a rational basis for valuing a company's return on investment and the stock price. The rate of return is expressed in terms of dividend payments, which return to investors a proportion of the profits of the company. Efficient markets theory takes things further because it is suggested that the share price actually anticipates the level of dividends and thus constitutes a valuable tool for forecasting which way corporate profits are heading.

In summary, efficient markets theory suggests that the real value of shares is determined by the level of dividends. This will come as a bit of a surprise to most stock market investors because nowadays few of them are primarily interested in dividend levels when making investment decisions. The reality is that they tend to base investment decisions on how much they can make by liquidating their investments rather than by sticking with them.

Let us, however, assume that efficient markets theory is correct and that there is a distinct correlation between the movement of stock prices and dividends. Some research shows that the correlation holds true. For example, Gary Santoni and Gerald Dwyer have looked at price and dividend movements in the last century and can trace a connection, although they found that the correlation does not hold for the 1970s.[1]

Other research has come up with very different conclusions. Robert Shiller is one of the prominent opponents of the efficient markets theory; he maintains that 'this argument for the efficient markets hypothesis represents one of the most remarkable errors in the history of economic thought'.[2] Shiller points to a crucial weakness of this theory as a means of explaining why share prices move. 'Returns on speculative assets are nearly unforecastable,' he argues. That being so, it is suggested that 'the real price of stocks is close to the intrinsic value, that is, the present value with constant discount rate of optimally forecasted future real dividends'. However, this does not happen.

Shiller's research on stock prices and earnings of American companies (as opposed to dividends, which represent only the share of earnings that companies wish to distribute) shows that stock prices have consistently run well ahead of earnings since the later part of the nineteenth century. However, for obvious reasons, as share prices plunge, dividends, assuming companies are in a position to pay them, rise rapidly in proportionate percentage terms. This was dramatically seen during the 2008 crisis when, as Figure 9.1 shows, there was an almost complete reversal of the position in which share prices outstripped dividend growth in a pronounced manner. Only in the depressed 1940s and 1950s did share prices and dividends move in tandem.

What Figure 9.1 makes clear is that there is no basis for arguing that share prices anticipate dividend price movements. This was not so a century ago (although there was a closer relationship between dividends and prices), and it is even less so now.

Fabio Canova and Gianni De Nicolo have conducted research that suggests that dividend yields and stock price movements are even less closely related in Europe. However, they argue that in both the United States and Europe a correlation can be found between stock prices and production growth rates.[4] This seems to be another way of saying that economic growth and stock prices have a close relationship and thus expresses the rationality of the stock market.

The problem for advocates of the efficient markets model is that they argue that stock prices anticipate future earnings (and hence dividends) and do not hark back to historic earnings. This, they say,

Figure 9.1 **Stock prices and dividends, 1871–2008**

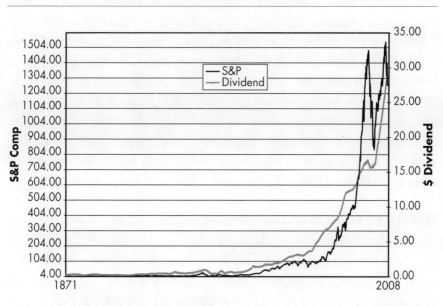

Source: Robert Shiller, www.irrationalexuberance.com

explains why the price–dividend ratio is low when dividends are high. However, there is no trend line showing how this anticipation works, besides which the discrepancy between dividends and share prices is too large to be explained away.

There is an even more fundamental problem with efficient markets theory, as Stephen LeRoy has observed. He wrote, 'If capital markets are efficient in this sense [that they reflect the discounted value of expected future dividends] changes in stock prices should be associated exclusively with new information leading to revisions in expected future dividends: when dividend prospects improve, stock prices rise.'[5] And the converse should occur when dividend prospects decline. We know that this does not happen, although over time stock price trends may well be consistent with dividends.

John Maynard Keynes did not directly take part in the efficient markets debate. However, as we have seen, he made the shrewd observation that investors are more interested in guessing what other investors will think about any given stock. The ability to guess changing perceptions over a stock's valuation ahead of other investors is the key to making money. It may well be that the guess is correct and that changing perceptions also reflect the change in fundamental values attached to a particular stock, but all this happens well before the changed fundamentals are known to the investing public. The reality is that it matters little in the short term whether perceptions are right or wrong, it is the perceptions that move markets.

What is rational stock market behaviour?

To assume that markets behave rationally is to assume that the participants behave rationally. This is a shaky assumption, particularly at times when markets become overheated and attract many players who have no real idea about what they are investing in. Nor should rationality be assumed for investment professionals, who are supposed to have better access to information but are not necessarily going to use it in a purely rational manner.

Was it, for example, rational for stockbrokers' analysts to be recommending shares trading on price–earnings ratios exceeding 100 during the height of the 1990s dotcom boom? Almost certainly not, because the earnings record suggested that it would take 100 years for the price of these stocks to be matched by the dividends they were paying. One of the more extreme examples of the dotcom madness were the valuations placed on Yahoo! Inc., which at one time was trading on a price–earnings ratio of around 500 and still remained high on brokers 'buy' lists. The dotcom boom was a heady period in which the much more upbeat subject of earnings potential replaced talk of boring old earnings.

In this light it is easy to see why an influential study by Lawrence Summers could conclude that 'even a cursory examination suggests that there are many traders pursuing strategies not closely related to fundamental valuations. There are no grounds for assuming either that irrational traders will be eliminated, or that they will be unable to move market prices.'[6]

In the sense that most investors are not looking for profit in the form of dividend payments but hoping to make money by way of capital gain, they can be described as rational in buying shares likely to register big price rises regardless of their fundamental value. This is the crucial point. However, as research by Peter Spiro suggests, capital growth has, over time, added far less to the value of shares than dividend payments. He found that in the thirty-year period from 1957 to 1986, the compound real annual growth in the Standard & Poor's 500 Index was only 0.9 per cent, whereas average dividend yields over the same period were 3.9 per cent.[7]

More recent advances in share prices are more than likely to have changed the picture painted by Spiro, but his research remains of historic interest because the high growth of share prices in recent times has made many people forget how much investors used to be preoccupied by dividend yields. Gains considerably in excess of 0.9 per cent could have been be made from share trading in the 1990s boom. This is what matters to most investors and explains why they were paying so little regard to dividend yields.

What actually moves prices is far more likely to be rumour, changing sentiment or new information that has an impact on the fortunes of a company. Stock prices tend to move most spectacularly at times when mergers, real or imagined, are underway. They move when rumours circulate in the market about changes in corporate leadership and a host of other things which have little to do with dividends in the short run.

Another way of looking at the irrationality of market behaviour is to examine longer periods of quite remarkable stock price movement which do not result in panics but, precisely because of their tenacity and duration, are more damaging to investors and provide far fewer opportunities than panics for making a profit. The market's attention is so focused on dramatic one-day price falls and rises that few people now remember the worldwide market decline of 60–75 per cent in the three years from 1972 to 1975. This was a miserable period for investors, but because it was an orderly fall and because it lacked drama this huge decline is not seen as a time of financial crisis. Nor, for that matter has the dramatic slide in the Japanese stock markets, starting in the 1990s and lasting for more than a decade, been viewed as a panic. It is spoken of as a crisis, but a long-term one that ultimately will be resolved.

The fact that markets appear to be rational over the longer term may provide comfort to advocates of market rationality and the supremacy of unfettered markets, but is of limited use in considering investment strategy. This is because short-term irrationality helps explain why panics break out and why those who are not swayed by short-term sentiment stand to profit as good sense returns.

The god of shareholder value

Any outbreak of good sense has, however, been severely curtailed by the rise of the new god of shareholder value. It was not until the late 1980s that this concept started gaining currency, and what a limited currency it turned out to be. Shareholder value sounds like a great idea until it is appreciated that it really means just two things. The first is percentage earnings growth and the second is share price rises, which come from earnings growth. Percentage earnings growth performance is not only a very limited way of viewing corporate strength but the manner in which it is judged is even more limiting and distorting.

Relying on just one criterion to judge company performance is dubious at the best of times and positively dangerous if that criterion is flawed. This is why more sensible investors like to consider other factors, such as a company's ability to generate a return on capital, or they may look at the state of cash flow and work out the amount of cash a business manages to retain. Most importantly, fundamental company research pays greater attention to the longer-term performance record rather than differences in earnings recorded at annual or even quarterly intervals.

The problem that arises from focusing on the share price and aligning the interest of company directors to the performance of shares is that the objective of raising share prices becomes an end· in itself. Thus the people running companies are rewarded when the share price goes up, even though the actual business of their companies might be going down. At the height of the dotcom boom some of the corporate managers who received the highest rewards were running businesses that were producing hardly any revenue at all. Indeed, their success was measured not by the revenue they were generating but by the level of the company's share price. As this had little to do with revenues the new economy managers were also applauded for diminishing the so-called burn rate, in other words the rate at which investment funds were being consumed. Those schooled in more old-fashioned accounting methods would simply describe this as loss reduction, but this ugly term was shunned in the bright, born-again world of the new economy.

The earnings game
Meanwhile stock market investors started making unreasonable demands on company managers. In the bull market of the 1990s there were demands for double-digit earnings growth. Penalties, in the form of lower share valuations, were dished out to companies that failed to deliver returns of this order.

Companies enthusiastically played the earnings game, promising continued earnings growth. There were enormous pressures to do so. Media coverage of their affairs focused on earnings. An influential website called WhisperNumber.com attained a large following as it published unofficial earnings forecasts and rumours about where earnings were heading. In the United States Thomson Financial/First

Call's average of analysts' predictions for each company's earnings was widely reported. Every other major stock market had its own consensus forecast mechanism, all of which commanded considerable attention. A survey of questions asked by analysts at company briefings compiled by Baruch Lev of New York University found that the overwhelming bulk of questions related to earnings.

Unsurprisingly this obsession with earnings formed the centrepiece of analysts' work. They then pumped out earnings forecasts. When companies reported earnings beating these forecasts they were rewarded with sharp spikes in their share price. A failure to meet consensus forecasts was rapidly followed by share price falls.

The almost religious belief in earnings led to a lack of sensible discussion of earnings quality. Nor was there discussion of the differences that should be expected from companies at differing stages of development. The markets were ignoring the fact that it is quite unreasonable to expect the same level of earnings growth from a mature company compared with a new entity that needs to grab market share and aggressively expand in order to establish itself. The fixation on percentage growth figures means that earnings growth from, say, $100 to $1,000 looks quite wonderful in percentage terms, but $1,000 remains a small amount of money. Conversely, a company generating a modest earnings growth in percentage terms of, say, 5 per cent, might well be returning earnings in the eight- or nine-digit bracket, which is real money by any standards.

The reality of the 1990s was that annual average earnings growth among American companies was around 7 per cent. However, the fact that some aggressive wonder-stock companies managed to report earnings increase figures well in excess of this average suggested to some investors that this was the norm. They did not stop to ask themselves how these large leaps in earnings were achieved, or, more importantly, if they were likely to be good for the long-term health of those companies. Writing in the *New York Times* Harris Collingwood reported that,

Left to their own devices, corporate managers during the boom weren't about to abandon the earnings game. The rewards for playing were too great and the penalties for nonparticipation too severe. But in theory at least, two groups of professionals – audit firms and securities analysts – had a duty to investors to restrain corporate managers' most self-serving impulses and subject their actions to sceptical scrutiny. Instead, far too many analysts and auditors connived with management to conceal the true condition of some of the market's most dysfunctional companies.[8]

The earnings game was played by a number of rules, only a few of which included expanding business by means of organic growth or adding real value as opposed to shareholder value to the business. As the 1990s boom came to an end it became clear that some of the players were so desperate to improve their earnings figures that they simply broke the rules altogether. The end of the boom gave way to an unprecedented crop of corporate scandals, discussed more fully in Chapter 5. What they had in common was an attempt to rig the accounts so that it appeared that the companies in question were enjoying spectacular earnings growth. Some of the means of producing these figures were downright fraudulent, others suggested a very questionable manipulation of the accounts that may not have been downright illegal but certainly produced a false picture of earnings.

The story of how the US appliance maker Sunbeam managed to dress up its earnings figures by 'borrowing' sales from one period and adding them to another in 1997 and early 1998 is instructive in revealing how this was done. There was nothing illegal about the company's activities, although they did result in a class action brought by shareholders. They alleged that the company misled them by getting dealers to stock up on barbecue grills in the winter, when they were in poor demand, and thus shipping them from Sunbeam's warehouses and therefore 'selling' them to make Sunbeam's first-quarter earnings forecast look accurate. However, the dealers did not pay for their stock so that when the time came for payment to be made it had already been recorded and the second- and third-quarter earnings figures looked terrible. The investors, for whom this manoeuvre was designed, took fright and sold off Sunbeam stock. The company then fled to the federal bankruptcy court for protection against its creditors. The Sunbeam saga, far from being the tip of the iceberg, was somewhat way down the list of corporate accounts manipulation scandals and involved sums far less than those that disappeared from WorldCom or Tyco or any of the other big corporate failures of the post-1990s boom.

The M&A game

Sunbeam is also a minnow compared to General Electric. GE rode the crest of the earnings wave under the leadership of Jack Welch, who became nothing short of a Wall Street hero for consistently producing impressive earnings. It now seems that most of the increase came not from real business growth but from an orgy of acquisitions financed at increasingly high cost to the company. Welch was buying a hundred companies a year over a five-year period.

Meanwhile WorldCom bought more than seventy-five companies in less than five years, the biggest acquisition being MCI in 1998 at a cost of $37 billion. Like GE, WorldCom was able to report fantastic earnings growth as a result of these purchases. As it did so its share price rose, enabling it to buy yet more companies.

GE and WorldCom were not unusual in doing what they did; indeed, a sharp rise in merger and acquisition (M&A) activity is a typical product of a stock market boom. It was seen ahead of the 1929 crash and again in the 1960s when investment banks (or merchant banks at they are known in Britain) first began to realise that working on M&As would provide an important source of revenue. In the 1980s the price falls in the stock market left many companies with very low stock valuations, making them vulnerable to corporate predators such as T. Boone Pickens in the United States and Sir James Goldsmith in Europe. They swooped down and promised to release hidden potential by making company assets work more efficiently.

Such activities led to two unsavoury developments that proved more enduring than any business synergies or other successes that they managed to produce. First they created the leveraged buy out, which allowed predators to secure loans on the back of future earnings of the companies in their sights. Secondly, they encouraged companies to use their resources to buy back their own shares. When this failed, the hapless corporations had to pay so-called greenmail to the predators to get them to back off. Both forms of defence ate up money that could have been much more usefully deployed in making real capital investments.

The dubious era of the 1980s takeover spree was followed by a pause as the disastrous results of these mergers and attempted mergers were disentangled. However, as the stock markets started rising again in the early 1990s all was forgotten. The quite absurd situation arose in which companies that were making tremendous losses or, at best, very small amounts of profit were able to acquire much bigger companies with a genuine earnings stream simply because the level of their stock market capitalisation was much higher than that of the profitable companies. This allowed them to offer their higher priced stock in return for the assets of these corporations.

What is different about the 1990s era of mergers is their sheer size. According to a survey by *Newsweek* the merger frenzy peaked in 2000, when a global total of $3.4 trillion was spent and every seventeen minutes a deal was being made somewhere in the world. The magazine quotes Hans Schenk, an economist at Tilburg University in the Netherlands, saying that 'since the 1960s, merged companies have typically performed 17 per cent worse than independent rivals in terms of productivity, profitability, new patents and growth in market share'. Schenk calculated that US and European mergers valued at $9 trillion, carried out between 1996 and 2000, resulted in some $5.8 trillion of waste as the deals failed to create or actually destroyed economic wealth.[9]

Schenk's findings are echoed in a survey by AT Kearney, the business consultancy, which looked at 24,000 companies spread over fifty-three countries. The survey, covering the period 1988–2000, found that only 20 per cent of mergers between companies resulted in an increase of turnover above the industry's average. Where shareholder value had actually increased, 60 per cent of the growth was attributable to internal growth; the rest was because of M&A activity.[10]

One of the more spectacular failures of the 1990s merger boom was the takeover of the Time Warner media company by the Internet service provider America Online (AOL). At the time of the takeover AOL had the higher market capitalisation but had earnings amounting to less than half those received by Time Warner. Moreover, Time Warner was expected to provide over 80 per cent of the revenues of the merged company, and some 70 per cent of its cash flow in the period following the merger. Yet Time Warner was the company being acquired. When the deal was struck it was widely described as a masterstroke. The combined market value of the two companies amounted to $290 billion; two years later, when all market valuations were well down, AOL Time Warner's valuation was even more depressed. The merged company's valuation stood at $135 billion, less than the $146 billion AOL had paid for its acquisition. By 2009 the name AOL had been removed from the company's title and capitalisation stood at around $35 billion.

If mergers are so consistently unsuccessful, why are they so popular? The usual rationale for mergers is given in terms of economies of scale, cost savings, synergies and better opportunities for competition. One of the few pieces of research supporting this point of view comes from Susanne Trimbath, a research economist at the

Milken Institute. Her book, *Mergers & Efficiency: Changes Across Time*, looked at 276 mergers of listed Fortune 500 companies over a five-year period ending 1995, just before the height of the 1990s merger boom. She found that two-thirds of the mergers did indeed increase efficiency and produce cost savings. The 100 companies making the biggest efficiency improvements registered gains averaging 5 per cent, measured by reductions in costs entailed in generating revenue. However, it seems that the smaller mergers worked best and as the scope of her research does not cover the period which has seen some of the more unsuccessful mergers, it is not possible to say if the verdict would have been different had the time period been extended.[11]

Trimbath's findings remain very different from those of other researchers who have reached the blunt conclusion that mergers are not producing better companies. If this is so other answers need to be found to discover the motivation for mergers. At one level the answer may simply reside in the giant egos of CEOs who want to control bigger and bigger companies. This certainly cannot be discounted, nor is it possible to discount the material rewards that come to company managers running larger companies and the rewards that come as a result of increased remuneration following mergers which boost both earnings and share prices.

There is no question that CEOs can earn large bonuses as a result of completing mergers. Take, for example, the $26 million special payment made to Joseph Nacchio, the CEO of Qwest Communications, which acquired US West in 1999. On the other side of the deal Solomon Trujillo earned $15 million for making the sale. The fact that the merger turned very sour indeed and Nacchio was forced out of his job says a great deal, but only in retrospect.

In addition, there is always a herding effect when M&A activity intensifies. Companies start to worry that they are missing the action as their competitors group together to form what superficially appear to be stronger entities. As one industrial sector experiences a wave of mergers it is almost inevitable that competitors within that sector start consulting their investment bankers for advice on how to replicate these arrangements.

At best, mergers are the route to rapid corporate growth, but the experience of some of the biggest mergers shows that the growth is not only hard to sustain but in many cases illusory. Before anyone finds this out, the merged company has usually managed to issue seemingly better earnings figures and, if they are nimble, the executives who have executed these mergers can quickly make an exit clutching a golden parachute. The fact that all this nonsense is encouraged by shareholders (until things go wrong) and has become an integral feature of bull stock markets suggests something rather worrying about the nature of the markets.

Paying shareholders, robbing companies

Having demanded rises in earnings, by whatever means they were achieved, shareholders were disappointed when earnings growth slumped and became positively alarmed when they realised that gearing levels were becoming dangerously high as a result of the acquisition activity. As share prices went into retreat in the new millennium questions started to be raised about the nature of the 1990s boom. Was it really all that it was cracked up to be?

Edward Chancellor makes a compelling case for the sceptics.[12] First he questions the US productivity figures which suggested very considerable gains during the 1990s. He argues that adjustments made for improvements in technology added 0.5 per cent to the figures at the end of the decade. This left annual productivity rises in the 1990s only marginally above those seen in the 1970s and 1980s but well below the impressive annual rises of some 3 per cent witnessed in the 1960s.

Secondly, he believes that returns on equity were greatly exaggerated during this decade because the figures were calculated minus the large amount of debt incurred during this period. This means that instead of the reported average 22 per cent return on equity, a more realistic figure was around 13 per cent if allowance is made for debt.

The pressure to increase earnings also compelled managers to look for cost savings, which is commendable until it reaches the point of hampering a company's ability to grow or provide the income needed to adequately service its own business. Stories pouring out from employees of the failed Enron group revealed the extent to which cost cutting was actively preventing the carrying out of their work at the time that the stock price was rising because shareholders were so enthused by earnings growth. Moreover, companies find it hard to produce impressive earnings figures when heavy allowances have to be made for capital investment which produces long-term results but a short-term reduction on the bottom line of the balance sheet. This provides a major disincentive to contemplate the kind of long-term investment needed to grow businesses. A survey by the New York research company Sanford Bernstein found that in the second half of the twentieth century shares in American companies with the highest levels of capital expenditure significantly underperformed the share prices of companies which spent less.[13]

In the 1990s major US companies were cutting the proportion of capital spending in relation to revenues and spending the money on such things as share buybacks. In this way they undermined their competitiveness both internally and in overseas markets, where major US corporations are operating with capital equipment far older than that deployed by European rivals. In the paper industry, for example, US producers' equipment is on average seventeen years old, twice the age of the equipment used by European companies. In the steel industry US producers are working with plant which is so much older than that of overseas competitors that the Bush administration had to launch a rescue plan for the industry in 2002 by imposing protective tariffs.

Stock markets can hardly be said to have helped make companies more competitive, yet share prices rose tremendously and the rise in corporate profitability provided considerable reassurance that all was well.

How the markets batter economies

But what happens when stock markets move into decline? Researchers at the Organisation for Economic Cooperation and Development (OECD) attempted to answer this question. They found that, particularly in the United States, a sharp downturn in stock prices, amounting to 20 per cent, had the effect of reducing household consumption by 1.2 per cent in the first year and 1.1 per cent in the second year. This translated itself into 0.8 per cent falls in gross domestic product (GDP) for both years. In Britain, however, the effect was less damaging, causing a small 0.2 per cent decline in consumption in the first year and 1 per cent in the second year, leading to no change in GDP in the first year and a 0.4 per cent drop in the second year. The British experience, according to this study, was mirrored in other European countries. In Japan there was a slightly bigger impact, with private consumption falling by 0.6 per cent in the first year and 0.7 per cent in the second year. Meanwhile Japanese GDP suffered a 0.5 per cent fall in the first year and 0.4 per cent in the second year. It seems that a less sharp fall in share prices – 10 per cent in Japan as opposed to 20 per cent in the US – produced a more or less proportionally similar impact on consumption. In other words, the impact, roughly speaking, was half as damaging.

The OECD research did not examine falls in corporate investment consequent on share price declines but quoted other studies suggesting that the impact on capital investment expenditure could be four times higher than that on private consumption. However, the fact that capital investment is only a quarter of the level of household expenditure in OECD countries suggests that the overall impact on economic growth is likely to be the same.[14]

Anyone who believes that stock markets play a positive role in the economy must accept that there are periods when they detract from economic growth, but the argument being made here is more fundamental and more damaging. It is that it is very hard to argue that stock markets are making capitalism work better, or indeed that the markets are giving businesses the means to create bigger and better companies. It seems quite reasonable to argue that, instead of providing a means of enhancing corporate activity and providing support for corporate growth, stock markets are increasingly responsible for detracting from business growth. Moreover, the markets are creating diversions for company managers, who are focusing too much on financial markets and not enough on improving their businesses.

Entrepreneurs shunning stock markets

There is clear anecdotal evidence that many entrepreneurs running worthwhile companies are deterred from applying for stock market listings because they fear that the unrealistic demands of stock market investors will detract from business growth. The owner of a successful company that supplies one of my companies said bluntly, 'If you think I'm going to have some pimply stockbrokers' analyst with two MBAs and no commonsense telling me how to run my company, you must be bloody mad.' The irony is that many successful entrepreneurs prefer seeking funds from the growing number of venture capital outfits who then tend to encourage stock market listings for successful companies because this gives the fund managers a way of realising gains from their investments.

Private placements of equity are also becoming more widely used among companies seeking new capital but anxious to obtain cash from investors prepared to stick with their equity stakes for a longer period and who understand that pay-back may take some time.

Although it seems unlikely that non-stock market forms of capital raising will remain at current levels, any complacency about the superiority of stock markets as equity markets should be tempered by the thought that some of the better equity issues are bypassing stock markets altogether.

Maybe they would not do so if Western stock markets adopted some of the mindset that prevails in the much maligned Japanese stock markets. Japanese investors understand that companies need to reinvest a large proportion of their earnings in order to grow. They do not demand high dividend payments but look instead for capital growth. Secondly, most of Japan's listed companies come to the market with the participation of their bankers, suppliers, customers and other business partners. In one sense this is unhealthy because it creates market cabals, but in another it means that shares are held by entities with a concrete interest in the growth of the underlying business and not an obsessive concern with the share price.

The hired hands versus the controlling shareholders

Differing attitudes to share ownership and the sale of shares in Japan are but part of a more complex international picture that is often overlooked when markets are judged from a Wall Street perspective. On Wall Street, and in other well-established markets, the control of most major corporations has already passed from the company founders and their families into the hands of professional managers. Such has been the state of corporate development in the United States that there was some surprise when someone bearing the name Ford resumed control of the Ford Motor Company.

Most people running big listed companies in the West hold an amount of equity that is substantial, but rarely sufficient for control. The consequence is that even CEOs can be hired and fired at the will of the board. This in turn means that independent company directors tend to be more assertive and more likely to question the activities of the management.

There are positives and negatives here. Among the positives is a more professional and objective approach to management. Secondly, directors who do not have majority shareholdings are more likely, although hardly guaranteed, to bring a genuinely independent mindset to tackling the company's affairs. On the other side of the coin, managers who are hopping from one corporation to the next are likely to be less committed. A survey published by the management consultants Booz Allen Hamilton in 2002 examined management changes in Europe and America's 2,500 largest companies. It found that in 2001, 231, or almost 10 per cent, changed their CEOs. This is more than 50 per cent up on the number of management changes recorded in 1995. The average length of tenure of CEOs declined from 9.5 to 7.3 years in the same period.[15] Management changes just below the top are even more frequent.

Most senior executives will strongly reject suggestions of lack of commitment to their companies but they are hardly likely to be as committed as the company founders. Moreover, they will argue that their loyalties lie with the shareholders, most of whom, like them, may well be temporary equity holders anxious to realise capital gains. This explains why corporate managers often focus on short-term gain. Such gains are most likely at times of mergers. Managers can argue that they have a responsibility to facilitate such activity for the share-holders' benefit. Their interest in such situations is hardly likely to be undermined by the prospect of earning fat bonuses as a result of a merger. In these circumstances the longer term prospect of whether a merger is actually good for business is likely to get lost among all the other more alluring short-term benefits being laid on the table.

These are complex matters, touched upon here only for the purpose of considering what this means for stock markets and investors. In brief it seems possible to argue that the increasing detachment of management from ownership of companies makes corporations more like tradable entities. Confirmation of this assertion is provided by the steady growth of M&A activity in well-established markets.

It is possible to take this argument a stage further and suggest that if corporate entities themselves have become more tradable, it follows that their shareholders will be more interested in the companies as tradable entities. They will be looking to make capital gains from companies being bought and sold rather than having an interest in the incremental gains achieved by steady improvements in corporate profitability. At the height of the dotcom boom (reflecting exactly the events that occurred during the mid-1800s railway boom) this mindset reached its logical, or arguably illogical, conclusion. Companies with no earnings at all could still be bought and sold for great sums of money on the promise of earnings to come. The shares of these no-earnings companies could also be traded at great profit. In effect, what was happening was not merely that the companies had become tradable commodities but, because they had little asset value, what was actually being traded were concepts or ideas.

The contrast between listed companies in developed markets and those in emerging markets is sharp. In most emerging markets the listed companies are still run by their founders, or at least by the founding families, who retain overwhelming control of the equity. In the Asian region, most listed companies place only a very small percentage of their equity in the hands of the public, sometimes as little as 10 per cent. Some countries impose a lower limit, as in Hong Kong, where at least a quarter of the equity must be in the hands of the public for a company to retain its listing.

Unsurprisingly M&A activity in Asia is very modest when compared with Britain or the United States. When mergers take place they are usually the result of distress selling. Healthy corporate entities tend not to even consider mergers.

The plus side of family control and family management is that the listed companies enjoy considerable continuity and the owners rarely consider engaging in merger activity. Because they own such a large proportion of the equity they are less likely to be swayed by unreasonable investor demands for higher dividends or whatever. However, most of these entrepreneur owners obtain the bulk of their incomes from dividends as opposed to salaries or fancy share option schemes (discussed more fully in Chapter 5), so may have a vested interest in high dividend payments. The CLSA Emerging Markets brokerage looked at share options in Asian blue chip corporations and found that of the eleven companies studied, eight provided share options to staff. Where stock options were in place and not treated as expenses they had the effect of overstating earnings by an average of 6.8 per cent, which is less than a third of the distortion that typically affects US blue chip companies.[16]

Companies controlled by family groups are also much less likely to engage in the accounting shenanigans seen in the United States because if they were to do so they would be cheating no one but themselves. The strength of owner managers is that they maintain a focus on growing the business as opposed to boosting the share price.

However, the negatives of family control are daunting. These companies typically suffer from a lack of professional management born of nepotism. Although they are in theory public companies, the owners continue to behave as though they are running private companies. This means the conduct of business is far from transparent and the concept of accountability to shareholders is practically alien.

Worse still is the way that the assets of the majority shareholders' private companies are shuffled in and out of the public companies at the expense of minority shareholders. If they protest, they are simply told to invest in another company. Sometimes this asset shuffling is so detrimental to the interests of minority shareholders that they finally make a dash for the exit and the listed companies have to be privatised. However, the damage will already be done by the time this happens.

Investors in emerging markets appreciate that even the biggest businesses are driven by individual personalities to a far greater degree than in the United States, where some business personalities become media stars but the companies they run manage quite well after they have departed. This is not so in Asia, where big companies are synonymous with their big bosses. In Hong Kong investors will buy shares in any company controlled by Li Ka-shing, or 'Superman' as he is known locally. In Indonesia anything run by Liem Sioe Liong (or Sudono Salim, his Indonesian name) was a guaranteed buy while the Suharto regime remained in power. In this instance the close links between politics and business, highly characteristic of emerging markets, was underlined as Liem's star soon fell when Suharto was toppled. In practically every emerging market there are clutches of tycoons who dominate the stock market in much the same way as the so-called robber barons controlled the US market at the end of the nineteenth century when it was still in its infancy.

Despite everything – the case for stock markets

Inevitably the development of stock markets was never going to take place without diversions from the path of perfect markets and without other distortions entering the picture. But is it really the case that they have now developed to an extent that they are dragging down the very businesses they have helped to build?

It can be argued that in mature markets people running companies appear to be held to ransom by the short-term desires of shareholders, while in emerging markets the company bosses largely ignore their shareholders but nevertheless cater to their short-term interests. In neither instance can it be said that the presence of shareholders is adding to the value of the underlying companies whose shares are being traded.

However, this simplistic characterisation of the situation ignores many of the beneficial effects of stock markets which get lost under the weight of the large swirls of money that mesmerise many market observers. It remains the case that corporate development tends to be better served by raising equity capital rather than taking on large loan burdens. Moreover, the willingness to exchange equity for financing implies the taking on of responsibilities to shareholders who may have unreasonable expectations but at the end of the day respect business growth and will reward companies that achieve it. The markets in their often perverse ways nevertheless instil a degree of discipline on managers. At times the discipline points in the wrong direction, but at other times it works.

Stock markets also have an important role to play in providing incentives for the employees of listed companies. This is because they provide a mechanism for distributing equity. The abuses connected with share option schemes have overshadowed the great benefits of giving employees an equity stake in their companies. Away from the boardrooms, where share options are distributed wholesale, many companies hand out options much further down the line and thus provide their employees with an enhanced stake in their place of work.

A rather more tongue-in-cheek case for stock markets as a means of redistributing wealth was made by the London-based business journalist Patrick Hosking. He argued that 'sometimes the stock market can be more revolutionary than any socialist'. Discussing the sharp price falls following the end of the 1990s boom he wrote, 'The share market's slide is nature's way of distributing wealth from the haves to the have-nots of the next generation, and it's all done without a penny of inheritance tax being forked out.'[17] Hosking's point is that new investors entering a depressed market have a great opportunity to buy cheap shares at what he describes as 'sensible' prices. Of course there is nothing to stop existing investors doing exactly the same, assuming that their wealth has not been wiped out by forced share selling in a depressed market.

Stock markets are also useful devices for quantifying the state of companies and, in some senses, the state of the economy. Winston Churchill's famous remark about democracy being a deeply flawed system but better than all the others could well be applied to stock markets. They are far from perfect quantifiers of value but in the long run they pretty much reflect the state of economies in general and companies in particular. The problem with stock markets is that they are erratic and so when they are forward looking, which is their nature, they can be both good and lousy indicators of movements in economies.

There is also a case to be made for stock markets in terms of public policy, particularly in nations where legal structures are shaky and governments are prone to arbitrary changes to the rules of the business game. A World Bank study says that, 'if nothing else, the potentially large economic benefits of a vital stock market highlight the cost of government efforts to impede market development by policy or law. Conversely, a national programme that encourages both markets and banks to thrive can have dramatic effects.'[18]

At the end of the day the best case for stock markets is made by questioning what business would do without them. No doubt other means of raising equity could be created and no doubt other ingenious means of financing would be found, but it is likely that they would end up establishing new markets where equity can be traded. These markets would require sufficient transparency and liquidity to facilitate trading. If stock markets did not exist it is more than likely that they would be created in some form very close to their current incarnation.

Taking a stand for or against stock markets is really rather pointless: they are most unlikely to disappear and, if past history is anything to go by, they provide the most consistently reliable means of preserving and increasing wealth. Even people of modest means have good cause to pay attention to stock markets if they have the smallest interest in making the best of whatever assets they possess.

Understanding the contradictions

Potential investors should be aware that they are entering a battlefield with many live shells littered about the place. Only starry-eyed idealists believe they can pick their way through without the risk of injury. The unwary can lose far more money than they hope to gain, and they will do so if they persist in the belief that the market is some kind of wholly objective mechanism.

As we have repeatedly seen in this book, objectivity is not a marked characteristic of stock markets. This is primarily because markets are run by human beings. To understand markets involves knowing how people interact with financial markets. This often means gaining an appreciation of contradictions.

The hedge fund manager George Soros sees this as the crucial way of understanding markets. He writes: 'I believe that market prices are always wrong in the sense that they present a biased view of the future. But distortion works in both directions: not only do market participants operate with a bias, but their bias can also influence the course of events. This may create the impression that markets anticipate future developments accurately, but in fact it is not present expectations that correspond to future events but future events that are shaped by present expectations.'[19] This circular pattern of influence and distortion is what Soros describes as 'reflexivity'. It is a compelling theory not least because it reminds us of the lack of objectivity in the way that markets work. It also explains the way in which the perceptions that form the basis of stock market valuations are very much the product of human bias rather than the objective criteria which market enthusiasts believe in so strongly.

If Soros is right he challenges the very basis of efficient markets theory, which contends that stock prices both properly reflect underlying values and are capable of predicting the fortunes of companies. His point is that the distortion in stock prices, caused by the very way stock markets operate and participants behave, influences the price of stocks and inserts distortions that lead stock prices away from fundamental valuation. The market thus becomes a player in its own right. Soros argues that while 'the stock market is generally believed to anticipate recessions, it would be more correct to say that it can help to precipitate them'.[20]

Like revolutions, markets kill their babies

The arguments advanced by Soros are persuasive and have gained greater currency during the 1990s boom. This dotcom boom, like all other booms, bears eloquent witness to the way that markets not only fail to predict the future but encourage the growth of companies that have little staying power. As we have seen, most if not all the railway companies that fuelled the railway stock boom of the nine-teenth century went into liquidation. At the end of that century and the beginning of the next as many as 1,500 automobile companies were founded in the United States. Just three survived: Ford, General Motors and Chrysler, which had to be bailed out in 1979 and is now controlled by the German Daimler Benz group. At the time of writing their survival is again in question.

Who survived the dotcom wipeout? Very, very few companies, as few as survived other booms, which provided vital advances in industrial technology but did so by killing off the companies that were the pioneers in the field. As Pierre Vergniaud, one of the better known chroniclers of the French Revolution, observed, 'there was reason to fear that, like Saturn, the Revolution might devour each of its children in turn'. The fear was realised in both France and Russia, and in the business world exactly the same phenomenon has followed each big business revolution connected with stock markets.

Although living without computers and the Internet is every bit as unimaginable as living without automobiles, life goes on quite merrily without the continued existence of the companies that made these technological developments possible. It can even be argued that their demise was in large part caused by the very success they achieved when the companies were floated on stock markets. The markets lavished them with funds and drove their share prices way above any sustainable level. The companies were then punished for having flown too high and for having consumed too much investors' money. It is quite conceivable that many of the companies that perished would have survived had the source of their funding been outside stock markets and the amounts of money channelled into their coffers been more modest.

Stock markets nurture the strong
While stock markets both help to nurture the babies of business revolutions and then kill them off, they also help to make a very small

number of companies much stronger. Investors love a winner, and their support makes the winners that much stronger. In recent times investors clustered around the stock of Microsoft, unquestionably the most successful computer operating system and software developer. When Microsoft first went into business the market was flooded with potential competitors, particularly in the software field. Now Microsoft is so powerful that it faces allegations of anti-competitive practices stemming from its domination of the market. Microsoft is only repeating a pattern seen in the automobile industry, which was whittled down to the three dominant players in the American market.

It is in the nature of capitalist enterprise to strive for market dominance. Stock markets provide more than just the financial support to achieve this objective. They help to create the momentum that pushes some companies to the front of the line while others are pushed out altogether.

Obviously, investors who have correctly identified which companies are set to prosper will make gains, but they can also do well by investing in companies that will not run the course. The trick, as ever, lies in knowing when the window of opportunity for investing in these new industry companies is about to close and when to exit the market.

There is no need to be a true believer in dotcom companies, biotech companies or whatever is the next big thing. Simply knowing that shares in these companies are perceived as the new wonder stocks is sufficient. As Keynes said, markets are moved not so much by the intrinsic value of shares but by what investors perceive that value to be. The successful investor is the one who can predict how perceptions will change.

Shutting out market noise

The people running the businesses listed on stock markets should in theory be able to shrug off share price movements, pausing only occasionally to consider whether a healthy share price might provide better access to low-cost funding. After all, once capital has been raised in the market, the price at which shares change hands should be neither here nor there. Some of the most successful companies are run by managers who remain largely indifferent to their shareholders. Marks and Spencer, which for many years was Britain's most successful retailer, was famous for its indifference to the shareholders, even though the founding families had long ceased to control the bulk of the company's equity. In her fascinating book about the company Judi Bevan quotes Sir Richard Greenbury, the Marks and Spencer chairman, saying he was not 'prepared to spend my life, or even any of my time, on buffing up the company's image or its share price'.[21] In making these remarks Sir Richard was merely echoing the views of the Marks family, who saw the shareholders as a class of people ranking well behind the customers and staff of the company. When Marks and Spencer was performing well, shareholders were prepared to accept this kind of treatment. However, when it started to falter, as it did during the period of Sir Richard's chairmanship, the shareholders piled on the pressure.

Few executives are as indifferent to the share price as the people who ran Marks and Spencer, not least because, as we have seen, such a large proportion of their remuneration is tied up in the performance of the company's shares. They are both wise and foolish to behave in this way. They are wise because the share price quite often does not reflect the fundamental value of the company and it should not affect the running of the business. On the other hand, they are foolish if they ignore the share market completely because to do so may not only bring punishment at a personal level but may well also cause a loss of confidence in the company. The judgements passed by shareholders in the valuations they give to companies might be unrealistic reflections of earnings, but they do reflect market perceptions, which it is dangerous to ignore.

The Wall Street guru Benjamin Graham described the stock market as being 'in the short run a voting machine but in the long run it is a weighing machine'. He believed that over time the market would reflect the true value of companies, even though in the short term it may do little more than reflect their popularity. He may be generous in his assessment but the history of stock markets shows that they do, in fact, get it right ... eventually.

10

Opportunity

I F STOCK MARKETS were entirely rational places, populated by people committed to the implementation of efficient markets theory, they would offer fewer exciting opportunities to investors. Fortunately, signs of an outbreak of stock market rationality are no more than intermittent.

It may be that stock markets are less irrational than they were in the past but this only serves to underline the fact that irrationality still plays a major role in the operation of equity markets. This persistent fact of stock market life can be summed up in just one word – opportunity.

Bear markets produce the greatest opportunities

The best opportunities are commonly believed to occur in bull markets, when prices are steadily rising and, so it seems, making money is easy. However, one of the strongest lessons from history is that investors rarely know when to get out of a bull market and thus end up seeing the bulk or possibly all of their gains wiped out. It seems more realistic to argue that the best opportunities are found when markets are under the greatest pressure. This gives the inspired investor a chance to turn away from the crowd and follow a different strategy.

At times of pressure, when prices are falling, stock markets become very perverse places. Thankfully the people who operate in and around them are masters of perversity. How else to explain why they are so busy advocating the benefits of buying stocks when their prices reach the highest levels and are so anxious to sell when prices are falling? Moreover, they consistently follow this behavioural pattern despite the fact there has been no time in history when a sudden and deep fall in stock prices has not been followed by recovery.

John Kenneth Galbraith quotes the famous statement by Professor Joseph Lawrence of Princeton University, who said before the 1929 crash, 'the consensus of judgement of the millions whose valuations function on that admirable market, the Stock Exchange, is that stocks are not at present over-valued ... Where is that group of men with the all-embracing wisdom which will entitle them to veto the judgements of this intelligent multitude?'[1] The answer is that they are numbered among the investors most likely to make money in stock markets. The extent to which this is so is illustrated by Figure 10.1, which shows the speed with which markets have recovered in the wake of the biggest one-day falls on Wall Street over the past hundred years.

Speculating on recovery

What is most striking about Figure 10.1 is that recovery periods have become shorter since the second half of the last century. However, even in the depths of the 1930s recession, and just after the Great Crash of 1929, investors who were bold enough to challenge 'the judgements of this intelligent multitude' would have quickly profited by so doing. This figure builds on Figure 8.4 (page 202); it shows how long it took for the market to make gains of 10 per cent and 20 per cent. Investment gains of this order are generally associated with bull market periods but, as the figure shows, they are generally achieved with some ease during the depths of bear markets. In the period following the 1929 crash, which gave way to the worst bull market of the last century stretching over three decades, the market still threw up windows of opportunity for great profit.

Figure 10.1 **A century of panic and recovery on Wall Street**

Date	Percentage DJIA fall	Time taken to regain 10%	Time taken to regain 20%
19 Oct 1987	22.60	2 days	5 months
28 Oct 1929	12.80	5 months	233 months
29 Oct 1929	11.73	1 day	6 months
6 Nov 1929	9.90	3 months	4 months
12 Aug 1932	8.40	10 days	21 days
26 Oct 1987	8.04	4 days	8 months
15 Sept 2008	7.87	20 days	*
21 July 1933	7.80	20 days	6 months
18 Oct 1937	7.75	8 months	12 months
1 Dec 2008	7.70	7 days	*

* data not available at time of writing

Figure 10.1 shows that in the wake of the ten biggest one-day declines on Wall Street the market usually made a 10 per cent recovery within a month. What is even more striking is that with one exception the market rose by 20 per cent within a year. Sometimes the market fell back again after recovering, but investors who came into a very depressed market would have reaped fairly rapid gains in all but one instance. Apart from occasional traumatic periods, the American stock market, alongside other well-established markets, has consistently shown resilience.

The pattern of resilience is repeated on a much wider scale when looking at longer periods of depressed market activity, as opposed to the dramatic one-day market falls shown in Figure 10.1. An examination of the Standard & Poor's 500 Stock Index, instead of the Dow Jones Industrial Average, shows that in the second half of the twentieth century (from 1941 to 1999), the index fell in only twelve years. In all but one of these years the fall was followed by a substantial rise in the next year averaging 24 per cent. The one year which did not show a recovery was 1974, a dire time for investors caught between recession, inflation and an oil crisis, compounded in the United States by the political turmoil that accompanied the forced resignation of President Nixon. However, in the two years that followed the nightmare of 1974 stocks were up 70 per cent.

Further back in time, even after the four years of downturn that followed the 1929 crash there was a tripling of stock prices in the next four years, despite the persistence of the worst recession of the century. An even longer term survey of the US stock market, covering the years 1790 to 1985, shows that for 71 per cent of the period the total return on equities (i.e. price appreciation plus dividend payments) was positive. The biggest concentration of annual market rises was of the order of 10 per cent, with almost as many of around 20 per cent. The market even managed an annual rise of around 30 per cent on thirty-five occasions.[2]

In part, stocks have always bounced back in the United States because the economy has always bounced back, but even weaker economies have seen their stock markets move more or less in line with Wall Street. It is difficult to argue that the resilience of stock prices is purely attributable to the state of the economy, and hence corporate profitability. Account must also be taken of market herding, of market overreaction to events and subsequent correction and of the absence of more attractive investment opportunities for the vast sums of money in search of a home.

Understand the bias – understand the market

It is crucially important to understand the biases which influence the market if investors are to have a chance of dealing with them and learning how to profit from the way the market really operates. I use the term 'bias' in a value-free sense, suggesting not prejudice as much as propensity. Understanding bias means understanding the likely market response to events, which is not the same thing as understanding the events themselves.

This becomes even more important at times of market panic when irrationality takes firm command and investors need to step back from the market mayhem in order to make sense of what is happening.

Doubts may be raised about the value of particular stocks and the value of the market as a whole, but this does not mean that profits cannot be made. Indeed, some of the more cynical investors believe that greater profit potential exists when the market is behaving most irrationally and when stock valuations are pushed seriously out of line. This fits well with the consistent theme of this book that the greatest opportunities arise at moments of panic.

Jack Schwager's *Market Wizards* records the stories of some successful fund managers who understood and acted upon this basic point. Paul Tudor Jones, the head of the Tudor Futures Fund, made spectacular profits in the wake of the October 1987 crash. He did so both by buying shares as prices tumbled on 19 October and by buying bonds, having correctly anticipated the US government's response to the panic in the share market. He realised that the government would try to support the market by lowering interest rates. This, in turn, would lower the yield on bonds and bond prices would therefore rise. Tudor was exactly right and made a great deal of money for himself and his clients.[3]

Another bigtime beneficiary from the 1987 crash was Bruce Kovner, a major player in currency and futures trading. Like Tudor he sat back and thought about what the United States government would do in response to events on Wall Street. He saw the US government taking a role in trying to instil new confidence in the markets and acting to stimulate economic growth by lowering interest rates. This would cause the value of the dollar to fall while there was little likelihood of other governments coming in to defend the US currency. Betting against the dollar in these circumstances proved to be very lucrative.[4]

Both Tudor Jones and Kovner demonstrated the benefits of looking beyond what was happening as market turmoil hogged the headlines. The information in their possession was no different from that held by others. All they did was to think beyond the information and predict the reaction of the markets. By doing what other investors were not doing they emerged triumphant. Both are sophisticated fund managers with access to large sums of money but even small, relatively unsophisticated investors could have made considerable gains by simply refusing to follow the crowd and buying shares and other assets when others were selling.

It is a brave person who can close his or her ears to the rising crescendo of stock market noise, particularly at times of panic. However, that, essentially, is what successful investors have to do if they are to outperform the market.

Timing

Because of the many uncertainties in stock markets investors are always asking when they should get in and when they should get out. The financier Nathan Rothschild, whose very name is synonymous with successful investment, explained his strategy by saying, 'I never buy at the bottom and I always sell too soon.' In other words, he did not spend his time searching for the elusive market peaks and troughs. On the contrary, he ignored them and focused on buying when he saw good value and selling when he made what he considered to be an adequate profit.

It seems to me that it is easier to know when to buy rather than when to sell. Buying at times of stock market panic has consistently proved to be a good strategy, but there are killings to be made every time that quality stocks, i.e. those with a consistent record of improving earnings and achieving high returns on assets, fall to bargain prices. This often happens even when there is no panic underway.

But when is a good time to sell? There is no magic rule for determining when markets are getting too exuberant and vulnerable to a sharp fall, although attempts have been made in Chapters 2 and 4 to identify the signs of instability in a bull market that usually presage a decline. Given the absence of a foolproof method for predicting when a bull run will end, it seems more sensible to focus investors' minds on their own particular circumstances, which are quite possibly not the same as those prevailing in the general market. Focusing on the general state of the market rather than on the state of an individual's portfolio often confuses investment decisions. The barrage of conflicting information makes it hard to make sense of what is really happening.

However, investors can easily gauge what they should be doing within their individual portfolios simply by examining the performance of those portfolios: when and at what price were the shares purchased and how they have performed since then?

Market performance judgements are typically made by, for example, looking at how shares have fared over a twelve-month period, or since the beginning of a given year. This is largely irrelevant to a shareholder who purchased a share two or three years ago. Far more important is the comparison between the share's original purchase price and its current value. If it has risen by, say, 25 per cent since the time of purchase, the decision whether to sell or hold should be dependent on an assessment of the profit to be realised over the time of ownership. Every shareholder knows exactly when they bought shares and at what price (if not, they are careless to the point of stupidity), and this information provides a far better indication of what to do than any general judgement on the state of the market.

An investor may examine the state of his or her portfolio and conclude that an acceptable profit has been made, or that the time has come to cut losses and move on. If the latter, any losses will be personal ones, not some abstract fall over an arbitrary period that has triggered a sell signal more relevant to the portfolios of other investors.

There is a great deal of debate over whether it is better to cut losses or simply wait for the market to make good the drop. George

Ross Goobey, a well-known investor in the City of London during the 1960s, is strongly on the loss cutting side of the argument. He wrote, 'unfortunately … human nature being what it is this cost factor seems to play the most important part and one is much more ready to sell an investment standing above the price paid for it than vice versa'. He thinks this is sheer folly and advises investors to 'run profits and cut losses'.[5]

Goobey also has some amusing things to say about the practice of averaging, or 'dollar cost averaging' as it is now more widely known. This usually kicks in when the price of a share is falling and the investor buys more shares at a lower price so as to average down the cost of acquiring these stocks. Goobey describes this as 'a sort of human vanity which cannot admit that the original purchase was wrong and that therefore it must be an even better investment to purchase more shares at a cheaper price'.

The biggest nightmare for those who hang on tenaciously to shares that are rapidly losing value is that the price will fall beyond the point of recovery. This is the worst case scenario, but well before it is reached investors have to think about their level of loss tolerance, a subject much less discussed than risk tolerance. Most investors are more tolerant of losses than they are of risk, partly because their attitude towards loss is influenced by the need to reverse a decision previously taken. In other words, if they have invested in a stock that turns out to be a dud performer they have to revise their opinion of that stock and admit that their initial judgement may have been poor. On the other hand, in a rising market investors often take the view that their perspicacity in selecting stocks has led to their rising value and they are therefore loath to relinquish those stocks while the prospect remains of making further gains.

Setting targets

Assuming that an investor is inclined to trade stocks, particularly after they have registered gains, what criteria should be employed in deciding when to sell? It is quite impossible to establish general rules, but every investor can establish personal targets for profits and limits for losses. These will reflect their personal tolerance of risk and loss. There is no other way of establishing a workable stratagem for share trading; like all strategies it may change but if it is truly to be a stratagem as opposed to a mere reflex response, it should not change that often.

To follow this approach requires a great deal of discipline, as the share trader Warren Primhak pointed out in Chapter 6. However, this essentially was the approach followed by Nathan Rothschild, whose fortune speaks for itself.

Discipline and setting targets are especially vital during bull market periods, when the euphoria generated induces the notion that prices will keep rising for ever. Although more sensible market participants know that this cannot happen they are loath to make an exit while prices are still rising and the search for the elusive top of the market is underway.

Yet a better case can be made for selling stocks in a bull market than in a bear market. This, of course, assumes that the individual investor has made a reasonable amount of money from stocks during a bull run. At this point they may wish to pause for breath and leave the market with their profits in hand and park the cash elsewhere for a while.

Individual definition of 'reasonable profit' is likely to vary a great deal. Some people think that earning 10 per cent every year, or indeed any sum that beats the rate of inflation, is more than reasonable while others are far more ambitious. Again there is no general rule here, only a question of risk appetite.

Even the most ambitious investors will find it hard to take rational decisions without setting targets for the performance of their assets. If these targets are high, and they are happy to take the accompanying risks involved in achieving them, then they will stay in the market longer than those with a lower tolerance for risk. However, targets need to be set with some regard for history, since any target too far out of line with previous records is likely to be unrealistic. This is especially so in circumstances where developed markets are becoming less volatile over time while also showing an ability to sustain longer bull runs than before. The scope for more ambitious targets is therefore present but still constrained by the art of the possible.

Once these targets have been achieved investors need to exercise the easier-said-than-done discipline of acting without the fatal restraint of regret for forgone profit. They must also neither dither nor delay; to do so is to engage in nothing less than an act of avoidance. An investor brave enough to stick to their own programme of stock disposals may forgo a certain amount of profit, but will nearly always avoid the danger of much bigger losses.

Some wise investors simply believe that there is no case for selling stocks in order to buy other investments, even after impressive gains have been registered in share prices. They believe that there is no better asset class for investment and that selling good stocks does little more than incur unnecessary costs without providing a good alternative home for the money raised after the sale.

This may be so, but surely taking profits on stock price gains makes sense when there is a high probability that the very same stocks will be available at some time in the not too distant future at much lower prices. One of the few certainties in the world of equities investment is that prices are subject to cyclical behaviour. The likelihood of a downward price trend being replaced by an upward trend and vice versa is quite high enough to give investors confidence of the recurrence of both buying and selling opportunities.

The gains made by selling after taking decent profits and buying again at times when prices fall far outweigh transaction costs, although they may not outweigh the cost of paying capital gains taxes in jurisdictions where such taxes apply. This suggests that selling should only be contemplated at a point where the real profit (i.e. net of transaction costs and taxation) is sufficiently large to justify the risk of forgoing even greater profits. However, in the kind of bull markets seen towards the end of the last century and quite likely to recur in this one it is hard to believe that opportunities will not arise.

The brave investor

If investors were to follow the logic of evidence presented by over a century of investing history they would almost certainly put all their funds into stocks, particularly US equities. Not only has this investment class delivered better returns than any other but it has also proved itself to be ultimately less risky and increasingly less volatile. However very, very few investors are prepared to put all their eggs in one basket. Most continue to believe that diversification is the only prudent investment strategy. This is not so much because diversification offers the best returns but because it offers the prospect of fewer losses.

It matters not that it can be empirically demonstrated that investment in shares is by far the best form of investment because most investors would not be comfortable with such high exposure to just one asset class, even if it were to be hedged by parallel investments in equity derivatives. As an investor I cannot argue with the logic of focusing entirely on equities but I simply cannot bring myself not to invest in other asset classes. I also gravitate towards markets that I know best because I like to have the sense of having some control over my investments based on knowledge. I do so in the full awareness that other asset classes offer larger returns and that some of the markets I happen to know well are not likely to be the best performing, but at least I have some idea how they work.

In other words, I cannot claim to be a totally logical investor. On the one hand I am not brave enough to follow the logic of empirical evidence and on the other I take investment decisions that are heavily influenced by my need for comfort, a need that sometimes overcomes the desire for gain. Like most active investors I am ultimately risk averse and therefore not brave enough to act on the logic of the evidence that the overwhelming bulk, if not all, of my investments, should be in US equities.

There is no point in holding investments that cause anxiety or in constructing a portfolio which leaves its owner with a sense of discomfort. This is why some investment options might not have the best track record but happen to suit the risk tolerance of the investor and fulfil that person's concept of what is secure. This emphasises the great importance that psychological factors bring to bear on the world of investment. Investments are made by people, not by spreadsheets or by machines that can be said to be wholly objective. Indeed, as we saw during the 1987 crisis, the computers that were supposed to be generating objective portfolio insurance management were simply overridden by fund managers who wanted to sell whatever their programs were telling them to do.

Understanding investment psychology and the likely response of people to events is, as John Maynard Keynes strongly believed, the key to making money in stock markets.

Predicting extreme behaviour

Even the supposedly unpredictable human element is not that unpredictable when it comes to forecasting how investors will respond, especially at times when markets move to their bullish and bearish extremes. Benjamin Graham, the famous American investor quoted elsewhere in these pages, liked to say that investors behaved like manic depressives when things went wrong on the stock market. He could have added that investors behave like manic optimists when things are going well. The markets tend to produce exaggerated behaviour, which can also be described as irrational, but fortunately they do so consistently.

The consistent record of investor response to crisis may well change in the future but there is no sign of it changing right away. Far too much nonsense is talked about human irrationality in stock markets and far too much unnecessary fear is generated by conjuring up visions of great unpredictability in the markets. To redress the balance requires an understanding of stock market psychology, which is not half so complex a subject as some academic studies would suggest.

This book is mainly concerned with understanding stock markets when they reach extreme points. One of the central arguments is that investors have nothing to fear from stock market panics and everything to gain. I have started from the assumption of a reasonably high degree of irrationality, but hope I have shown that this irrationality falls into discernible patterns and thus becomes manageable. The history of stock markets is a history of cycles. It is not a history of so-called random walks through time meandering in unpredictable directions.

While it is not possible to pinpoint when panics will emerge, it is certainly possible to identify a number of telling signs that almost always give forewarning of what is about to happen. In Chapter 4 these signs were examined and in Chapter 5 I have attempted to show why markets, while becoming less volatile, are becoming more prone to panic. Moreover, panics are becoming more dangerous as stock markets move further and further away from the companies that underlie the markets and from the economies which house these companies.

New markets – old patterns

As stock markets increasingly inhabit a world detached from the economies they are supposed to reflect they are also growing at a fantastic rate. Even well-established stock markets are still managing to register impressive growth levels, while new stock markets are popping up in practically every country in the world. Some of these newer markets are expanding at such an extraordinary rate that they threaten to overtake their more established counterparts. In 2002, for example, the Taiwanese stock market moved close to overtaking Japan in terms of volume. There are many ironies here, not least that Taiwan was a Japanese colony until 1945 and considered a backward sort of place with only limited prospects of being much more than a reasonably well-off agricultural province.

China, which is still under the control of the Communist Party, has some of the fastest growing stock markets in the world and they are receiving active government support. Meanwhile former communist states, such as Russia, are busy building new stock markets, which are seen as symbols of their liberation from the old days of centrally planned economies. Every self-respecting nation wants its own stock market and can supply large numbers of local investors to keep them in business.

The global growth of stock markets means that it can no longer be said that equity markets are the exclusive preserve of the industrialised West. Even when most countries did not have stock markets of their own they were affected by sharp movements on Western exchanges; now the linkage is much closer. Most markets follow Wall Street but, as we have seen, often manage to move in an upward direction when American shares are treading water, although they rarely manage to detach themselves from sharp downward movements on Wall Street. This, in part, is a consequence of the global reach of large investment funds that can easily allocate money anywhere in the world and can cause considerable ructions when they shift allocations from one market to another. Although the power of international fund managers is an article of faith among anti-globalisation campaigners and some of Wall Street's more arrogant market players, it is frequently overstated. Closer examination shows that these funds are not as global as they often appear to be and that most movements in emerging markets are a consequence of activity by domestic investors. However, because of its size and its dominant position in equity markets, movements on Wall Street have a considerable psychological impact on other markets which are quickly translated into price falls when American stocks go into steep decline.

The stakes are higher

What all this means is that the stakes are much higher these days. The amounts of money in stock markets and the global reach of equity markets have increased by an enormous amount, particularly over the past two decades. This in turn has led to a situation where stock markets, instead of providing financial backing for business, are themselves dictating the way that business is carried out and as stock markets move up and down their movements have an impact on the performance of economies.

Not only are the stakes higher but more and more people have a direct and indirect interest in the fortunes of the stock market. In the United States the number of individual shareholders rose from 27 million in 1989 to 33.8 million in 1998. However, if all direct shareholders are combined with those invested in the stock market through mutual funds and pension schemes, the number of people with a stake in the stock market showed an even more rapid rate of increase from 52.3 million in 1989 to 84 million in 1998.[6]

Stock markets therefore have become far too important to remain the preserve of a small band of investment professionals, yet relatively small numbers of people control the fate of these markets. I have met several people in this group, and their lack of self-doubt and patchy knowledge of the world outside financial markets is a matter of concern.

A conflict of interest

Stock markets show remarkable resilience in the face of crises, scandals and all other forms of extreme behaviour. Investors who learn to take all this in their stride will profit greatly.

At the time of writing investors are understandably nervous. The new millennium is shrouded in uncertainty. Not only has the biggest bull run in history finally come to an end but it has done so with a spectacular flurry of corporate failures, allegations of enormous corporate fraud and a strong sense of distrust surrounding all those who play a role in the world of corporate finance. No wonder share trading volumes are down.

Yet none of this should dismay the savvy investor. On the contrary, the potential for profit is greatest when fear, irrationality and extreme behaviour dominate stock markets.

It occurs to me that by writing this book I have created a conflict of interest. If more people understand the opportunities arising from markets at their supposedly weakest moments, the potential for profit will diminish. Obviously everyone wishes for more rational behaviour, at least in theory, but in practice it would mean a distinct loss of opportunity.

Stock markets provide some of life's few genuine opportunities; it is a continuing mystery that they are so consistently squandered.

Notes

Chapter 1   **The panic of 2008**

1 I recommend looking at the following link for an explanation of the model and its background: http://bradley.bradley. edu/~arr/bsm/model.html, 'A Study of Option Pricing Models' by Kevin Rubash.

2 Bank of England, *Financial Stability Report*, Bank of England, London, 2008.

3 Gerard Caprio, Jr., Asli Demirguc-Kunt and Edward J. Kane, 'The 2007 Meltdown in Structured Securitization: Searching for Lessons Not Scapegoats', Policy Research Working Papers. World Bank, Washington, DC, October 2008.

4 Robert Shiller, 'Price–Earnings Ratios as Forecasters of Returns: The Stock Market Outlook in 1996', Yale Department of Economics, 1996. http://www.econ.yale.edu/~shiller/data/ peratio.html.

5 Laura Pavlenko Lutton, 'Does Your Fund Manager Feel Your Pain?', Fund Spy, *Morning Star*, 19 June 2008. http://news. morningstar.com/articlenet/article.aspx?id=241755.

6 Daniel Ren, Enoch Yiu and Jonathan Yang, 'Funds face brain drain fallout', *South China Morning Post*, Hong Kong, 27 May 2008.

7 Credit Suisse, *Research Weekly*, Zurich, 10 January, 2008.

8 International Monetary Fund, *World Economic Outlook*, Washington, D. C., April 2007.

9 Kyung Bok Cho, 'Global Stock Market Rout May Continue, Rogers Says' (Update 1), *Bloomberg News*, 12 November 2008. http://www.bloomberg.com/apps/news?pid=newsarchive&sidcaXD.ktb8insw.

10 *BBC News*, 'World credit loss £1.8 trillion', 28 October 2008. http://news.bbc.co.uk/2/hi/business/7694275.stm.

11 Joanna Slater, 'Stocks appear cheap world-wide', *Wall Street Journal*, New York, 3 November 2008.

12 Mark Pittman and Bob Ivry, 'U.S. Pledges Top $7.7 Trillion to Ease Frozen Credit', *Bloomberg News*, New York, 24 November 2008.

13 Noreena Hertz, 'The death of Gucci capitalism', *New Statesman*, London, 23 October 2008.

14 Mark Maremont, John Hechinger, and Maurice Tamman, 'Some CEOs took money off the table', *Wall Street Journal*, New York, 21 November 2008.

Chapter 2 **Preparing for panics and profiting from them**

1 John Kenneth Galbraith, *The Great Crash 1929*, Houghton Mifflin, Boston, 1988, p. 99.

2 Quoted in Eugene White, 'When the Ticker Ran Late: The Stock Market Boom and Crash of 1929', in Eugene White (ed.), *Crashes and Panics: Lessons from History*, Dow Jones/Irwin, New York, 1990.

3 'Warren Buffet on the Stock Market', *Fortune*, New York, 10 Dec 2001.

4 White, 'When the Ticker Ran Late', p. 240.

5 Galbraith, *The Great Crash 1929*, p. 90.

6 Gary Santoni and Gerald Dwyer, 'Bubbles of Fundamentals: New Evidence from the Great Bull Markets', in White, *Crashes and Panics*.

7 Charles Kindleberger, Manias, Panics and Crashes: *A History of Financial Crises (1978)*, John Wiley & Sons, New York, 2000 edition, p. 25.

8 Jeremy Siegel, Stocks for the Long Run: *A Guide to Selecting Markets for Long-Term Growth*, Irwin, Homewood, Ill., and New York, 1994, p. 249.

Chapter 3 **Types of panics**

1 David Cutler, James Poterba and Lawrence Summers, 'What Moves Stock Prices', *Journal of Portfolio Management*, Vol. 15, No. 3, 1989.

2 Peter Garber, 'Who Put the Mania in the Tulip Mania?', in Eugene White (ed.), *Crashes and Panics: Lessons from History*, Dow Jones/Irwin, New York, 1990.

3 Larry Neal, 'How the South Sea Bubble Was Blown Up and Burst: A New Look at Old Data', in White, *Crashes and Panics*, p. 34.

4 E. S. Browning and Greg Ip, 'Six Key Myths that Led the Boom in Tech Stocks – Growth Slows, Monopolies Erode, And Yes, Business Cycles Matter – Mr. Blodget's New Prescription', *Asian Wall Street Journal* (Hong Kong), 17 Oct. 2000.

5 George Soros, *The Alchemy of Finance*, John Wiley & Sons, New York, 1994. Soros' views on the crash as a whole can be found in Chapter 20.

6 Quoted in Stephen Vines, *The Years of Living Dangerously: Asia from Financial Crisis to the New Millennium*, Texere, London and New York, 2000, p. 11.

7 Ibid., p. 13.

8 Ibid., p. 239.

9 International Monetary Fund, *International Capital Markets Report*, IMF, Washington, DC, 1995.

10 Jeremy Siegel, *Stocks for the Long Run: A Guide to Selecting Markets for Long-Term Growth*, Irwin, Homewood, Ill., and New York, 1994, p. 198, emphasis in original.
11 Jeremy Grantham, writing in *Outstanding Investor Digest* (Boston), Vol. 15, Nos. 1–2, 31 July 2000, emphasis in original.

Chapter 4 **The panic cycle**
  1 'A Successful Operator', 'How to Invest and Speculate Safely in Railway Shares', in Ellis Charles and James Vertin (eds.), *Classics II: Another Investor's Anthology*, AIMR Business One/Irwin, Homewood, Ill., 1991.
  2 Sean Beckett and Gordon Sellon, 'Has Financial Market Volatility Increased?', in Robert Kolb (ed.), *Financial Institutions and Markets: A Reader*, Kolb Publishing, Miami, 1991, Article 14.
  3 Jeremy Siegel, *Stocks for the Long Run: A Guide to Selecting Markets for Long-Term Growth*, Irwin, Homewood, Ill., and New York, 1994, Chapter 15.
  4 C. P. Jones, R. Sylla and J. W. Wilson, 'Financial Market Panics and Volatility in the Long Run, 1830–1988', in Eugene White (ed.), *Crashes and Panics: Lessons from History*, Dow Jones/Irwin, New York, 1990.
  5 Milton Friedman, 'After the Boom', *Asian Wall Street Journal* (Hong Kong), 23 Jan. 2002. Friedman's views are expanded at greater length in his *Monetary History of the United States, 1867–1960*, co-authored with Anna Jacobson, Schwartz, Princeton, 1971.
  6 Peter Spiro, *Real Interest Rates and Investment and Borrowing Strategy*, Quorum Books, Westport, Conn., 1989, Chapter 9.
  7 John Kenneth Galbraith, *The Great Crash 1929*, Houghton Mifflin, Boston, 1988, p. 21.

8 Charles Kindleberger, *Manias, Panics and Crashes: A History of Financial Crises (1978)*, John Wiley & Sons, New York, 2000 edition, Chapter 2.
9 Ibid., p. 177.
10 The IMF's record during the Asian crisis is discussed in more detail in Stephen Vines, *The Years of Living Dangerously: Asia from Financial Crisis to the New Millennium*, Texere, London and New York, 2000, pp. 198–203.
11 Kindleberger, *Manias, Panics and Crashes*, p. 73.
12 Galbraith, *The Great Crash 1929*, p. 133.
13 E. S. Browning, 'Stock History Repeats Itself', *Wall Street Journal*, 11–13 Feb. 2002.
14 David Wessel, 'Boardroom Sins Continue to Emerge', *Wall Street Journal*, 21 June 2002.

Chapter 5   **A new age of panics**
1 'Warren Buffet on the Stock Market', *Fortune*, 10 Dec. 2001.
2 'Stock Markets and Economic Growth', *World Bank Research Bulletin* (Washington, DC), Vol. 6, No. 2, March–April 1995.
3 World Bank, *Global Development Finance 2001*, Washington, DC, May 2001, Table 2.6.
4 Stephen Vines, *The Years of Living Dangerously: Asia from Financial Crisis to the New Millennium*, Texere, London and New York, 2000, p. 131.
5 World Bank, *The Emerging Asian Bond Market*, Washington, DC, June 1995, Table 1.4.
6 World Bank, *Global Development Finance*, Table 3.1.
7 Robert Shiller, *Irrational Exuberance*, Princeton University Press, Princeton, NJ, 2000, pp. 119–20.
8 *OECD Observer* (Paris), 7 Nov. 2001, p. 69.
9 International Monetary Fund, 'Asset Prices and the Business Cycle', *World Economic Outlook*, Washington, DC, May 2000, Chapter 3.

10 Richard Pettway and Craig Tapley, 'Efficiency of World Capital Markets: The Case of Japan and the United States', in Carl Beidleman (ed.), *The Handbook of International Investing*, Probus, Chicago, 1987.

11 Bernice Cohen, *The Edge of Chaos: Financial Booms, Bubbles, Crashes and Chaos*, John Wiley & Sons, Chichester, 1997, p. 339.

12 Both quotations are taken from Edward Chancellor, *Devil Take the Hindmost: A History of Financial Speculation*, Farrar, Straus and Giroux, New York, 1999, p. 335.

13 Ibid., p. 333.

14 Franklin Edwards, 'Historical Perspective and Proposed Changes', in Eugene White (ed.), *Crashes and Panics: Lessons from History*, Dow Jones/Irwin, New York, 1990.

15 Eugene Moriarty, Douglas Gordon, Gregory Kuserk and George Wang, *Statistical Analysis of Price and Basis Behavior: October 12–26, 1987, in S&P 500 Futures and Cash in the Stock Market: Bubbles, Volatility and Chaos*, Kluwer Academic, Boston, 1988.

16 A full account of this incident can be found in Vines, *The Years of Living Dangerously*, pp. 208–18.

17 *Report of the Presidential Task Force on Market Mechanisms,* US Government Printing Office, Washington, DC, 1998, p. 69.

18 Ibid., p. v.

19 Robert Shiller, Market Volatility, MIT Press, Cambridge, Mass., 1989, p. 395.

20 New York Stock Exchange, *Shareownership 2000*, NYSE, New York, 2000, pp. 53–4.

21 Ibid., p. 62.

22 New York Stock Exchange press release, 22 Feb. 2002.

23 New York Stock Exchange, *Shareownership 2000*, p. 34.

24 Ibid., p. 15.

25 Richard Brealey, 'Can Professional Investors Beat the Market?', in Charles Ellis and James Vertin (eds.), Classics: *An Investors' Anthology*, Dow Jones/Irwin, Homewood, Ill., 1989.

26 Lars Tvede, *The Psychology of Finance*, Norwegian University Press, Oslo, 1990, p. 149.

27 Burton Malkiel, *A Random Walk Down Wall Street*, W. W. Norton, New York, 1996, p. 184.

28 Robert Sobel, *The Pursuit of Wealth: The Incredible Story of Money Throughout the Ages*, McGraw-Hill, New York, 2000, p. 299.

29 Ibid., p. 300.

30 Elena Moya, 'UK Brokers Recommend Clients', *Bloomberg News Service*, London, 18 Feb. 2002.

31 Shiller, *Irrational Exuberance*, p. 30.

32 Elroy Dimson and Paul Marsh, 'An Analysis of Brokers' and Analysts' Unpublished Forecasts of UK Stock Returns', *Journal of Finance*, Vol. 39, No. 5, Dec. 1984.

33 Neil Barsky, 'Getting Out of the Wall Street Game', *Asian Wall Street Journal* (Hong Kong), 10–12 May 2002.

34 David Reilly, Philip Segal and Jonathan Weil, 'Stock-Option Accounting Colors Earnings Pictures', *Asian Wall Street Journal* (Hong Kong), 17 July 2002.

35 Jeremy Grantham, writing in *Outstanding Investor Digest* (Boston), Vol. 15, Nos. 1–2, 31 July 2000.

Chapter 7 **The psychology of panics**

1 Peter Garber, *Famous First Bubbles*, MIT Press, Cambridge, Mass., 2000, p. 124.

2 George Soros, *The Alchemy of Finance*, John Wiley & Sons, New York, 1994, p. 33.

3 Ibid., pp. 54–5.

4 Peter Bernstein, *Against the Gods: The Remarkable Story of Risk*, John Wiley & Sons, New York, 1996, p. 300.

5 Charles Mackay, *Extraordinary Popular Delusions and the Madness of Crowds (1841)*, Harmony Books, New York, 1980 edition, p. xx.

6 Ibid., p. 91.

7 Ibid., p. xx.

8 Gustave Le Bon, 'General Characteristics of Crowds: A Psychological Law of Their Mental Unity', in Charles Ellis and James Vertin (eds.), *Classics: An Investors' Anthology*, Dow Jones/Irwin, Homewood, Ill., 1989, p. 88.

9 Ibid., p. 91.

10 Lars Tvede, *The Psychology of Finance*, Norwegian University Press, Oslo, 1990, p. 179.

11 John Kenneth Galbraith, *A Short History of Financial Euphoria*, Whittle Books, New York, 1993, p. 10.

12 Werner DeBondt and Richard Thaler, 'Does the Stock Market Overreact?', *Journal of Finance*, Vol. 40, No. 3.

13 Manmohan Kumar and Avinash Persaud, 'Pure Contagion and Investors' Shifting Risk Appetite', IMF Working Paper, Washington, DC, Sep. 2001.

14 Amos Tversky, 'The Psychology of Risk', in William Sharpe (ed.), *Quantifying the Market Risk Premium Phenomenon for Investment Decision Making*, Institute of Chartered Financial Analysts, Charlottesville, Va, 1990, p. 75.

15 Robert Shiller, *Market Volatility*, MIT Press, Cambridge, Mass., 1989, Table 23.2.

16 Findings of research cited in Bernstein, *Against the Gods*, p. 264.

17 Tvede, *The Psychology of Finance*, p. 165.

18 Ibid., p. 243.

19 Robert Shiller, *Irrational Exuberance*, Princeton University Press, Princeton, NJ, 2000, pp. 154–5.
20 Ibid.
21 Ibid., p. 91.
22 Shiller, *Market Volatility*, Table 23.2.
23 Sushil Bikhchandani and Eric Clifton, 'Herd Behaviour in Financial Markets: A Review', IMF Working Paper, Washington, DC, March 2000.
24 Arnold Wood, 'Behavioral Risk: Anecdotes and Disturbing Evidence', in Association for Investment Management and Research, *Investing Worldwide*, VI, AIMR, Charlottesville, Va, 1996.
25 William Reichenstein and Dovalee Dorsett, *Time Diversification Revisited*, Research Foundation of the Institute of Chartered Financial Analysts, Charlottesville, Va, 1995.
26 Galbraith, *A Short History of Financial Euphoria*, p. 13.
27 Ibid., p. 5.
28 Quoted in Tvede, *The Psychology of Finance*, p. 139.
29 Galbraith, *A Short History of Financial Euphoria*, p. viii.

Chapter 8 **Does diversification provide protection against stock market fluctuations?**

1 Peter Bernstein, *Against the Gods: The Remarkable Story of Risk*, John Wiley & Sons, New York, 1996, p. 253.
2 Ibid., p. 285.
3 Warren Bitters, *The New Science of Asset Allocation*, Glenlake, Chicago, 1997.
4 Stacy Sirmans and C. F. Sirmans, 'The Historical Perspective of Real Estate Returns', *Journal of Portfolio Management*, Vol. 13, No. 3, Spring 1987.
5 Peter Spiro, *Real Interest Rates and Investment and Borrowing Strategy*, Quorum Books, Westport, Conn., 1989, esp. Appendix.

6 Eugene Sherman, *Gold Investment: Theory and Application*, Prentice-Hall, New York, 1986, p. 178.

7 *Barclays Capital Equity–Gilt Study*, Barclays, London, 2002.

8 Robert Shiller, *Irrational Exuberance*, Princeton University Press, Princeton, NJ, 2000, pp. 194–5.

9 Jeremy Siegel, *Stocks for the Long Run: A Guide to Selecting Markets for Long-Term Growth*, Irwin, Homewood, Ill., and New York, 1994, p. 12.

10 Ibid., Figure 1-1.

11 Ibid., p. iv.

12 Don Chance, *Essays in Derivatives*, Frank J. Fabozzi Associates, New Hope, PA, 1998, pp. 16–17.

13 Greg Beier, 'Understanding the Difference Between Hedging and Speculating', in Robert Klein and Jess Lederman (eds.), *Derivative Risk and Responsibility*, Irwin, Chicago, 1996.

14 Merton Miller, *Merton Miller on Derivatives*, John Wiley & Sons, New York, 1987, pp. 80–81.

Chapter 9 **Is the market always right?**

1 Gary Santoni and Gerald Dwyer, 'Bubbles or Fundamentals: New Evidence from the Great Bull Markets', in Eugene White (ed.), *Crashes and Panics: Lessons from History*, Dow Jones/Irwin, New York, 1990.

2 Robert Shiller, *Market Volatility*, MIT Press, Cambridge, Mass., 1989, p. 8.

3 Robert Shiller, *Irrational Exuberance*, Princeton University Press, Princeton, NJ, 2000, pp. 5–7.

4 Fabio Canova and Gianni De Nicolo, 'Stock Returns and Real Activity: A Structural Approach', in *International Stock Returns and Business Cycles*, CEPR Conference Report No. 5, Centre for Economic Policy Research, London, 1994.

5 Stephen LeRoy, 'Capital Market Efficiency: An Update', in Robert Kolb (ed.), *Financial Institutions and Markets: A Reader*, Kolb Publishing, Miami, 1991, Article 15, p. 157.
6 Lawrence Summers, 'Does the Stock Market Rationally Reflect Fundamental Values?', *Journal of Finance*, Vol. 41, No. 3, July 1986, p. 599.
7 Peter Spiro, *Real Interest Rates and Investment and Borrowing Strategy*, Quorum Books, Westport, Conn., 1989, p. 173.
8 Harris Collingwood, 'The Earnings Cult', *New York Times*, 9 Sept. 2002.
9 Karen Lowry Miller, 'The Giants Stumble', *Newsweek*, 8 July 2002.
10 AT Kearney, *Merger Endgames*, Chicago, 2000, see http://www.atkearney.com.
11 Associated Press Report, 'Finally, Some Kind Words for Corporate Takeovers', *International Herald Tribune* (Paris), 8 August 2002.
12 Edward Chancellor, Perverse Incentives, *Prospect*, London, 2002.
13 Ibid.
14 'Recent Equity Market Developments and Implications', *OECD Economic Outlook*, OECD, Paris, Dec. 1998, Chapter 5, pp. 168–9.
15 George Melloan, 'CEO's Face the Music for Irrational Exuberance', *Asian Wall Street Journal* (Hong Kong), 30 July 2002.
16 David Reilly, Philip Segal and Jonathan Weil, 'Stock-Option Accounting Colors Earnings Pictures', *Asian Wall Street Journal* (Hong Kong), 17 July 2002.
17 Patrick Hosking, 'The Business', *New Statesman*, 24 June 2002.

18 'Stock Markets and Economic Growth', *World Bank Policy Research Bulletin*, Washington DC, Vol. 6, No. 2, March–April 1995.

19 George Soros, *The Alchemy of Finance*, John Wiley & Sons, New York, 1994, p. 14.

20 Ibid., p. 49.

21 Judi Bevan, *The Rise and Fall of Marks & Spencer*, Profile Books, London, 2001, p. 96.

Chapter 10 **Opportunity**

1 John Kenneth Galbraith, *The Great Crash 1929*, Houghton Mifflin, Boston, 1988, p. 70.

2 Gary Brinson and Roger Ibbotson, 'US Equity Returns from Colonial Times to the Present', in Charles Ellis and James Vertin (eds.), *Classics II: Another Investor's Anthology*, AIMR Business One/Irwin, Homewood, Ill., 1991.

3 Jack Schwager, *Market Wizards: Interviews with Top Traders*, New York Institute of Finance, New York, 1989, pp. 132–4.

4 Ibid., pp. 73–4.

5 George Ross Goobey, 'Human Foibles', in Charles Ellis and James Vertin (eds.), *Classics: An Investor's Anthology*, Dow Jones/Irwin, Homewood, Ill., 1989.

6 New York Stock Exchange, *Share Ownership*, NYSE, New York, 2000.

Select bibliography

Arbel, Avner and Albert Kaff, *Crash: Ten Days in October ... Will it Strike Again?*, Longman, USA, 1989

Beckett, Sean and Gordon Sellon, 'Has Financial Market Volatility Increased?', in Robert Kolb (ed.), *Financial Institutions and Markets: A Reader*, Kolb Publishing, Miami, 1991, Article 14

Beidleman, Carl, *The Handbook of International Investing*, Probus, Chicago, 1987

Bernstein, Peter, *Against the Gods: The Remarkable Story of Risk*, John Wiley & Sons, New York, 1996

Bitters, Warren, *The New Science of Asset Allocation*, Glenlake, Chicago, 1997

Brady, Nicholas (chairman), *Report of the Presidential Task Force on Market Mechanisms*, US Government Printing Office, Washington, DC, 1998

Chancellor, Edward, *Devil Take the Hindmost: A History of Financial Speculation*, Farrar, Straus and Giroux, New York, 1999

Chote, Robert, 'International Stock Returns and Business Cycles', in *International Stock Returns and Business Cycles*, CEPR Conference Report No. 5, Centre for Economic Policy Research, London, 1994

Cohen, Bernice, *The Edge of Chaos: Financial Booms, Bubbles, Crashes and Chaos*, John Wiley & Sons, Chichester, 1997

Dimson, Elroy and Paul Marsh, 'An Analysis of Brokers' and Analysts' Unpublished Forecasts of UK Stock Returns', *Journal of Finance*, Vol. 39, No. 5, Dec. 1984

Galbraith, John Kenneth, *The Great Crash 1929*, Houghton Mifflin, Boston, 1988

Galbraith, John Kenneth, *A Short History of Financial Euphoria*, Whittle Books, New York, 1993

Garber, Peter, 'Who Put the Mania in the Tulip Mania?', in Eugene White (ed.), *Crashes and Panics: Lessons from History*, Dow Jones/Irwin, New York, 1990

Garber, Peter, *Famous First Bubbles*, MIT Press, Cambridge, Mass., 2000

Hubbard, Glen (ed.), *Financial Markets and Financial Crises*, University of Chicago Press, Chicago, 1991

Kindleberger, Charles, *Manias, Panics and Crashes: A History of Financial Crises (1978)*, John Wiley & Sons, New York, 2000 edition

Kleidon, Allan, 'Stock Market Crashes', Research Paper 1262, Jackson Library, Stanford University, Jan. 1994

Le Bon, Gustave, 'General Characteristics of Crowds: A Psychological Law of Their Mental Unity', in Charles Ellis and James Vertin (eds.), *Classics: An Investor's Anthology*, Dow Jones/Irwin, Homewood, Ill., 1989

LeRoy, Stephen, 'Capital Market Efficiency: An Update', in Robert Kolb (ed.), *Financial Institutions and Markets: A Reader*, Kolb Publishing, Miami, 1991, Article 15

Mackay, Charles, *Extraordinary Popular Delusions and the Madness of Crowds (1841)*, Harmony Books, New York, 1980 edition

Miller, Merton, *Merton Miller on Derivatives*, John Wiley & Sons, New York, 1987

Miskin, Frederic, 'Asymmetric Information and Financial Crises: A Historical Perspective', in Glen Hubbard (ed.), *Financial Markets and Financial Crises*, University of Chicago Press, Chicago, 1991

Miskin, Frederic, 'International Capital Movements, Financial
Volatility and Financial Instability', National Bureau of Economic
Research Working Paper 6390, Cambridge, Mass., 1998

Moriarty, Eugene, Douglas Gordon, Gregory Kuserk and George
Wang, *Statistical Analysis of Price and Basis Behavior:
October 12–26, 1987, S&P 500 Futures and Cash in
the Stock Market: Bubbles, Volatility and Chaos*, Kluwer
Academic, Boston, 1988

Morris, Charles, Money *Greed and Risk – Why Financial Crises
and Crashes Happen*, Times Books, New York, 1999

Pierce, Phyllis (ed.), *The Dow Jones Averages*, Business One/
Irwin, Homewood, Ill., 1991

Santoni, Gary and Gerald Dwyer, 'Bubbles or Fundamentals: New
Evidence from the Great Bull Markets', in Eugene White (ed.),
Crashes and Panics: Lessons from History, Dow Jones/Irwin,
New York, 1990

Schwert, William, 'Stock Market Crash of October 1987', in
Peter Newman, Murray Milgate and John Eatwell (eds.), *The
New Palgrave Dictionary of Money and Finance*, Macmillan,
London, 1992, pp. 577–82

Sherman, Eugene, *Gold Investment: Theory and Application*,
Prentice-Hall, New York, 1986

Shiller, Robert, *Market Volatility*, MIT Press, Cambridge, Mass.,
1989

Shiller, Robert, *Irrational Exuberance*, Princeton University Press,
Princeton, NJ, 2000

Siegel, Jeremy, Stocks for the Long Run: A Guide to Selecting
Markets for *Long-Term Growth*, Irwin, Homewood, Ill., and
New York, 1994

Sill, Keith, 'Predicting Stock Market Volatility', in Peter Rose
(ed.), *Readings on Financial Institutions and Markets*, Irwin,
Homewood, Ill., 1994–5, Article 20

Sobel, Robert, *The Pursuit of Wealth: The Incredible Story of Money Throughout the Ages*, McGraw-Hill, New York, 2000

Soros, George, *The Alchemy of Finance*, John Wiley & Sons, New York, 1994

Spiro, Peter, *Real Interest Rates and Investment and Borrowing Strategy*, Quorum Books, Westport, Conn., 1989

Summers, Lawrence, 'Does the Stock Market Rationally Reflect Fundamental Values?', *Journal of Finance*, Vol. 41, No. 3, July 1986

Tvede, Lars, *The Psychology of Finance*, Norwegian University Press, Oslo, 1990

Vines, Stephen, *The Years of Living Dangerously: Asia from Financial Crisis to the New Millennium*, Texere, London, 2000

White, Eugene (ed.), *Crashes and Panics: Lessons from History*, Dow Jones/Irwin, New York, 1990

Index

Optimism, vii, 33–4, 48–9, 155, 164, 177
Organization of Petroleum Exporting Countries (OPEC), 20, 60
Over trading, 80
Overend, Gurney, 38

P

Pacific Century CyberWorks, 113–4
Panics, v–vii, xi, xiii–xix, xxiv–xxv, 3–5, 13, 15, 17–23, 26–30, 32, 35–6, 38–41, 43–5, 47–50, 53, 56–7, 59–61, 63–4, 66–9, 71, 74, 76, 78–9, 81–4, 86–9, 92, 94, 97–9, 114, 126, 137, 139, 144–6, 150, 152–7, 161, 164–5, 167, 172, 179–181, 183–5, 195, 198, 200, 202–3, 208–9, 219–220, 247, 249–250, 257, 261–7, 270, 274–6
causes of, 99
contagious, v, 43, 56–7
cycle stages, 79
end-of-cycle, 47
phoney, v, 27, 43–4, 49–50
real, vi, 43, 63, 67
self-induced, 50, 53
Pearl Harbor, 46
Persaud, Avinash, 165, 268
Pettway, Richard, 111, 266
Philippines, stock market, 91, 106, 204
Pickens, T. Boone, 225
Pioneer Group, 147
Playboy, 80

Political impact
Ponzi, Charles, 102
Ponzi schemes, 103
Portfolio insurance, vi, 68, 117, 120–123, 160, 256
end of, 124, 160
Poterba, James, 48, 263
Pound, John, 171
Price-earnings ratios, 10, 15, 18, 21
Pricing, 6, 55, 108, 140, 195, 261
Prime Computer, 147
Primhak, Warren, vii, x, 137, 253
Procter and Gamble, 206
Productivity, US, 228
Program trading, vi, 100, 117, 123
Property investment, 188, 190–1
vs stocks, 190
Proprietary trading, 132, 133
Prospect theory, 165–6

R

Radio Corporation of America (RCA), 54
Railway shares mania, 53
Recessions, 73, 239
Reichenstein, William, 175, 269
Research and development, 107
Returns on equity, US, 228
Risk aversion, 166–7, 184
Risk tolerance, 252, 256
Rogers, Jim, 14
Rothschild, Nathan, 250, 253
Rubinstein, Mark, 121
Russian investors, 101

S

Sadler, Simon, 42